VOTING BEHAVIOUR IN THE REPUBLIC OF IRELAND

Voting Behaviour in the Republic of Ireland

A Geographical Perspective

M. A. BUSTEED

CLARENDON PRESS • OXFORD
1990

Oxford University Press, Walton Street, Oxford OX2 6DP
Oxford New York Toronto
Delhi Bombay Calcutta Madras Karachi
Petaling Jaya Singapore Hong Kong Tokyo
Nairobi Dar es Salaam Cape Town
Melbourne Auckland
and associated companies in
Berlin Ibadan

Oxford is a trade mark of Oxford University Press

Published in the United States
by Oxford University Press, New York

British Library Cataloguing in Publication Data
Busteed, M. A. (Mervyn Austen) 1944–
Voting behaviour in the Republic of Ireland : a
geographical perspective.—(Oxford research studies in
geography).
1. Ireland (Republic). Electorate. Voting
behaviour, history
I. Title
324.9417
ISBN 0–19–823276–4

Library of Congress Cataloging in Publication Data
Busteed, M. A. (Mervyn Austen) 1944–
Voting behaviour in the Republic of Ireland : a
geographical perspective/M. A. Busteed.
p. cm.—(Oxford research studies in geography)
Includes bibliographical references and index.
ISBN 0–19–823276–4
1. Elections—Ireland. 2. Voting—Ireland. 3. Ireland—Politics
and government—1949– 4. Geography, Political. I. Title.
II. Series.
JN1541.B87 1990 324.9417'0824—dc20 90–40178

Typeset by Graphicraft Typesetters Ltd., Hong Kong

Printed and bound in
Great Britain by Bookcraft (Bath) Ltd.
Midsomer Norton, Avon

To Helen, still my best political adviser

PREFACE

The years 1981–6 proved a decisive period in the political geography of the Irish Republic. During that time there were three general elections and two referenda. Taken together these events provided an intriguing opportunity to discover the dominant influences on Irish opinions, their relative strength, and spatial patterns. What was revealed was a dual Ireland. Traditionalist influences of history, family, locality, and Catholic Church emerged as still dominant, especially in the rural and small-town districts of the west and the midlands, but also to some extent in the long-established, urban, working-class areas of Dublin and Cork. But there also emerged a quite lively, liberal, secular Ireland, strongest in the urban areas and especially in the more middle-class districts of the Dublin region.

Such duality is not new in Ireland, nor is it confined to political and social geography. There have long been contrasts between rural and urban Ireland, and structural and geographical contrasts are also notable in industry and agriculture. However the political cleavages may be the most serious, because this study reveals that the country must somehow fully integrate a significant, vocal, liberal minority. Not since 1927 when the Fianna Fáil party, the political representatives of republicanism, decided to participate fully in the parliamentary system has the Irish state faced such a challenge.

ACKNOWLEDGEMENTS

I would like to express my thanks to all who have assisted in any way in the production of this book. Several generations of undergraduates in the School of Geography at Manchester University have been subjected to some of the material and have endured with patience and humour. My colleagues in the same department and the University authorities kindly agreed to allow me sabbatical leave for Summer and Michaelmas Terms 1987 and this enabled me to complete the research and writing up. The University Committee on Staff Travel Funds for Research in the Humanities and Social Sciences provided a grant which was used for a short stay in Dublin in July of that year when I was able to fill some gaps in data. I would like to express my thanks to the staff of the National Library in Kildare Street and the Government Publications Sales Office in Molesworth Street, Dublin, for their patience and assistance during that period. Various friends and acquaintances too numerous to mention individually also helped with suggestions and ideas. The maps and diagrams were drawn by Graham Bowden of the Drawing Office and the text was produced by the secretarial staff in the Manchester Geography Department. I appreciate all their work.

Finally I would like to thank my wife Helen for providing the index and constant encouragement. The dedication is no mere flattery.

Hale, Altrincham, Cheshire   M.B.
June 1988

CONTENTS

LIST OF FIGURES

LIST OF TABLES

Introduction

Between June 1981 and June 1986 the Republic of Ireland held three general elections and two referenda. These five events provided the raw material for a unique insight into the spatial patterns of public opinion. Never before in the history of the state had so many elections occurred within such a short time, to be followed within four years by two referenda. The opportunities for study were increased by the fact that all five polls used virtually the same pattern of constituency boundaries—indeed the first two elections were conducted using the same electoral register. In addition, there had been a census of population in 1981 and, with some adjustments (Appendix), parts of this data could be used in association with the election and referenda results.

In their studies of elections political geographers have concentrated on four features (Busteed, 1975; Johnston, 1979; Taylor and Johnston, 1979). First, the allocation of parliamentary seats and the drawing of constituency boundaries. These provide the basic spatial framework within which elections and referenda are organized and conducted. The way in which this framework is set up can influence the outcome of elections, either intentionally or by accident. In the Irish Republic redrawing of such boundaries was until 1977 in the hands of the incumbent government and it will be shown there is good prima-facie evidence to suggest that the process was gerrymandered, or manipulated for partisan ends. After 1977 however it was given over to a non-partisan commission and their scheme of seat and boundary allocation was the spatial framework for all five campaigns. The principles they followed and the way in which they interpreted them in practice are discussed in Chapter 2, along with the workings of Ireland's virtually unique electoral system.

A second preoccupation of electoral geographers has been the spatial pattern of seats and votes won by the various parties and the opinions expressed in referenda results. These in turn are related to aspects of the socio-economic milieu of the constituencies as revealed by census data and to the personal links of candidates to the localities and kinship networks of the constituencies they are contesting. Discussion of these factors is greatly assisted by the Irish electoral system, the variety of Proportional Representation known as the Single Transferable Vote (usually referred to simply as PR-STV). This will be outlined in Chapter 2, but its crucial feature for present purposes is that it allows voters to distinguish not merely between parties but also between candidates. When voters do this, a vast variety of factors come into play, including ideology, personality, kinship linkages, age, gender, and links with places within the constituency. The transfer of votes at various stages of the counting can reveal the impact of such factors. These spatial patterns will be discussed in Chapter 5. A further factor which can influence electoral choice is the spatial allocation of government expenditure. Sometimes this is allocated strictly by need or in accordance with non-political criteria, but there are also occasions when it is distributed as a reward to government supporters or to induce voters to look on the government more favourably. In particular, areas which are politically marginal may be encouraged to swing towards the government by judicious allocation of resources. In Ireland it has long been a widely accepted fact that both individual Dáil deputies (TDs) and governments do try to ensure that supporters or potential supporters are rewarded in this way. This will also be discussed in Chapter 5.

Constitutional change in Ireland can usually only occur after a referendum and in the period under review two referenda were held. They both concerned matters which were highly sensitive, especially in Catholic Ireland, namely abortion and divorce. Not only did they touch on personal values and behaviour, they were also matters on which the Catholic Church, to which 90% of the population claimed allegiance, had strong and distinctive teaching. Consequently, the referenda were significant as a test of the nature of the Church–state relationship in Ireland. The campaigns and their results showed how the majority of the population viewed that relationship, the balance of opinions within the country, the geography of those opinions, and the links with other aspects of Ireland's social, cultural, and economic geography. These are discussed in Chapter 6.

Elections and referenda in any country occur within a national context forged by historical experiences, both distant and more recent. Chapter 1 outlines the origin and nature of the Irish party system, placing it in the context of the Civil War of 1922–3 and the unwinding of events since then. These formative experiences have given the whole Irish party system a distinctive ethos, some of which persists, but each party has also experienced changes of emphasis over the years and these will also be examined. Such changes have largely been in response to changes in Irish society as a whole. Chapter 3 will look firstly at that society as it evolved in its rather insular and introverted fashion until the late 1950s, and then at the various forces which eroded this isolation and introduced a wider range of value systems and viewpoints. In Chapter 4 the events of

1977–83 will be discussed in particular detail since they provide the immediate context against which the three elections and two referenda campaigns were fought. In the Conclusion there will be an attempt to summarize the state of opinion in Ireland in the aftermath of these contests, with particular reference to their spatial patterns and their implications for the future of the Irish political system.

1

The Irish Party System

INTRODUCTION

The political parties of the Irish Republic have long provided a puzzle for outside observers because it seems that only one, the Labour Party, is instantly recognizable by West European norms, and it is by far the weakest of the three main parties. The normal reaction has been to regard Ireland as a deviant case not really fitting into any classification scheme (Carty, 1981).

Closer examination, however, reveals that this is not so. Many of the forms of Irish political life such as universal suffrage, free elections, parliamentary government, and the alternation of parties in office are close to West European models. Complication arises from the fact that they are found in association with a historical experience highly unusual by West European standards. The Irish republic experienced a long period of colonial rule, and only finally became an independent state as the result of a violent political revolution. This traumatic experience coincided with a massive extension of the franchise and provided the mould in which the country's political system was cast.

The Irish party system actually originated in a bitter difference of opinion over the form that independence should take and the nature of the new state's future political relationships with its former colonial master, Great Britain. The treaty setting out the terms of Ireland's independence was signed in December 1921. It gave the 26 counties of southern Ireland the status of a dominion within the British Commonwealth with the title 'Irish Free State'. Great Britain retained the right to occupy three naval bases and to use them in time of war, and the six north-eastern counties of Ulster were given the right to opt out of the Free State and remain within the United Kingdom, a right which they promptly exercised.

When the Irish delegates returned home with the Treaty the ensuing debate revealed a deep division of opinion within the hitherto united Sinn Fein party, which had carried the banner of the political campaign for Irish independence since 1917. Dáil Éireann voted in favour of the Treaty on 7 January 1922 by the rather narrow margin of 64 votes to 57, and only after protracted and at times bitter debate which saw erstwhile colleagues and comrades-in-arms accuse each other of treason (Lyons, 1973). Supporters of the

Treaty argued that it was the best agreement they could get under the circumstances. They pointed out that the alternative was a continuation of the warfare of 1919–21, a conflict which Irish forces were in no condition either to resume or to win. Moreover, they maintained, an immense amount had been gained: most of Ireland would now be free from British administration for the first time since the twelfth century, and while the precise form of that freedom was not ideal, it was sufficiently flexible to permit further evolution to a more satisfactory status.

The opponents of the Treaty directed their opposition on three levels. On purely pragmatic grounds they argued that it was a moot point whether Ireland would ever be able to stay out of any war in which Britain was involved when three Irish ports were being used as British naval bases. Moreover, 6 of the 32 counties were to remain under British rule. But their arguments were also voiced on grounds of almost mystical principle. For many in Sinn Féin the Irish Republic had come into existence when it was formally proclaimed at the outset of the 1916 Easter Rising, and the sufferings of both insurgents and civilians in battle and in prison during the rising and the war of independence had virtually sanctified the republic in blood (Fanning, 1983). Consequently, any settlement which left Ireland with less than full republican independence was seen as betrayal. These reactions focused in particular on the symbolic significance of the Oath of Allegiance to the British monarch which all members of Dáil Éireann would be required to take.

Despite strenuous efforts to avoid it, southern Ireland drifted towards civil war in the early months of 1922. The divisions over the Treaty sundered not merely Sinn Féin but also the Irish Republican Army which had waged the military campaign against British forces. When civil war did break out it lasted from June 1921 until May 1922 (Hopkinson, 1988; Younger, 1970). There were some notable casualties on both sides, the most outstanding being the Commanders-in-Chief of the pro- and anti-Treaty forces, Michael Collins and Liam Lynch. At a humbler level, the war is estimated to have caused 4,000 casualties and damage costing almost £50 million (Lyons, 1973). The most enduring legacy was probably created by the guerrilla warfare which the rapidly weakening anti-Treaty forces launched in August 1922. Their ambushes, assassinations, and destruction of government and private property angered the Free State government. They responded in Draconian fashion with internment of over 11,000 suspects and summary execution of 77, including some who had been notable in the recent war of independence against the British. The feelings roused by these events were to polarize and embitter Irish political life for generations (Manning, 1972), provoking uproar on the floor of the Dáil as late as the 1960s (Ayearst, 1971), and receiving mention by at least one candidate in the general election of November 1982 (Trench, 1982). The events of this period, the personalities involved, and their views and attitudes were to become heroic bench-marks for successive political generations on both sides and were to provide the crucible in which the main elements of the Irish party system crystallized (Fig. 1.1).

FIANNA FÁIL

Fianna Fáil, the dominant group in the Irish party system, is directly descended from the elements of Sinn Féin which opposed the 1921 Treaty with Great Britain and took the losing republican side in the civil war which followed (Fig. 1.1). The subsequent history of the party shows a remarkable evolution from what was originally a marginalized, fundamentalist political group with a militant and militaristic background into a political party with a broad pragmatic national appeal and an enviable record in winning elections (T. Gallagher, 1981). Between first entering the Dáil in August 1927 and November 1982 the party fought 19 general elections and formed the government after 13. On two occasions (1938 and 1977) it won an outright majority of the popular vote, a rare and difficult achievement in democratic politics.

The fifty-seven TDs who had voted against the Treaty in January 1922 subsequently withdrew from the Dáil under the leadership of Éamon de Valera on the grounds that it was no longer a legitimate assembly. They briefly attempted to set up an alternative administration but it drew little support. In the general election of June 1922 they gained 21.6% of the vote and 36 seats; in a further election of August 1923 they had 27.5% of the vote and 44 seats. In both cases however they refused to take up their seats.

At this point the more pragmatic elements in the anti-Treaty group began to reconsider their position. The attempt to set up an alternative government had failed and their electoral support seemed stagnant. Abstention began to appear a blind alley. Meanwhile the Free State government was proceeding to build up the new Irish state and the only opposition in the Dáil was coming from the small Labour and Farmers' Parties and independents. De Valera and his supporters began to consider the possibility of entering the Dáil if the need to take the Oath of Allegiance to the British monarch could be circumvented.

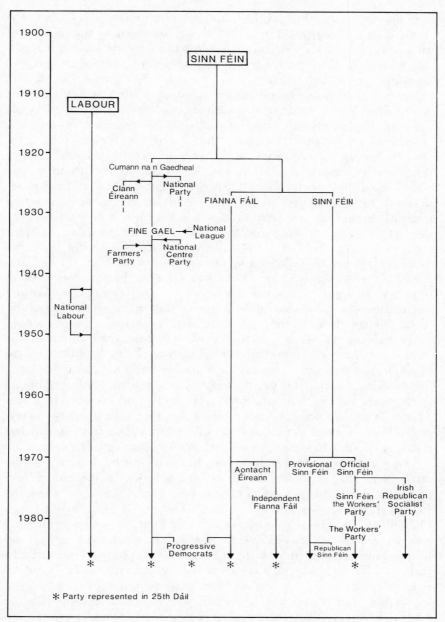

FIG. 1.1 Genealogical table of Irish political parties

However, when this proposition was put to the party's *ard-fheis*
(annual conference) in March 1926, it was wrecked by the passage of
an amendment which declared participation in the Dáil incompat-
ible with republican principle. Shortly afterwards de Valera resigned
from Sinn Féin and in May 1926 founded a new party, Fianna Fáil
(Soldiers of Destiny). Significantly, it was subtitled in English 'The
Republican Party' because although it represented the more flexible
wing of the movement, de Valera and his colleagues were still
convinced republicans, believing that all 32 counties of the island
should become a republic totally independent of Great Britain,
though if necessary associated with the Commonwealth in a way
which would not compromise Irish sovereignty. Alongside the prag-
matists some elements in the party had an evangelistic sense of
mission, believing they were engaged in an almost holy crusade to
save the nation's republican soul. Others were stiffened in their
resolve by memories of sufferings and hardships during both the
War of Independence and the more recent civil war (O'Faolain,
1980). Having set up the new party, it now had to be given a
nation-wide organization. In the next few years the party's leading
personalities criss-crossed the country setting up the party structure.
They benefited from their accumulated experience of ten years'
perpetual campaigning, and being able to take over much of the
existing infrastructure and personnel of Sinn Féin. Prominent local
republicans were key elements in founding the new party (Boland,
1982). Once won over to the idea of a constitutional republican
party their personal reputations plus family links were often sufficient to form a local branch (*cumann*) whose area usually corres-
ponded to the local parish. As a result Fianna Fáil, from its earliest
days, has had an extensive national grass-roots organization.

From the outset de Valera was the undisputed leader. As the
senior surviving officer of the 1916 Rising, former President of Sinn
Féin, the Irish Volunteers and the first Dáil, he was a towering
figure in the republican movement. (Dwyer, 1980; Longford and
O'Neill, 1970). Though he had many able lieutenants, his leadership
was never seriously questioned, and public solidarity, unity, and
unquestioning obedience to the leader became part of Fianna Fáil's
tradition. This could well have been the result of the party's military
and militant origins. Certainly the combination of strong central
leadership and thorough grass-roots organization became Fianna
Fáil trademarks. They were probably best seen during election campaigns when the party machinery became a byword for thorough
efficiency and, some would say, ruthlessness.

Just thirteen months after its foundation the party fought the election of June 1927, winning 26.1% of the vote and 44 seats. It had clearly captured the lion's share of the republican vote since Sinn Féin had only 3.6% of the vote and 5 seats. However, Fianna Fáil's total was still little better than the anti-Treaty vote of August 1923 and moreover it still could not enter the Dáil because of the Oath. The solution to this problem was taken out of the party's hands when Kevin O'Higgins, vice-president of the Executive Council, was assassinated in July 1927. The government responded with several pieces of legislation one of which declared that all Oireachtas (Dáil and Senate) candidates had to swear that if elected they would take any oath prescribed by the constitution or forfeit their seats. Fianna Fáil then formally entered the Dáil in August 1927 having signed the appropriate Dáil register. The election of September 1927 seemed to ratify their decision since their vote rose to 35.2% with 57 seats.

The government survived until 1932 with the votes of minor parties and independents but Fianna Fáil put the interim period to good use. Party organization was still being built up, funds were collected at home and supplemented by donations from Irish Americans and in September 1931 the pro-government monopoly in newspapers was broken when the *Irish Press* was founded (Longford and O'Neill, 1970). The opportunity was also taken to broaden the party's appeal. Hitherto it had largely been known for its stand on constitutional issues such as the demand for a republic, an end to partition, and abolition of the Oath. Now a broader appeal was planned. The result was a carefully crafted package of policies which had a philosophical and dynamic coherence and managed to appeal to almost everyone (Mansergh, 1934). The overarching emphasis was Irish independence on all fronts, political, cultural, and economic with the aim of enabling Ireland to live off her own material and spiritual resources. The resulting programme displayed an astute combined appeal to both patriotism and self-interest. Mindful of its strong support amongst the small farmers and Irish-speakers Fianna Fáil promised to encourage small-scale, family-based, arable farms and to pursue more rigorously the revival of Irish culture, especially the language. Farmers still buying out their holdings under the old British Land Acts would in future make their loan repayments to the Irish rather than British government. The same dual appeal to patriotism and self-interest was seen in industrial policy. It was proposed to apply the ideas of Arthur Griffith, founder of Sinn Féin, and stimulate Irish industrial development by imposing tariffs on all imported goods which Irish industry did, or could, produce. The prospect of producing for a guaranteed, protected market clearly appealed to the Irish business community. In addition, there were proposals to enable rural labourers to buy their own cottages, to keep rents low in urban areas, increase old-age pensions, accelerate the electrification programme, and reduce electricity charges (Moss, 1933).

The harvest of these preparations was to be seen in the general election of 1932. To some extent the outcome was the result of a tired government, barren of new ideas, losing the contest, just as much as of an aggressive and radical Fianna Fáil winning it. It is equally possible that no incumbent Irish government would have been re-elected against the background of the world economic depression. It is also true that since a world trend towards economic protection had set in, Fianna Fáil's economic programme seemed appropriate to the time. Whatever the reason, the party won 44.5% of the vote and 72 seats, not an overall majority but a considerable improvement on 1927 and enough to make it the largest party. Fianna Fáil therefore took office for the first time, with Labour support.

The new government set about putting its programme into action. It proceeded to abolish the Oath, downgrade the post of Governor-General, and suspend land annuity payments to Britain. The British government responded to this last measure by imposing a 20% tariff on all Irish goods entering Britain in order to recoup the money; the Irish government responded with a 20% tariff on British goods, and what was called the 'Economic War' had begun. It had unexpected results: by checking pastoral exports it reinforced the Irish government's appeal for more tillage. In political terms it stoked anti-British feeling and enabled de Valera to reappear in his original role of 1917–21, the champion of Irish interests against Britain (Williams, 1978). This may help explain the fact that when he suddenly called an election in January 1933 Fianna Fáil gained 49.7% of the vote and 77 seats, just enough for their first overall majority.

It was probably during this period that de Valera and Fianna Fáil were able to take the initiative and acquire a virtual monopoly in what became known as 'the national question', namely constitutional issues and relations with Britain. They continued with their task of dismantling the Treaty, abolishing the right of appeal to the British Privy Council in 1933, the Senate for a short period in 1936, and the post of Governor-General in June 1937. In the same year a new constitution was introduced which was republican in all but name. A general election at the same time as the referendum on the constitution saw Fianna Fáil's support decline to 69 seats and 45.2% of the vote but with independent support it remained in power. In spite of this electoral slippage, de Valera was becoming a truly national figure, personifying the historic Irish demand for national self-determination and Fianna Fáil was successfully presenting itself as the party of all true Irishmen dedicated to achieving total freedom for their country. Events of the next few years reinforced de Valera's status and the nationalist credentials of his party. Settlement of the 'Economic War' in 1938 brought considerable credit. There was no movement on partition, but it was agreed that the 20% tariffs should be lifted, Ireland should make a final payment of land annuities, and Britain should give up the three naval bases and all other facilities she had retained under the Treaty (Fisk, 1985). On the strength of this de Valera again went to the country and scored a major triumph, when Fianna Fáil gained 77 seats and a record 51.9% of the vote, its best ever. It also represented a significant stage in the party's development. By now its record in government had reconciled it to significant elements in Irish society. The years since 1932 had shown that in spite of its roots on the republican side in the Civil War and its radicalism on constitutional issues, the party consisted for the most part of people who were notably conservative on social and economic issues (Williams, 1978), were devout practising Catholics, and had totally distanced themselves from the extraparliamentary violence of Sinn Féin. Irish industry for its part experienced modest prosperity in this period and certain elements began to develop a close, enduring relationship with Fianna Fáil. The Catholic Church was more than happy to be unofficially consulted when the 1937 constitution was being drawn up (Chubb, 1982), to see some of its articles clearly based on Church teaching, and to see the government impose censorship on books, newspapers, and films (Whyte, 1980).

The stature of both de Valera and Fianna Fáil were further enhanced by Ireland's experiences during 1939–45. Eire remained neutral during the war but nevertheless it was a time of tension and strain, known as 'The Emergency'. There was no formal coalition though the opposition parties did take part in the National Defence Conference which dealt with problems arising from the situation. However, these years inevitably worked to the advantage of the incumbent government. It is generally believed that the policy of neutrality had widespread support across the political spectrum (Fisk, 1985). There was a tendency in this national crisis to close ranks; opposition could seem treasonable and in any case the opposition parties were somewhat compromised by membership of the Defence Conference.

But there is also evidence that during this period both Fianna Fáil and de Valera broadened their appeal to become almost national institutions. A general election in 1943 did see the party drop 10 seats and 10% of its record 1938 vote but another poll the next year took advantage of opposition disarray and saw the party back to 48.9% first preference votes and 76 seats, an overall majority of 7. Examination of this period reveals a decisive realignment of Irish electoral behaviour with the party extending out of its traditional regional stronghold of the west and rural areas to make substantial gains in urban and eastern Ireland (Garvin, 1981*a*), though there is evidence that progress in this direction had been made in the early 1930s. De Valera for his part gained enormously in prestige as the personification of Irish neutrality and the national leader whose diplomatic agility enabled the country to stay aloof from the conflict despite pressures from both the German and Allied sides (Murphy, 1975). By the mid-1940s therefore Fianna Fáil had established a remarkable position in Irish political life. It was now a truly national as well as a nationalist party, drawing strong, though not unvarying, support across the country from all groups, regardless of age, gender, class, occupation, or region. Moreover, it had also established the political equivalent of a moral ascendency in that it seemed to be the party of every true Irishman. Somehow not to vote Fianna Fáil seemed vaguely un-Irish and disloyal.

Nevertheless 1948 saw the party voted out of office for the first time since 1932. The explanation lies partly in the accumulated grievances of the war years, partly in the feeling it was time for a change, and partly in the loss of Fianna Fáil votes and seats to a new party, Clann na Poblachta (Manning, 1972; Murphy, 1975). However by 1951 the inter-party coalition which had replaced Fianna Fáil was visibly disintegrating (Lyons, 1973) and in the election of that year Fianna Fáil returned to power with the support of independents. It lost office again in 1954 and another coalition came to power. By 1958 however a combination of economic difficulties and the withdrawal of Clann na Poblachta support caused this second inter-party government to call an election which returned Fianna Fáil to power.

The party was now to be in office for another period of 16 years and during this time experienced some significant changes in personnel and emphasis. As in most revolutions, the generation of men who had come to prominence in the period 1916–26 had been relatively young and had dominated the subsequent political scene for generations. However, by the 1950s they were beginning to fade from politics. The transition was symbolized by the retirement of de Valera to the presidency in 1959 and his replacement as party leader and Taoiseach by Sean Lemass. Though himself a 1916 veteran and founder member of the party, Lemass took a pragmatic, managerial approach to affairs (B. Farrell, 1983) and it was under his leadership that significant changes occurred in Irish life and outlook (Lee, 1979*b*). The Republic began to lose its preoccupation with the Anglo-Irish relationship and relate more to the outside world at large. In 1958 the first of a series of plans for economic expansion was launched and the traditional policies of protection were steadily dismantled. Strenuous and successful efforts were made to attract foreign investment; Ireland applied to join the EEC and finally succeeded in 1973; a free trade agreement was signed with the United Kingdom in 1965; and a contingent of Irish troops was sent to serve with the United Nations in the Congo in 1960.

At home Fianna Fáil fought three elections between 1959 and 1969 and though only the last produced an outright majority, the governments of 1961 and 1965 were able to rely on the steady support of independents. During this period the nature and ethos of the party altered. The significance of the traditional nationalist appeal began to fade and was gradually replaced by a more pragmatic emphasis on economic management. The party laid increasing emphasis on a claim to superior skills in managing the Irish economy and its ability to provide stable one-party government (M. Gallagher, 1985). There appeared a new generation of government ministers (Manning, 1972) who had proved their skills in commerce, industry, and finance and were sometimes scathingly referred to as 'the mohair suit brigade' (D. Walsh, 1986). Close links were forged with some of the new industries which developed after 1958 but when efforts were made to institutionalize the relationship in a fund-raising group called Taca ('support'), suggestions of corruption caused the idea to be abandoned (Boland, 1982).

At a humbler level Fianna Fáil had always combined nationalist fervour with a realistic acknowledgement that voters required material provision as well as rhetoric. Its nationalist ideology did not really predetermine any attitude towards economic and social affairs beyond vague commitments to develop national resources and care for the population. Consequently, the party had no ideological inhibitions about launching state initiatives in economic development and constructing a welfare state. Some groups may have supported Fianna Fáil simply because it was so successful at winning elections and it was gratifying to be on the winning side. There is also some evidence that the rewards could be of a more substantive nature. It came to be widely believed that in the making of government appointments and placing of contracts, party supporters were favoured (Manning, 1972). The party thereby developed a certain

earthy populism and a strong voter orientation in all its policies
and this, together with its electoral success, gave it a reputation
for political astuteness which became a matter for some pride
and self-congratulation in being the only party which really understood the plain people of Ireland (D. Walsh, 1986). It also led it
to look upon its opponents with some contempt as political
amateurs.

Lemass had retired in 1966 and was replaced by Jack Lynch, a
compromise choice to avoid outright conflict between three powerful
contenders, Charles Haughey, George Colley, and Neil Blaney. In
some ways Lynch was well suited to the new ethos in the party. He
had no family background in the 1916–26 period or indeed in
politics at all: his early reputation was made as an outstanding
hurley player and gaelic footballer. His pleasant, affable, pragmatic
style was well suited to the broad-based, catch-all nature which the
party had evolved (Murphy, 1979). He led the party to a notable
electoral victory in 1969 when it gained 45.7% of the vote and 75
seats, an overall majority of one. However, in 1970 there occurred an
event which was to reverberate through Fianna Fáil for years to
come. In 1968 Northern Ireland had begun its long slide into political chaos. The response in the Republic was compounded of sympathy for the Irish nationalist minority and a reluctance to become
involved. However the crisis reminded some of the more traditionalist elements in Fianna Fáil of their party's roots and the unfinished
business represented by partition. Some party members were suspected of more than sympathy. On 5 May 1970 Lynch dismissed two
of his most powerful Cabinet Ministers, Blaney (Agriculture) and
Haughey (Finance), on the grounds that they had been involved in
illegally importing arms for use by nationalists in Northern Ireland.
The Minister for Justice, Michael O'Morain, had already resigned
48 hours previously and the same day as the dismissals the Minister
for Local Government, Kevin Boland, resigned in sympathy with
Blaney and Haughey and shortly afterwards his parliamentary
secretary followed his example.

It was an unparalleled trauma for Fianna Fáil, the party which
had made such great play at elections of its discipline, internal
solidarity, and faithfulness to its leader. In future such claims would
ring hollow. Of the dismissed ministers O'Morain disappeared from
public life when he lost his seat in 1973; Boland formed the strongly
republican Aontacht Éireann (Irish Unity) Party but made no electoral progress; Blaney and Haughey were later acquitted in court of
charges of illegally importing arms in October 1970. Blaney was
expelled from Fianna Fáil in November 1971 and was subsequently

returned as an independent for his constituency of Donegal North-East. Charles Haughey for his part stayed within the fold, keeping his own counsel, quietly working his way back into favour. By 1972 he had been elected a vice-president of the party, became honorary secretary in 1974, and in opposition was finally restored to the front bench when Lynch made him spokesman on Health also in 1974. In the course of his rehabilitation his cultivation of the grass roots and indeed his record in the Arms Trial had made him something of a hero for the party activists and the more traditional nationalistic elements in Fianna Fáil.

The 1973 general election saw Fianna Fáil gain votes over 1969 but lose seats and go out of office largely thanks to an agreement between Fine Gael and Labour over the exchange of lower preferences (Busteed and Mason, 1974). While in opposition Lynch carried out a thorough overhaul of party organization, finances, and policy, including the appointment of a new general secretary and the creation of a Fianna Fáil youth wing. The most significant policy change came on the economic front. Under the guidance of Dr Martin O'Donoghue the party went into the 1977 general election with an alluring, expansionist manifesto. It included attractive items such as the abolition of rates on dwelling houses and road tax on most cars and motor cycles. Economic expansion was to be financed initially by increased borrowing abroad but it was also assumed that the need for this would decrease as the 'pump priming' became effective and the private sector recovered to take up the new opportunities provided. Largely on the strength of this attractive programme and the revamped party machine, Fianna Fáil seized the initiative right from the outset in 1977 and won a startling victory with 50.6% of the vote, its second highest total, and 84 seats, to give a record majority of 20 over all other parties. In the new government Haughey was restored to favour, becoming Minister for Health and Social Welfare and O'Donoghue headed a new Department of Economic Planning and Development.

Overall, Fianna Fáil can be viewed as a remarkably successful party. From its foundation in 1926 until 1977 it fought 17 general elections and formed the government on 12 occasions. From first taking office in 1932 until 1977 its popular support only fell below 44% in 4 elections, it gained over 50% twice, it never lost a presidential election, and although it did not always have an overall majority in the Dáil, it never had to enter a formal coalition in order to form a government. Even when in opposition it was always the largest party in the Dáil and it never lost two successive elections.

The key to this glittering series of electoral successes lies in the party's ability to contain a vast range of potentially conflicting groups within its ranks. In its earliest days Fianna Fáil was noted for the strength of its support amongst the more traditionalist elements of rural, especially western, Ireland. Between 1933 and 1943 it broadened its base until by the latter date it was pulling in significant support right across the country (Garvin, 1978, 1981a). The party was able to hold this extraordinary coalition together even though it could legitimately be criticized for not really delivering on many of its original aspirations such as unification of the island, restoration of the Irish language, economic self-sufficiency, and preservation of the traditional, small-farm basis of Irish agriculture (T. Gallagher, 1981). This extraordinary achievement can be attributed to several factors, but above all perhaps to the enduring appeal of historic Irish nationalism, especially to the more traditionalist, conservative elements in Irish society. It is hard to imagine any force other than nationalism appealing across differences of class, age, gender, occupation, and region. The party has exploited this appeal with regularity and energy and successfully conveyed an image of standing in direct line of descent from all who have been involved in the historic Irish struggle for national independence. As such it has not hesitated on occasions to impugn the nationalist credentials of its opponents and to play upon anti-British sentiment. But the party has also realized that electors need more material inducements than nationalist rhetoric. It has never hesitated to supply these and the result is a party that is every bit as populist as nationalist. It has readily endorsed state intervention in the economy, embraced the welfare state, and been able to give such activities an appropriate nationalist gloss as examples of maximizing the use of native Irish resources and caring for the nation's people. The party has also contained in its ranks successive generations of deputies who have been masters of the art of clientelist politics, who have bound voters to themselves and the party by judicious application of pressure and influence upon the government bureaucracy, though just how effective such measures can be both in influencing allocation of resources and securing votes will be discussed later. The party has also been remarkably effective in mobilizing activists and voters at election times, thanks to an organizational structure which combines strong national leadership and a high level of committed, deferential grassroots activism. Overall, Fianna Fáil conveys an image of energy, efficiency, and experience together with an air of knowing self-confidence, secretiveness, and political cunning. It perceives itself, and is perceived, as being more in touch with the everyday realities of Irish voters than any other party.

FINE GAEL

The second most important party in the Irish system is Fine Gael. Like Fianna Fáil, it is a nationalist party, born out of the dispute over the 1921 Treaty and the subsequent Civil War, and it too still bears the marks of its early history.

The party had its roots in that more moderate element of Sinn Féin which had always been uncomfortable with some aspects of the 1919–21 military campaign (Lyons, 1973; Bell, 1979). Its deep-seated desire for a return to civic peace was a significant element behind support for the Treaty in the Dáil, in December 1921 and January 1922. When the Treaty was accepted and de Valera and his supporters resigned, the provisional government of the new Irish Free State was drawn entirely from Treaty supporters and, after the deaths of Arthur Griffith and Michael Collins in August 1922, was led by William T. Cosgrave.

When the Dáil met in September 1922, one of the new government's first acts was to appoint a whip to oversee passage of its parliamentary business and organize its voting strength. Strictly speaking there was still no formally organized party but this appointment encouraged government supporters to behave and think as if there were, and certainly there were frequent references in press and conversation to 'the Cosgrave party', 'the Ministry party', or 'the Treaty Party' (Manning, 1972). In December 1922 it was decided to begin organizing a formal party and it was launched in April 1923 under the title Cumann na n Gaedheal ('League of Gaels') (M. Gallagher, 1985).

The new party fought its first election just four months after its formal inauguration. It gained 39% of the vote and 63 seats, almost exactly comparable with pro-Treaty support at the 1922 election. It is difficult to be precise about the nature of its support base, but it is significant that in comparison with 1922 its vote declined in Connaught and the three Ulster counties and increased in the Dublin region. Most of its support seems to have come from groups who had most to lose from rejection of the Treaty and renewal of the war with Britain and most to gain from the restoration of peace and stability. Consequently from its earliest days the party gained support amongst the more prosperous elements in the community: the large farmers, those involved in commerce and trade, the urban middle-classes (Manning, 1972). They were to give the party a characteristic emphasis from the outset.

Cumann na n Gaedheal was to provide the governments of the young Irish Free State for the first ten years of its existence, and its experiences and responses during this period were to be as formative for the party as for the country. One of the most significant problems centred on the question of law and order. The party had been founded in the middle of a civil war, when both a new army and a police force were still being created, and during which it saw Arthur Griffith and Michael Collins, its two most able leaders, struck down, one by illness and the other in ambush. The government responded with a fearful ferocity. Believing the whole political and social fabric of Irish society to be under threat, it used internment and summary execution on a scale even the British had not dared employ between 1919 and 1921 (Lyons, 1973). Nor did the succeeding years bring total stability. The Civil War ended in 1923, but the IRA remained in the background, contemptuous of all politics, refusing to recognize the new political structures in Ireland, and dedicated to ending them by force. As for the main opposition party, up until 1927 at least it seemed unsure whether it really believed in parliamentary methods and one of its senior members, Sean Lemass, put his finger on the ambivalent attitudes of many of his colleagues when the following year he described Fianna Fáil as 'a slightly constitutional party' (B. Farrell, 1983). On top of all this, the government was severely shaken in 1924 when some officers in the National Army, unhappy at their reduced peacetime status and numbers and the slow progress towards a full republic, staged a mutiny and the Minister of Defence resigned.

Against this background successive Cumann na n Gaedheal governments stressed the importance of security, law and order, and respect for the constitution and these became characteristics of the party outlook. Unfortunately on occasions it was also true that they over-reacted to perceived threats and introduced Draconian legislation which in the end seemed to threaten the liberty of the subject more than did the dangers they were trying to put down. This trend reached a climax in the early 1930s when a combination of economic distress and an IRA resurgence led, in October 1932, to the banning of twelve republican or left-wing groups and their publications and the setting up of a five-man Military Tribunal to deal with political crime. To the alarm of many it was given the right to pass death sentences and the only appeal was to the Executive Council (Cabinet). Even more alarming, as well as politically inept, was the decision just before the 1932 election to prosecute the editor of the pro-Fianna Fáil *Irish Press* for treason before the Military Tribunal. This tendency to overreact on such issues was to remain in the party ethos.

During these ten years successive governments were much taken up with constructing all the basic institutions of the new Irish state and the experience was to give the party a characteristic emphasis, even an obsession, with efficiency, economy, and balanced books. Following independence the Irish police force, armed forces, civil service, and judiciary were either organized for the first time or adopted from British predecessors. The new Irish state in these early days was not a wealthy country, and these tasks had to be achieved out of very limited resources and therefore with a minimal outlay. The economic orthodoxy of the day also preached the virtues of parsimony in public spending and this doctrine was followed faithfully by the new government. Part of the explanation for this emphasis may have lain in the personal backgrounds of government members in commerce and the professions, but part may have been due to the fact that the tasks at hand were so vast. Given the dimension of these tasks, it seems highly likely that ministerial oversight was cursory and the civil servants made many key decisions and set the precedents (Fanning, 1983). They may characteristically have taken a cautious line, because many had served under the old British administration and would simply follow established custom. Moreover, in the early days several were seconded from London to set up new departments such as Defence, External Affairs, and Industry and Commerce and in so doing followed orthodox British administrative models and values (Chubb 1982).

But it is also true that as time went on the new state's governments seemed to lack vision. The loss of Griffith and Collins so early on removed the two most imaginative and adventurous individuals from the pro-Treaty ranks and the assassination of O'Higgins in 1927 removed the only person who seemed to be graduating to such stature. Those who were left were able and sincere, but they lacked flair. As time went on they seemed to become preoccupied with administration and appeared to lose touch with political realities. This lack of political sensitivity could lead them into measures which offended significant sections of the electorate or appeared unfeeling. Just before the general election of 1932 for example the government proposed to reduce old-age pensions, to cut the salaries of the Garda Siochana (which had been in the forefront of the struggle against republican subversion), and to reduce the salaries of teachers and ban married women from the profession (Moss, 1933). At a stroke it had offended three vital interest-groups who normally supported it. It was evidence of a remoteness and lack of political common sense which were to become all too characteristic (Nowlan, 1978).

By the early 1930s the party had also lost the initiative to Fianna Fáil on all issues relating to the status of Ireland as an independent state, relations with Britain, and partition. It was widely known that Fianna Fáil wanted to proceed towards a full sovereign republic as quickly as possible: this message was simple, explicit, and easily comprehended. Potentially, Cumann na n Gaedheal had an equally dynamic message, that the Treaty settlement could be made to evolve towards greater independence and eventually a republic, as actually happened. However, the killing of Collins and O'Higgins removed the two most able exponents of this evolutionary interpretation of the Treaty. Increasingly, their colleagues adopted a defensive attitude and drew back to a view of the Treaty and Commonwealth membership as marking the furthest limits of Irish independence rather than as starting points for further progress. In adopting this stance they were at a double disadvantage. In the first place the Treaty was a compromise and even some of its supporters were not entirely happy with it. Compromises are always difficult to defend from passionate conviction since they are always second best. Opponents of the Treaty by contrast could attack without reservation, enjoying all the assurance and conviction of republican purity. But Treaty supporters were also at a disadvantage in that they were compelled to defend a continuing association with Britain, emphasized in such things as the Oath of Allegiance, appeal to the Privy Council, the post of Governor-General, and membership of the Commonwealth. In so doing, they cut themselves off from that vein of anti-British sentiment which has always been present in Irish nationalism and was now increasingly to nourish Fianna Fáil and give it the image of the only really nationalist party. Perhaps the point where Cumann na n Gaedheal began to lose the claim to be a legitimate spokesman for Irish national aspirations came with the fiasco over the Boundary Commission in 1925. The Commission had been set up under the 1921 Treaty to review the boundary between the Free State and Northern Ireland. Its inclusion seems to have been one of the key factors inducing Collins to sign the Treaty since it was widely expected to recommend the transfer of so much territory and population to the Free State that Northern Ireland would become unviable and compelled to merge with the 26 counties (Laffan, 1983). Just before its official report was presented, the Commission's findings were leaked to the Conservative *Morning Post* newspaper on 7 November 1925. The disclosure proved a grave embarrassment to the Irish government because it was claimed the Commission would recommend only minor border adjustments, including some transfers of territory to Northern Ireland. The British and Irish governments agreed to suppress the report, accept the existing border, and waive some financial payments that the 1921

Treaty had committed the Irish government to make to London (Andrews, 1960, 1968; Hand, 1969). It was a depressing and disillusioning experience for the Irish government. The last realistic chance of achieving reunification in the foreseeable future had gone and to some observers it seemed the Free State claim to the North had been bought off by the financial agreement.

Thus the party faced the challenge of Fianna Fáil in 1932 in a somewhat depressed, defensive mood, lacking in ideas and possibly exhausted by ten years of state-building. It also lacked discipline and organization. From quite early on Cumann na n Gaedheal had a tradition of independent-minded ill-discipline amongst its TDs. To some extent this was illustrated by the breakaway of nine deputies over the army mutiny in 1924 and a further three in 1926 over the Boundary Commission. But it was not unusual to find even Cabinet Ministers differing in public over more mundane matters, most notably tariffs. The reasons lay partly in the personal backgrounds of the party's personnel, partly in the party's origins. Many in the party were men of reasonable means, well educated, with notable records in the 1917–23 period. They therefore enjoyed security, confidence, and independence and carried these qualities into politics. But the fissiparous nature of the party was also increased by the lack of any overall political, social, or economic philosophy. The party was held together by only one central principle—support for the Treaty. Beyond that its members had little in common and it was hardly surprising that they went their own ways on many issues. In so doing, they established a tradition of ill-discipline which carried over into Fine Gael.

The lack of philosophical coherence was complemented by poor party organization at the grass roots, especially when it came to electoral campaigning. Unlike Fianna Fáil, Cumann na n Gaedheal originated amongst a group of individuals already inside the system who were heavily involved in state-building for the first nine years or so of the party's existence. This created a party organization which was élitist, haphazard, and personalized. The party machine was created from the top down, with greater emphasis on leadership than grass-roots organization, which always tended to be thin and patchy. There are indications that, whether from choice or preoccupation with government, leading members of the party were impatient with the comparatively mundane tasks of electioneering (M. Gallagher, 1985). What actually happened at election times was that government TDs and Ministers put together their campaign machinery only after the Dáil had been dissolved. The necessary workers and structures were supplied by personal friends and relatives. Once the contest was over the machinery went into abeyance and between elections the party organization at constituency level was almost non-existent. It also meant that whatever structure did exist was centred on the TD rather than the party and this in turn increased the personal independence of successful candidates since they could justifiably claim to have been elected by their own efforts rather than those of the party. The overall result of these tendencies was to give Cumann na n Gaedheal, and later Fine Gael, justified reputations for élitism and poor organization which lasted well into the 1970s. Too often the party seemed to consist of genteel, amateur part-timers. On occasion the contrast with the superbly co-ordinated Fianna Fáil machine was painfully obvious.

The party was defeated in both the 1932 and 1933 general elections. The latter experience acted as a catalyst on some suggestions which had been circulating that Cumann na n Gaedheal should link up with some of the other groups opposed to Fianna Fáil (Manning, 1972). In the end a union was achieved in September 1933 and the new party was named Fine Gael ('tribe of the Irish'). It consisted of Cumann na n Gaedheal, the Centre Party, some independents, and the National Guard, which supplied the new leader, General Eoin O'Duffy. This last group had grown out of the Army Comrades Association, formed in 1931 by ex-members of the Free State Army. It frequently provided stewards at pro-Treaty election meetings and often came into violent conflict with IRA supporters. They proved a dubious asset. As time passed they began to resemble continental fascist movements, both in their rhetoric and their adoption of a blue-shirt uniform (Manning, 1970; Thornley, 1978). O'Duffy proved himself unstable, unreliable, and totally lacking in political judgement. In September 1934 he was finally forced to resign and Cosgrave replaced him as leader in March 1935.

The whole episode severely damaged the new party. Its reputation as a party of law and order was badly dented and the fascist overtones of the Blueshirts were to become an uncomfortable historical legacy, raked up by opponents even in the 1980s. The party in fact lost the initiative in the 1930s. As Fianna Fáil proceeded to dismantle the Treaty and widen the parameters of Irish sovereignty Fine Gael was placed in a dilemma. It could not really endorse the constitutional changes because its opponents could then ask why they had not carried them out between 1922 and 1932. Nor could it condemn them because that would give the appearance of being pro-British and opposed to the extension of Ireland's freedom. Consequently, though Fine Gael's vote rose in the 1937 election, it came nowhere near being able to form a government and in any case it

lost ground in the 1938 election. The 'Emergency' of 1939–45 compounded the party's problems. Public opinion, and most members of
Fine Gael, supported the neutrality policy, but none the less as the
party of Treaty and Commonwealth there were conflicts of loyalty
for some. Furthermore, the party took part in the National Defence
Council and this also limited its freedom to criticize government
policy. But the most inhibiting factor was the national tendency to
close ranks behind the incumbent government in a time of crisis. It
made any criticism seem ill-timed and possibly disloyal. The result
was that this period became the absolute nadir of the party's fortunes. In the general elections of 1943 and 1944 its vote fell to 23.1%
and then 20.5%. Leading personalities lost their seats and one,
James Dillon, was forced to resign from the party in 1942 for advo-
cating that Ireland enter the war on the allied side. On some occasions the party actually had to refrain from contesting by-elections
because it could not find suitable candidates (M. Gallagher, 1985).

At the general election of 1948 the party suffered a further decline
in votes to 19.8% but its first experience of government in 16 years,
albeit as part of a multi-party coalition, was to mark the beginning
of a gradual revival in fortunes. The mere fact that Fianna Fáil had
been turned out of office checked the argument that a vote against
them was wasted. It also seems likely that since Fine Gael had 6 of
the 13 Cabinet posts it gathered the lion's share of the patronage and
publicity which came with office. But possibly the greatest long-term
boost came from the decision to declare a republic and leave the
Commonwealth in 1949. Henceforward the traditional Fianna Fáil
jibes that Fine Gael was unsound on the national question would
ring less true, though this was not to prevent them being heard even
in the early 1980s (Boland, 1984; Trench, 1982).

The 1951 election saw the defeat of the inter-party government,
though Fine Gael's vote actually rose to 25.8% and it gained 9 seats.
The 1954 contest saw a further gain of 10 seats. The party again
went into coalition but its increasing dominance of opposition ranks
was shown when it took 8 of the 13 Cabinet seats and when the
Department of Gaeltacht was formed in 1956 it took that portfolio as
well. However, the higher profile inevitably meant that when things
went wrong the party took the largest share of the blame. A worsen-
ing economic situation was met by some unpopular government
restrictions on expenditure and credit which helped produce record
unemployment and emigration. The outbreak of the 1956–62 IRA
campaign was met by strict security measures and caused the small
Clann na Poblachta Party to withdraw its support from the coalition. At the ensuing general election early in 1957 Fine Gael lost

5.4% of the vote and 10 seats, and went out of office. However, despite its undoubted defeat, the gradual erosion of the smaller parties which had emerged in the 1940s now left Fine Gael as the chief opposition party.

In October 1954 there was a change of leader. W. T. Cosgrave had been replaced by General Richard Mulcahy in 1944 but because of his controversial role in the Civil War he had not been nominated as Taoiseach in 1948 or 1954 and John Costello had served instead. The replacement as leader was James Dillon, son of the last leader of the old Irish Parliamentary Party, who had been readmitted to Fine Gael in 1952 after his wartime expulsion. Under his leadership Fine Gael settled comfortably into the role of the party of moderation and common sense. True to its traditions, it espoused the causes of law and order and sound, economical administration. Given this ethos, it gradually took on a conservative, right-wing image. In terms of policy ideas it lacked imagination or constructive thinking and seemed content merely to criticize Fianna Fáil and wait for the government to make mistakes. Consequently, while the party's total of votes and seats gradually drifted upwards in successive elections, there was little sign of a large-scale breakthrough. This ethos of comfortable, somewhat old-world stagnation spurred on a small group of liberals who had gradually been coalescing around John Costello's son, Declan. Described as social democratic in outlook, they were advocates of the application of current ideas on economic planning to the Irish economy. After vigorous discussion in May 1964 the party accepted some of those ideas as the basis for policy and set up a committee to work out details. However, this had not yet reported when the 1965 general election was called. A policy document 'Planning for a Just Society' which drew heavily on the committee's work was hurriedly accepted as the framework for Fine Gael's programme but some of the more senior elements in the party did little to hide their distaste for it (Lyons, 1973).

The 1965 general election saw another increase in votes but no gain in seats. Dillon resigned as leader and was replaced by Liam Cosgrave, son of the former Taoiseach. Initially things went quite well for the party. Its candidate in the 1966 presidential election, Dr T. F. O'Higgins, came within 10,568 votes of defeating de Valera and when the government tried to adopt the British first-past-the-post electoral system in a referendum in October 1968 Fine Gael campaigned vigorously and successfully against it. Some effort was also put into reorganization and recruitment. However, the 1969 general election was something of a disappointment. A recent resurgence in Labour strength, together with the new ideas circulating in

Fine Gael, led some to believe a Fianna Fáil defeat was a serious possibility. In fact, the government was returned with increased votes and seats and its first overall majority since 1957. Fine Gael gained three seats, but its vote was unchanged, which seemed meagre reward for all the hopes and efforts.

The experience had two results. Some elements in the party began to think of a change of leader. Cosgrave was very much in his family and party tradition, cautious, conservative, sceptical of social and economic reform, and much concerned with law and order (Arnold, 1984; Manning, 1979). At the party *ard-fheis* in 1972 he pointedly defied and threatened his critics (M. Gallagher, 1985). Later in the year he isolated himself when he supported government emergency legislation to deal with IRA activities in the Republic. For a time it seemed he was about to be toppled but when there were bomb explosions and serious casualties in Dublin itself in December 1972, the party swung in behind him and voted for the bill (Manning, 1979). The 1969 result had also revived serious thinking within Fine Gael about another coalition arrangement with Labour. Despite the party's progress since 1961 it was still nowhere near being able to form an alternative to Fianna Fáil on its own. Significantly, some elements within Labour were also beginning to think along the same lines and there were some tentative, desultory contacts between the two parties.

In February 1973 Jack Lynch called a snap general election, possibly hoping that the recent discontents within Fine Gael and the incomplete state of the negotiations with Labour would catch the Opposition on the wrong foot. However, the prospect of an election concentrated minds. Fine Gael and Labour produced a Joint Programme of 14 points concentrating on economic issues and campaigned as allies, each encouraging its supporters to give later preferences to the other. This joint approach had a decisive effect on the result; while Fianna Fáil's vote actually rose by 0.5%, the exchange of lower preferences between the two allies meant the government lost 6 seats, and Labour and Fine Gael gained 5 and went on to form a National Coalition with an overall majority of 2 (Busteed and Mason, 1974).

The new government had the advantages of considerable public goodwill and several very able people in its ranks. It steered Ireland through its first years of EEC membership and played a constructive role in the Sunningdale Conference of December 1973 which set up a short-lived Northern Ireland executive drawn from both nationalist and unionist representatives. However, external events soon created difficulties. In common with the rest of the western world, Ireland felt the impact of the trebling of oil prices by the end of 1973. Inflation and unemployment began to rise. The government struggled to cushion the effect on more vulnerable elements in society but it was also forced to bring in a capital gains tax and direct taxation of farmers, alienating two groups of traditionally staunch Fine Gael supporters.

In fact, many of the Coalition's troubles were of its own making. One of the most bizarre and damaging episodes came when the Minister of Defence publicly referred to the President as 'a thundering disgrace' because he had exercised his right to refer a contentious security bill to the Supreme Court before signing it into law. President O'Dalaigh resigned and was replaced by an unopposed Fianna Fáil nominee. The whole episode was deeply damaging to Fine Gael as a party which had made deference to state institutions one of its characteristic features. But more self-inflicted damage and ridicule were to follow. In 1973 the Supreme Court had ruled that the state had no right to intervene in the private life of a married couple, including their right to choose a means of family planning. In response to this decision, the Coalition decided to introduce a bill amending Ireland's restrictive laws on contraception and allowing the sale of contraceptives to married couples. To the total surprise of his Cabinet colleagues the Taoiseach voted with Fianna Fáil against his own government's bill. He was joined by another Cabinet member and five Fine Gael TDs and the measure was lost. It was an embarrassing public demonstration of disunity and lack of communication.

Traditional Fine Gael preoccupations with security and subversion also reappeared. The Northern Ireland power-sharing executive which had been agreed at Sunningdale collapsed in May 1974 and the troubles in the North occasionally spilled over into the Republic culminating in the assassination of the British Ambassador in July 1976. The government responded with a range of measures, including a declaration of national emergency, extension of the period for which people suspected of subversive activities could be detained before being charged, and more frequent use of road blocks and patrols in sensitive areas. But they also went beyond these rather orthodox measures into areas which caused concern about civil liberties. The section of the Broadcasting Act which forbade the Irish broadcasting service (RTE) to give publicity to members of illegal or subversive groups was vigorously enforced. At a more informal level, it was alleged that some members of the Garda, encouraged by the government's hardening line on security, became less scrupulous in their choice of suspects to arrest and in their treatment under interrogation. It was also alleged that a particular group of Garda officers were very robust indeed in their methods (Dunne and Kerrigan, 1984). The experience resurrected traditional fears about Fine Gael's authoritarian attitudes.

The Coalition entered the 1977 general election in confident mood, buoyed up by the first experience of office since 1957, a good series of by-election results, and some judicious redrawing of constituency boundaries (Arnold, 1984; Farrell and Manning, 1978). In fact, they were grotesquely ill-prepared and Fine Gael's traditional amateurism in electoral campaigning was seen at its worst. Preoccupied with government, the leaders had neglected the party machinery and positively discouraged organizational reforms or policy rethinking. The Coalition manifesto gave the impression of being hurriedly put together, consisting largely of a defence of the record since 1973, and containing few new ideas. The two parties had lost the initiative to Fianna Fáil who had spent a considerable time preparing both its campaign and its programme (Farrell and Manning, 1978). Liam Cosgrave's campaign epitomized the state of Coalition affairs: details of his speaking tour were not widely divulged and when he contracted laryngitis the tour had to be suspended half-way through.

Despite this situation, there was a general expectation that the Coalition would be re-elected. However this was to ignore the fact that successive opinion polls since January 1976 had shown a Fianna Fáil lead (Sinnott, 1978). The polls were proved correct. Fianna Fáil scored a famous victory and Fine Gael suffered a heavy defeat. Its vote fell by 4.6% to 30.5% and its seats to 43, the worst result since 1957. It lost particularly heavily in Leinster where it was believed the taxation of farmers had alienated many traditional supporters but ironically the redrawing of constituency boundaries had backfired. Many marginal seats had been created but the swing meant that they went to Fianna Fáil.

The extent of the party's defeat was such that the leadership inevitably came into question. One week after the election, Cosgrave abruptly announced his resignation. There was some vague discussion about several candidates but informal soundings quickly revealed that one stood out far above the others, namely Dr Garret FitzGerald, closely identified with the liberal wing of the party and fresh from outstanding service as the Minister for Foreign Affairs. On 1 July 1977 he was elected unopposed as leader of Fine Gael.

Such an overview of the fortunes of Fine Gael endorses Manning's (1972) comment that it could not really be described as a very successful party. In the years between 1933 and 1977 it had only been in power on three occasions and even then only as the senior partner in coalitions. Never in its history has the party formed a government on its own, though it is undoubtedly the largest single opposition party and an indispensable element in any non-Fianna Fáil administration. It has been dogged by problems of history and image. Given its background, it is hardly surprising that by the late 1970s it had a rather stuffy, old-fashioned, wealthy, middle-class air. Its outlook seemed dated, its organization amateurish, its attitudes authoritarian and indeed slightly contemptuous of ordinary people and the rough and tumble of politics. In policy terms it seemed sterile with no really exciting ideas capable of firing the imagination. Amongst the public at large it had no very clear image (T. Gallagher, 1981): it merely seemed a smaller, less clear-cut, less successful, shadow of Fianna Fáil. It also gave the impression that at times it was quite content with the status of chief opposition party since this provided opportunities for detached, olympian comment on the errors of the government. Overall the party seemed to lack the hungry drive for power which was so marked a feature of Fianna Fáil.

LABOUR PARTY

Labour is the oldest of the main Irish political parties, having been founded at the 1912 Conference of the Irish TUC, which passed a resolution declaring that the separate representation of Labour interests on public bodies was highly desirable (M. Gallagher, 1985). Of all the Irish parties it is the one most recognizable to British observers. In Ireland however, it is the weakest of the main parties, and its imminent demise is predicted at regular intervals (Magill, 1985; Van Hatten, 1985).

The Labour Party has been represented in every Dáil since 1922. To date its performances have varied from 5.7% of the vote (1933) and 7 seats (1932) to 17% of the vote (1969) and 22 seats (June 1927, 1965). It had served in three governments up to 1977, but always as the junior partner in coalitions. Despite its aspirations and conference rhetoric it has rarely seemed likely to replace any of the main parties. This relative weakness has attracted a volume of analysis disproportionate to the party's size and significance (e.g. B. Farrell, 1969–70; M. Gallagher, 1982; Mitchell, 1974; Mair, 1977–8). The chief explanation for the party's relative unimportance in the Irish political system lies in the basic nature of the Irish political culture. The primary historic cleavage in Irish politics has always been on nationalistic and constitutional issues. Consequently, a party which has always put economic and social issues to the forefront of its campaigning has very limited appeal. Labour has trouble even retaining that small section of the electorate who do vote for it against the nationalistic, populist appeal of other parties and Fianna Fáil in particular.

But it is also true that Labour is the party which has suffered most from partition and emigration. The partitioning off of the 6 north-eastern counties in 1921 removed Ireland's largest single concentration of industrial workers, the group which in most countries provides the natural electoral base for a Labour party. Moreover, those industries which were within the Free State boundaries were small-scale family firms, never a fertile breeding-ground for Labour politics. Even this group was further diminished when emigration set in during the late 1930s since it removed a disproportionate number of the unskilled and semi-skilled workers.

Labour also has to contend with an Irish social ethos which is at best conservative and certainly not conducive to radical ideas on social and economic change. The reason for such conservatism may lie in Ireland's lack of a classic nineteenth-century industrial revolution of the type which transformed the economy, social realtions, and intellectual atmosphere of much of Western Europe. It may also lie in the process of emigration which by definition drains away those elements of a population which are younger, more energetic, and least reconciled to existing economic conditions.

It has also been suggested that southern Ireland's devout Catholicism has reinforced the conservative bias of the political culture. Certainly the Roman Catholic Church has always been wary of revolutionary political movements, from the Fenians of the 1860s to the republicans of the Civil War. From 1917 onwards it was also intensely opposed to communism and by extension even the mildest form of parliamentary socialism came under suspicion. This created fertile ground for Labour's political opponents who as late as 1969 were happy to imply that the party was in reality a stalking-horse for sinister leftists. The result was to give Labour a recurrent identity problem. If it became too left-wing in outlook it risked condemnation from the Church; if it became too moderate it risked too close a resemblance to existing parties.

But to some extent Labour's difficulties have been self-inflicted. Its origin as a party created by and for trade unionists gave the impression that it was only concerned with advancing union interests and was not concerned with broader aspects of social and economic reform. This tended to repel people who, whilst of a radical disposition, did not necessarily identify with trade-unionism.

It was not until 1930 that the party became organizationally distinct from the ITUC. Some commentators have also argued that the party made grave tactical errors in its early days when it decided not to contest the general elections of 1918 and 1921 (B. Farrell, 1969–70). Since both contests were virtually referenda on the independence issue, Labour leaders argued that to put up candidates campaigning on social and economic issues would be unpatriotic and confusing. However, it has also been pointed out that in 1918 the franchise had just been extended to include all males over 21 and all women over 30 (Garvin, 1977–8). Consequently, Labour missed its chance to present its case at a vital formative stage in the evolution of Irish political culture.

But it is also true that the party has weakened itself by an endemic tendency to factionalism. For almost the first 30 years of its life it was divided by internal disputes between revolutionaries, personified by James Larkin founder of the Irish Transport and General Workers' Union and William O'Brien, the union's general secretary. So bitter did the quarrel become that between 1944 and 1950 Labour split into two distinct parties and reunification only came about with Larkin's death in 1947 and the experience of working together in the inter-party government of 1947–51. Though the personality clash was ended, differences over tactics persisted, particularly on the question of whether the party should serve in coalition governments.

Pro-coalitionists argue that while the aspiration of Labour to become a majority party is fine in the long run, for the foreseeable future it is likely to remain a minor third party. In such circumstances it is argued the only way the party can hope to influence governments and see at least some of its ideas translated into legislation is by entering coalition. Anti-coalitionists argue that such alliances are always dominated by the larger, more conservative parties, that they blur Labour's distinctive image, and that the party has little in the way of legislation to show for its periods in government. Indeed, they argue that the party has almost always lost votes and seats after serving in coalitions and that its greatest recent triumphs in terms of seats (1965) and votes (1969) have come when it has definitely pledged itself to stand alone. Conversely, they point to the fact that since the decision of the special conference of December 1970 to adopt a more open mind on future coalitions, the party totals of votes and seats have steadily declined.

The record of the Labour Party falls into a number of distinct phases. From the general election of 1922 until August 1927 Labour, in the absence of Fianna Fáil, provided the most sustained, coherent opposition to the Cumann na n Gaedheal governments (Manning,

1972; Nevin, 1978), constantly stressed economic and social issues, and played a key role in establishing the Dáil as a genuine forum of parliamentary debate (M. Gallagher, 1985). The second phase covers the period 1927–37. The entry of Fianna Fáil into the Dáil in August 1927 meant that it became the chief opposition party and Labour became the third and relatively minor party. The subsequent election of September 1927 polarized the electorate on the Treaty issue and all minor parties were squeezed. Labour was reduced to 9.1% of the vote and 13 seats. It also had to work out its attitude to Fianna Fáil. Partly because of the increasing conservatism and cost-cutting of the government and partly because it felt genuinely sympathetic towards some of the more populist socioeconomic elements in its programme, Labour generally tended to side with Fianna Fáil (Murphy, 1975). Indeed, when de Valera was first elected Taoiseach by the Dáil in 1932, the votes of the Labour TDs and some independents were necessary. Up until the late 1930s Labour generally continued to support Fianna Fáil on such measures as housing, income tax increases, tariffs, and constitutional reform (Manning, 1972; Nevin, 1978). Indeed, something like an informal pact seemed to develop and in the general election of 1933, Labour lost votes but gained a seat, thanks to the transfer of lower preferences from Fianna Fáil supporters (M. Gallagher, 1978–9).

But this closeness to Fianna Fáil was giving the party a long-term identity problem. Fianna Fáil's mixture of nationalism combined with populism on economic and social issues was stealing both Labour's thunder and its potential support base. It was during this period that Fianna Fáil managed to capture the largest share of the Irish working-class vote, a grip which has never significantly loosened. Partly in an effort to establish a more distinct identity, Labour adopted a new constitution in 1936 with more explicitly leftist aspirations, but the acceptable limits of socialism in Ireland were demonstrated when the Catholic hierarchy made clear its objections to some of the wording and it was amended in 1939 (Manning, 1978; Whyte, 1980).

The next period in Labour's development covers approximately 1937–57. Fianna Fáil's failure to deliver on some of its programme, most notably land redistribution, and the fact that it seemed increasingly comfortable with many of the established interests in Irish society, led to Labour distancing itself from its former associate. The 1937 general election marked a revival in the party's fortunes with a notable increase in both votes and seats. It slid back somewhat in terms of seats the following year and for the first time did not vote for de Valera as Taoiseach. The period of the Emergency between

1939 and 1945 initially gave Labour a considerable boost. Lacking Fine Gael's pro-Commonwealth background, it could be uninhibited in support of neutrality and was also able to capitalize on the grumbling public discontent about the inevitable shortages and rationing (Murphy, 1969). It was also able to capitalize on the resentment caused by the government's heavy-handed restrictions on wages and its efforts to curb trade-union activity. The revival of the party was seen in striking gains in the 1942 local elections, increased numbers of branches and members, and a marked rise in both votes and seats in the 1943 general election. For the first time voices were heard in Fine Gael suggesting a coalition with Labour (Manning, 1979).

However, the promise of this period was crushed when the dispute between Larkin and O'Brien entered its most virulent phase. Amidst accusations of a red take-over of the main party, five sitting Labour TDs broke away and formed National Labour. Noting this disarray and the fact that Fine Gael was in the throes of changing its leader, de Valera took the chance to call an election in 1944. Neither of the Labour parties was in fit state to wage a decent campaign and as a result the combined Labour total of seats and votes fell, and all the gains of 1943 were wiped out. In retrospect it is quite possible that these divisions in Irish Labour prevented the party from benefiting from the upsurge of support for left parties which was a common feature in Western Europe in the mid-1940s. In the case of Ireland the beneficiary was to be the new but short-lived Clann na Poblachta party.

The 1948 general election saw both Labour parties suffer a slight loss of votes but a gain in seats. By now disappointment and frustration with Fianna Fáil and the long years in opposition made Labour ready to enter the inter-party government. The Labour party took two Cabinet posts, with its leader as Tánaiste (Deputy Premier) and National Labour provided one Cabinet Minister. The experience of office was a mixed blessing but on the whole a positive one. The Labour ministers performed creditably under the disciplines of government, were able to claim some credit for the 1949 declaration of a republic and were not directly involved in the controversy over the proposed health-care scheme which was largely responsible for the government's demise. The experience of working together in government also had a therapeutic effect on the divided Labour movement though Larkin's death in 1947 doubtless helped. The two parties formally reunited in June 1950.

The general election of May 1951 defeated the inter-party government but of all the minor parties involved Labour sustained least damage, marginally increasing its vote but losing 2 seats. In the 1954 election it again increased its popular vote by 0.7%, gained 3 seats, and began its second period in coalition government. By now, however, as the smaller parties were fading and only three parties actually entered the government, Labour was emerging as the dominant element amongst the minor parties and this was seen in the share-out of posts. Four, including the post of Tánaiste, went to Labour. However, there were disadvantages in this higher profile— when things went wrong the party took a larger share of the blame. It was particularly unfortunate for Labour that this experience of office came when the Irish economy began to run into difficulties (Lyons, 1973), unemployment rose and, at Fine Gael's insistence, severe deflationary measures were imposed which in some ways merely exacerbated the problem (Walsh, 1979). For a party which had always set economic and social affairs at the top of its agenda it was a galling experience. The general election of 1957 depressed morale even further when Labour support fell by 3.0% to 9.1% and it lost 7 seats, finishing with a total of 12.

This defeat marked a turning point in the party's history and launched it on a third phase of its development which lasted from 1957 to 1970 (M. Gallagher, 1982). At its annual conference of June 1957 Labour turned its back on the coalition option and set itself the task of forming an Irish Labour government independent of all other groups. The new departure was reinforced in March 1960 when William Norton, leader for 28 years, was replaced by Brendan Corish. This staking out of an independent identity received encouragement at the 1961 general election when the party vote rose 2.5% and it gained 4 seats. Progress was maintained by the 1965 election, with further gains of 3.8% in the vote and 6 seats, to give the highest number of TDs since June 1927.

These gains help explain the extraordinarily euphoric state in which the party entered the 1969 election. Buoyed up by steady gains in votes, seats, membership and branches, and the recruitment of several leading personalities, the party put up a record number of 99 candidates and campaigned on a consciously radical manifesto for the return of a Labour government. In the event, it did make some progress but in the light of its heady expectations the overall result was a bitter disappointment. Its share of the popular vote rose by 1.6% to 17%, the highest ever, and there was notable progress in the Dublin region. However, party support in rural areas declined and it lost 4 seats overall, returning 18 TDs (Busteed and Mason, 1970). These results were to provoke years of debate, but the immediate outcome was a reassessment of the question of coalition and the start of the fourth stage of the party's history. In 1968 it had been so confident of gaining power on its own that it rejected overtures from Fine Gael proposing a working relationship against Fianna Fáil (Arnold, 1984). However the 1969 result had been a sobering experience and at a special conference in December 1970 it was decided by 396 votes to 204 to reopen the possibility of future coalition. The debate provoked a secession by 150 delegates and created strains between the parliamentary party, which was largely for coalition, and the Administrative Council (national executive) which was against.

Formal talks with Fine Gael on the possibility of co-operation did not take place until September 1972 and when the 1973 general election was announced they were nowhere near complete (Manning, 1978). However, they were spurred on by the prospect of the poll and, to the surprise of many, Labour and Fine Gael were able to campaign as allies on a joint programme of fourteen points, stressing economic and social issues and urging their supporters to continue their later preferences for their ally. The result was that although Labour dropped 3.3% of the vote to finish with 13.7%, it gained one seat, thanks to Fine Gael transfers.

The experience of government 1973–7 was as ever a mixed blessing for the party. Since there were now only two parties in the Coalition, Labour got a larger share of posts than ever before—5 out of 15 Cabinet places, 2 junior posts, and its leader Brendan Corish as Tanaiste. The party also had some solid achievements to its credit in the fields of social welfare, tax reform, house building, and labour legislation, but was disappointed at the slow progress in economic planning and the lack of any real movement on the questions of contraception and divorce law reform. Above all, unemployment and inflation began to rise. There was also some uneasiness at the government's heavy-handed approach to security. The 1977 general election saw Labour lose 2.1% of its votes and 2 seats overall. The party had now seen its total of votes and seats decline in two successive elections to the point where it was back to roughly its 1957 position. Voices began to be heard questioning the wisdom of coalition, but future strategy was to be the responsibility of a new leader because Brendan Corish resigned immediately after the election result became known, and after two ballots Frank Cluskey defeated Michael O'Leary.

Though Labour may seem to outside observers to be the most recognizable of the Irish parties, in the Irish context it is something of an exotic—long-established but always struggling to preserve itself in a rather inhospitable environment and on occasions, as in 1927–

38 or the late 1970s, appearing to lose its way. Its basic problem lies as already noted in the fact that the Irish political landscape was originally shaped by nationalistic and constitutional issues while Labour's appeal has been on social and economic grounds. Moreover, given the nationalist origins and pragmatic flexibility of the two main parties, but especially Fianna Fáil, they have been able to embrace ideas such as state intervention in economic activity and the creation of a welfare state which are usually characteristic Labour causes. As a result they have been able to capture elements of the electorate which would normally be expected to vote Labour. Labour is therefore hard put to hang on even to the voters it does have and elections since 1969 suggest its grip its slipping. One could almost conclude there is simply no room for Labour in the Irish political system, though it has recovered from unpromising times in the 1930s and 1950s. However, the party appears caught in a perpetual strategic dilemma. If it abandons coalition and becomes more consciously socialist it could be argued it will be even less successful, given the Irish political ethos. If on the other hand it is prepared to enter coalition its identity becomes blurred and it has no distinctive appeal: voters may as well support Fine Gael, the senior coalition partner. Since 1972 the dilemma has been resolved by entering coalition, attempting to moderate some of Fine Gael's policies and putting through as much Labour-inspired legislation as possible, but is has not proved an exciting approach and in view of electoral decline since 1969 not an entirely successful one either.

MINOR PARTIES

Aside from these three main parties, minor political parties have been represented in the Dáil after several general elections (Gallagher, 1985; Manning, 1972). Their successes have been particularly notable in two periods of Irish electoral history. They made a strong showing between 1922 and June 1927 when they may have provided an opportunity for some electors to opt out of the all-pervading arguments over the Treaty. It is also possible that their support came from people who, though unhappy with the Cumann na n Gaedheal governments, could not bring themselves to vote for Labour, which they saw as trade-union oriented and socialist, Sinn Féin, which was associated with violence and abstentionism, or even a Fianna Fáil which until August 1927 was also abstentionist and only doubtfully constitutional. The entry of Fianna Fáil into the Dáil in that year, however, polarized the Irish electorate and the elections of September 1927 and 1932 effectively ended this phase of minor party history. There was a brief revival in the shape of the Centre Party in the 1933 election but within a short time this had become one of the elements of Fine Gael.

The second great phase of minor party activity lasted from 1943 until 1951. In part the reappearance of the minor groups may have been a reaction against the relative stagnation of Irish politics during the Emergency. It may also have been a grumble vote against the rationing, shortages, and bureauratic planning of the period. But it could also have been an Irish version of the upsurge of support for radical parties which appeared everywhere in Western Europe during the 1940s. This was certainly the heyday of the minor party in Irish politics, since no less than two of them—three if National Labour is included—actually accepted office in the 1948–51 inter-party government. Even after this government's defeat in 1951 minor parties were to be quite strongly represented in the Dáil. One took part in the next coalition of 1954–7 and another supported the administration without taking office and indeed played a key role in its eventual downfall. However, it was clear that by the mid-1950s the electorate was drifting back to the three established parties. Support for minor parties fell at successive general elections until they returned only one TD in 1965.

The somewhat erratic history of these small parties has led one authority to designate them 'flash' parties (Carty, 1981). It is difficult to categorize such diverse groups, but they have generally fallen into three, sometimes overlapping, categories. The first may be broadly termed as 'centrist' in that it has tried to break away from the conventional historic alignment of Irish politics around the issues of the Treaty and Civil War. Into this category would come the National League, founded in 1926, strongly supported by Irishmen who had served in the British forces and which, since it was led by Captain Willie Redmond, son of the leader of the old Home Rule Party, probably pulled in many of that party's former supporters. It was formally dissolved in 1931 and most of its supporters found their natural home in Fine Gael. The Centre Party founded in September 1932 had, as its name suggests, aspirations to a new departure in Irish politics, but its rural and agricultural preoccupations made it more like a farmers' pressure group (M. Gallagher, 1985). It took 11 seats and 9.2% of the vote in 1933, but shortly afterwards coalesced with other groups to form Fine Gael. It was not until the formation of the Progressive Democrats in December 1985 that the idea of a centrist realignment resurfaced.

A second category of minor parties is the economic interest group. In the Irish context this, hardly surprisingly, has meant farmers' parties. Farming interests were represented by distinct groups in the Dáil in varying strength in 1922–32 and 1943–65. However, given the mixed nature of Irish agriculture, it is hardly surprising that these groups have varied significantly. Between 1922 and 1932 it was mostly the larger, more prosperous farmers of the midlands and south-east who were represented by the Farmers' Party. By 1933 however the all-pervading Treaty issue had squeezed this grouping out of existence; most of its supporters drifted into the National League and eventually into Fine Gael. The Centre Party hoped for a broad national appeal but its original title of the 'National Farmers' and Rate-payers' League', and its strong support amongst the pastoral farmers suffering from the 'Economic War' with Britain, revealed its rural roots and preoccupations.

The next farmers' grouping was significantly different in emphasis and support base. Clann na Talmhan ('Sons of the Soil') was founded in August 1939 to represent the interests of the small farmers of western Ireland who were beginning to feel resentful at Fianna Fáil's failure to redeem their 1932 manifesto pledges to raise the living standards of small farmers and ease their situation by redistribution of agricultural land. The party provided Cabinet Ministers for the inter-party governments of 1948–51 and 1954–7 but it had passed its electoral peak in 1948 and thereafter dwindled to extinction in 1965. Since then there have been no specifically farmers' parties represented in the Dáil, partly because all existing parties recognize the importance of the farming vote and go to considerable lengths to accommodate it, and partly because farming interests are well looked after by the various energetic farmers' organizations (Manning, 1979). However, T. J. Maher, an independent with a notable record of work in this area, was comfortably elected as a member of the European parliament in 1979, 1984, and 1989. Equally significantly, he failed when he stood as an independent for the Dáil in 1981.

The third group of minor parties consists of those which claim to stand for ideological purity, usually expounding a more fundamental version of an outlook already represented in the Dáil. Two traditions stand out here, and they have sometimes overlapped. Possibly the most enduring has been republicanism. This viewpoint argues that the unfinished business of creating a united 32-county Irish Republic has been neglected by the main parties and should be placed at the top of the political agenda and vigorous efforts made to terminate the British presence in Northern Ireland. Into this tradition could come the nine TDs who left Cumann na n Gaedheal in 1924 and formed the National Party and the three who departed in 1926 to constitute Clann Éireann. Both complained about the lack of progress towards an Irish Republic and both were destroyed at subsequent elections. A similar breakaway, though this time from Fianna Fáil, came in 1971 when Kevin Boland founded Aontacht Éireann ('Irish Unity') in order to push more strongly for an end to partition. This too suffered rapid electoral extinction.

Clann na Poblachta was an entirely new party which for a time seemed destined to transform Irish politics. Set up in July 1946, it was a combination of robust parliamentary republicanism and social and economic radicalism. It represented a certain disillusionment with Fianna Fáil's increasingly pragmatic approach to partition, and also expressed discontent with wartime rationing and shortages. It may also have benefited from the Irish equivalent of that upsurge of radical energies which elsewhere in Western Europe found its way into socialist parties. At the general election of February 1948 the party gained 13.2% of the vote and 10 seats, and entered the inter-party government. However, by 1951 it was fading fast and though it supported the Coalition of 1954–8 from outside the government, it was clearly a spent force, and was finally wound up in 1965.

Of all the representatives of militant republicanism who won Dáil seats, the most long-lived has been Sinn Féin which advocated the use of military force to end the British presence in Northern Ireland. This group has gone through various transformations. From its founding in 1907 until 1917 it was regarded as a fringe group for people with advanced nationalist ideas. From 1917 to 1921 it was effectively the political expression of the Irish demand for self-determination. Following the split over the Treaty, the party withdrew from the Dáil on principle and refused to occupy the seats it won in the 1923 general election. It kept to this policy even after the departure of de Valera to form Fianna Fáil, though its 5 seats and 3.6% of the vote in the election of June 1927 revealed it was no longer the main political exponent of Irish republicanism. Following this election the party abstained from electoral politics for 30 years. During that time it led a shadowy existence, was subject to left-wing schisms in the 1930s, and came strongly under the influence of the IRA. In 1957, on the strength of feelings roused by the ultimately unsuccessful IRA border campaign launched the previous year (Messenger, 1983; Coogan, 1984), it contested the general election winning 5.3% of the vote and 4 seats which it again refused to occupy. By 1961 however emotions had cooled and all 4 seats were lost.

This dual failure on the military and political fronts produced a radical rethink about strategy and tactics. Left-wing elements successfully argued that the party should build up popular support by campaigning on social and economic issues and even occupy any parliamentary seats they won. These developments were overtaken by serious rioting in Belfast in August 1969 when the Catholic community in the Falls Road district suffered badly. Traditionally, residents in the nationalist districts of Belfast had felt that in such a domesday situation the IRA would be their protectors. For the traditionalists in Sinn Fein, the failure to protect the Falls district was the final straw in their growing impatience with recent developments in the party. They took the opportunity to condemn the leftist ideas which had recently gained ground and the suggested abandonment of abstention and broke away in January 1970 to form a new party, Provisional Sinn Féin. This embraced traditional Irish republicanism and abstention from parliament, north and south. However the party was to drift through the 1970s with few real signs of progress until it underwent a remarkable transformation in the early 1980s.

The second variety of ideological puritanism which has inspired minor parties has been socialism in various forms. Periodically there are complaints that the Irish Labour Party does not preach a sufficiently muscular variety of socialism or indeed that it is hardly socialist at all. Until the early 1980s however, parties to the left of Irish Labour had little success, beyond electing Jim Larkin in September 1927 only to see him debarred as a bankrupt, and helping to elect an Unemployed Protest Committee TD in 1957. The National Progressive Democrats, who were quite leftist in their philosophy, elected two TDs in 1961 but they soon joined Labour (M. Gallagher, 1985).

The only firmly leftist group which has succeeded in putting down roots of any strength is the Workers' Party. When Sinn Féin split in January 1970 the left-wing elements renamed themselves Official Sinn Féin. Having parted company with their traditionalist colleagues they rapidly evolved into an avowedly socialist party and as time passed they left militant republicanism behind and put an increasing distance between themselves and the Official IRA. This evolutionary process reached the point where they dedicated themselves to campaigning throughout Ireland on a socialist programme aiming to raise working-class consciousness north and south, thereby leading to a non-sectarian 32-county workers' republic. The means were to be peaceful campaigning inside and outside parliament and any seats won were to be occupied and used to these ends. Thus they put up nine candidates in the 1973 General Election, though with little success. In January 1977 their new direction was epitomized by changing the party name to Sinn Féin the Workers' Party. However, in the general election of that year, though their vote rose marginally to 1.7%, they gained no seats.

Minor parties have some success in winning seats in Irish politics but not in retaining them and establishing a permanent presence in the Dáil. None of the minor parties has succeeded in growing into a major party and permanently displacing one of the existing political groups in the Dáil. With the passage of time they have disappeared, either because the voters deserted them or they have merged with existing parties. They may well have fallen victim to the superior campaigning resources of the big parties at election times but they may also have been victims of the inherent flexibility of the main parties. Given their pragmatic, non-ideological outlook they have been able to take over ideas from the minor parties or take action to defuse specific issues or causes which originally fuelled their success. Thus the farming interest is now easily accommodated by Fianna Fáil and Fine Gael. Moreover, the major party candidates are as astute as any in exploiting those features of Irish society and the voting system which sometimes assist minor parties.

INDEPENDENTS

Independent TDs have been present in every Dáil since the election of 1922. They were particularly numerous during two crucial periods, the first ten years after independence and the period immediately after 1945. It is hardly surprising that the period 1922–32 should see a large number of deputies unattached to the main parties. The Irish Free State was only recently established, and a basic party system was still evolving. Moreover, until Fianna Fáil was established and entered the Dáil, voting for an independent was one way for non-socialists to express constructive parliamentary opposition to the government. However, as soon as Fianna Fáil took its place in parliamentary politics and made the Treaty the dominant issue, the independents, like the minor parties, began to feel the squeeze. Their fortunes did not revive until the 1948 election when they reached double figures again, partly benefiting from the same post-war discontents, radicalism, and disillusionment which boosted Clann na Poblachta. The 1951 election saw a small increase in independents but their numbers declined to single figures thereafter to reach an all-time low of one TD in 1969. Subsequently there was a small increase but they never regained their former numbers.

Independents are by definition almost impossible to categorize:

they are very much individualists. However, many have originally belonged to one of the established parties. Some were deputies first elected on a party ticket but subsequently expelled or resigning, have fought and retained their seats as independents. In recent years the outstanding example is Neil Blaney, originally Fianna Fáil TD for Donegal North-East, sacked from the Cabinet over the 1970 Arms Crisis and finally expelled from the party in 1971 after vigorous attacks on the leadership. However, he easily retained his seat in subsequent elections. Other independents have been members of major parties who, failing to win a place on the party ticket at the constituency nominating convention, have successfully stood on their own.

Individuals with no party background at all have been rare and many independents have not lasted beyond one Dáil simply because when it comes to fighting elections they have lacked the resources of finance and personnel to compete with the major parties. Others however have managed to build up a personal vote solid enough to see them through a succession of elections. One such was Joseph Sheridan, first elected for Longford-Westmeath in 1961 and surviving through the four elections of the next 20 years until he retired in 1981. Like the minor parties, independent TDs can play a significant part in a finely divided Dáil. James Dillon, expelled from Fine Gael in 1942, actually served as Minister for Agriculture between 1948 and 1951. But more often than not independents have been content to bargain their support in return for specific pieces of legislation or particular favours for their constituency. Sean Lemass's two governments of 1961 and 1965 both lacked overall majorities and only survived through such independent support.

The role of the independent members in the Dáil is unusual in comparison with the United Kingdom experience but also by most West European standards. Their persistence and significance over such a long period are dependent on the two phenomena which may also be partly responsible for the success of minor parties, namely the enduring significance of locality and personality in Irish society and an electoral system which allows these factors full play and may even help perpetuate their significance.

THE SUPPORT BASES OF IRISH POLITICAL PARTIES:
AN OVERVIEW AND INTERPRETATION

It has virtually been accepted as a truism that one of the distinguishing features of the Irish political system is a lack of any clear-cut correlation between electoral behavior and socio-economic characteristics. One student of the Irish scene surveying political behaviour in the late 1960s for a comparative handbook on electoral choice entitled his essay 'Ireland: Politics without Social Bases' (Whyte, 1974) and much subsequent work has adopted this title as an assumption (Carty, 1981). The reason for this line of argument lies in the dominant position of Fianna Fáil in the Irish political system and the remarkable breadth of its appeal. As already noted, it is undoubtedly the largest and most successful party. Particularly since the early 1930s it has been able to draw significant support from every region of the country and every category of the population, regardless of age, gender, occupation, income, or social class. The same can be said of Fine Gael, the only difference being that its support overall is somewhat lower than for Fianna Fáil. Only Labour has a constituency largely confined to one socio-economic group, the unskilled working-class (Busteed and Mason, 1970). The remarkably broad spread of support for the two biggest parties has made such an impression on observers that there was a tendency to react by asserting that there was no patterning whatsoever in party support.

In actual fact, even the earliest studies revealed that there were some groups which gave greater-than-average support to particular parties. In the case of Fianna Fáil they seemed to attract extra support from Irish-speakers, small farmers, and the urban working-class, while Fine Gael support, though more difficult to categorize, seemed greatest amongst large farmers and the professional and middle classes. This was actually picked up in the earliest studies of Irish party support (Manning, 1972; Whyte, 1974) and confirmed in subsequent work (M. Gallagher, 1976; Sinnott, 1978). The great obstacle to a full understanding of Irish voting behaviour is the lack of an in-depth national survey of the type first conducted for Britain by Butler and Stokes (1969). However, recent work, particularly by Laver, on accumulated aggregate and opinion-poll data has gone some way towards filling the gap. Aggregate analysis confirmed that some correlations were variable over time, giving some support to the 'politics without social bases' thesis, and also that there was some definite social structuring to the Fianna Fáil vote, and in particular a close link with pastoral agriculture. The Fine Gael vote appeared to lack any firm pattern at the inter-county and constituency level. Labour's vote was easiest to predict, showing an association with rural areas specializing in tillage and horticulture and some urban areas, but also profoundly affected by local influences (Laver, 1986a). An overview of opinion-poll data since 1974 elaborated on these findings and hinted at more marked correlation between party choice and socio-economic background in recent years. Fianna Fáil was confirmed as an all-embracing party with a notable lead amongst small farmers and skilled and unskilled workers. Labour emerged with its strongest support amongst unskilled workers, though with definite signs of slippage in recent years. Fine Gael support was strongest amongst farmers owning more than 50 acres and with growing strength in the middle classes (Laver, 1986*b*, *c*). Subsequently Laver used survey analysis material from Galway West to mount a direct challenge to the 'politics without social bases' thesis. He argued that it may have been invalid all along due to the use of crude social categories and small samples by market researchers. He argues that by using more refined sociological categories for data collection and analysis a much more clear-cut structuring emerges. Fianna Fáil takes the largest share of the working-class vote, the routine non-manual workers and the petty bourgeoisie of small shopkeepers, self-employed tradespeople, and own-account workers. Fine Gael is strongest amongst the salaried professionals and routine non-manual workers while the new Progressive Democrats had an overall majority in the salaried group and the bourgeoisie of self-employed professionals and owners of medium and large businesses. Labour support was a steady 8–9% of all groups (Laver, 1987). The situation in Galway West may be unique of course and the emergence of the Progressive Democrats may have given rise to a more thorough social categorization of party support than previously—undoubtedly much subsequent research will be aimed at testing the validity of these findings at national level.

Comparative interpretations of the Irish party system have traditionally declared it to be a unique case (Whyte, 1974; Carty, 1981). Part of the difficulty may have lain in the widespread acceptance of the 'politics without social bases' thesis and the marked contrast with British electoral behaviour and the British party system. However, it has been argued (Sinnott, 1984, 1987) that the Irish case does conform quite well with some aspects of the Lipset and Rokkan (1967) model of state and party development. Using a historical analysis of West European states, this argues that present-day party systems and the social cleavages they represent are results of the stage of economic and social development of the state at the point when universal suffrage was introduced. Broadly speaking, it is argued that states have experienced four major conflicts in their historical development, two related to the process of state- and nation-building designated the National Revolution and two to the economic transformation known as the Industrial Revolution. The four categories of conflict and cleavage are first, a conflict between a dominant central culture and a subordinate peripheral culture. This reflects the fact that most modern states were created by a process whereby one group of people established a position of hegemony over others by military, diplomatic, or economic means and became the dominant element in the new state. However, no matter how successful this process, it is often incomplete. Remnants of the subject culture and peoples often persist in outlying areas peripheral to the centre of state power and provide the basis for separatist feelings and parties. A second form of cleavage is formed by conflicts between the state apparatus and the dominant church or between contending churches for the right to determine the cultural norms and ethos of the state. Education often provided the crucial battleground for conflict. Such struggles often led to the formation of secular radical, liberal, or anti-clerical parties on the one hand and church defence or confessional parties on the other. The third cleavage was a conflict between the primary and secondary economies. It usually arose from an industrial revolution which created a strong primary urban manufacturing sector whose interests clashed increasingly with the long-established rural agricultural sector. Finally, there was a workers-versus-employers cleavage. This emerged as the industrial revolution created an increasing employee class which became concerned over working conditions and wages and began to form first trade unions and then nation-wide socialist parties to improve their economic and social position. The final key element in this model concerns the creation of universal suffrage and its timing in relation to national development. Whatever cleavage dominates a country's politics when universal suffrage is introduced will decide the party alignments of the new voters when they are politically mobilized for the first time and, most important, the party system in the country for generations to come. Thus if a country is in the throes of a state-versus-church conflict at a time when large numbers are first enfranchised, then the voters will align themselves on one side or another in this controversy and support the appropriate parties. These parties in turn will continue to dominate the system for long periods, their personnel, preoccupations, and ethos profoundly affected by these formative years.

In the Irish case the 1918 election was the key date for the mobilization and politicization of Irish voters since the electorate had been almost doubled by the recent Representation of the People Act and the events of 1916–18 had created what was virtually a new, vibrant, militant nationalist sentiment which was articulated by Sinn Féin. Using the Lipset–Rokkan categories, the basic cleavage can be visualized within a British Isles context as a dominant central culture (Britain) versus a subject group in the periphery (most of Ireland), a conflict resolved by the secession of the 26 counties from the United Kingdom to form the Irish Free State. Thus at the formative stage of the Irish political system the key issues were nationalistic and constitutional and these were to dominate the ethos of the new state. Moreover, Labour deliberately stood aside from the 1918 election and there were no bases for alternative church–state, agrarian–industrial, or worker–employer cleavages because the overwhelming Catholic and agricultural sections of Ireland—and these largely coincided—simply broke away from Great Britain and the north-east of the island and created a state remarkable for its religious and economic homogeneity. Subsequently Irish political debate continued to be preoccupied with these nationalist and constitutional issues as the original Sinn Fein movement split over the precise degree of independence from Britain. One part of Sinn Féin, Cumann na n Gaedheal (Fine Gael) was more pragmatic and cautious and became preoccupied with the construction of stable, efficient, and economical state institutions. Consequently, though it found some support in every part of the country on the appeal of its nationalist roots, it particularly won the loyalty of those who had most to lose from the resumption of war with Britain and the consequent instability and damage, namely the better off, the large farmers, and the middle classes. The stress on efficiency and economy confirmed their allegiance and the economic policy of the first decade of independence, with its stress on large-scale pastoral production for export (Meenan, 1978), confirmed their support. That support became rock-solid after the change of government in 1932 when Fianna Fáil switched the agricultural policy to support for tillage, and pasture suffered severely in the subsequent Anglo-Irish 'Economic War' of 1933–8.

The republican–Fianna Fáil groups which were eventually to dominate the Irish political system took a purist, ultra-nationalist stance from the outset, stressing continuity with historic Irish aspirations for national self-determination. This unequivocal stance had a powerful emotional appeal to voters regardless of age, gender, occupation, and class. Their capture of much of the symbolism of Irish nationalism and invocation of traditional Irish cultural values and self-sufficiency had a particular appeal to Irish-speakers, small farmers, and small-scale businessmen, but also became part of the national ethos to the point where it was claimed that Ireland was a state where the values of the periphery dominated those of the centre (Garvin, 1974, 1977–8, 1978). Encouragement and protection of industry and arable agriculture won over some of the more prosperous elements in Irish society and after 1932 the drive to provide better housing and welfare services gained the support of large sections of the rural and urban working class. Judicious allocation of patronage by both parties when in office helped them retain their supporters.

The implication of this perspective is that while the early years of a political system have a profound and long-lasting effect on the nature of the parties and the basis of their support, change does occur either as a response to more widespread change in society as a whole or as a result of government activity itself (Mair, 1978). In the present work the electoral events of the early 1980s are being examined to provide a snapshot of the spatial patterns of Irish opinions and values after a period of such change.

CONCLUSION

Studies which have regarded the Irish party system as unique suffer from using an inappropriate geographical context. In some ways Ireland belongs both to the developed and to the Third World. It is located in Europe and shares some of its social and economic characteristics and many of its cultural values, and yet it has a history resembling the experiences of a Third World country, having been a colony of a major West European power, drawn into a dependent economic relationship with the metropolitan centre, and only coming to sovereign statehood as the result of a nationalist resurgence and a successful, violent, political revolution.

This is a highly unusual set of experiences for a European state and consequently the parties created out of this formative experience are unusual by European standards. However, if the comparison is broadened to consider Third World states which have also had to free themselves from colonial rule then the Irish party system becomes more comprehensible.

Like all parties, Irish political groups still bear many of their birthmarks, even several decades after their foundation. They have been kept going partly by the power of the original nationalistic impulses which brought them to birth and, as these have faded, by a mixture of inertia, adroit management, patronage, and their inherent adaptability. One of the distinctive features born in the formative period of graduation to independence is the Irish electoral system, and this too has contributed to the inherent flexibility of the political system and will now be examined.

2

The Irish Electoral System and the Spatial Framework for Elections

INTRODUCTION

The outcome of elections is not only decided by the total votes cast for particular parties and candidates. Two other influential factors are the system of voting used and the spatial framework of constituency boundaries and seat allocation.

Since 1922 southern Ireland has used the form of proportional representation known as the Single Transferable Vote (STV) in multi-member constituencies. It is almost, though not quite, a unique system. In the mid-1980s it was also used to elect the senate in Australia, the lower house in Malta, and the Tasmanian legislature (Bogdanor, 1984). In Northern Ireland it was employed in local elections until 1922 and in voting for the Stormont parliament until 1929 but was later abolished. However, it was restored in the 1970s for local government, provincial assembly, and European, though not Westminster, elections. In the United Kingdom the Liberal Party has argued for the adoption of a PR electoral system since 1922 and at their foundation in March 1981 its electoral allies the Social Democrats endorsed this viewpoint. Indeed, in July 1982 the two parties produced a joint document in which they argued that the STV system of PR should be adopted for all British elections with some modification for rural areas (*Guardian*, 23 July 82; *Electoral Reform*, 1982).

THE VOTING SYSTEM: ITS HISTORY

The basic elements of the Single Transferable Vote electoral system were originally devised by Thomas Wright Hill (Bogdanor, 1984) but the details were worked out by a Danish politician, Carl Andrae, and an English barrister, Thomas Hare, in the mid-nineteenth century (Hare, 1857, 1859). Hare's intention was to create as close a relationship as possible between the proportion of votes and seats won by each party in a general election on the grounds that this made a national parliament more truly representative of the division of political opinion in the country. His ideas won a notable convert in John Stuart Mill, and in 1884 the Proportional Representation Society was formed to campaign for adoption of Hare's system. Its first successes came when it was adopted for elections to the Tasmanian legislature in 1907 and the South African Senate in 1909 (C. O'Leary, 1979). However, in the United Kingdom progress was less sure. A Speaker's Conference on Electoral Reform in 1917 reported in favour of proportional representation, but the proposal was manœuvred out of the 1918 Representation of the People Act. Private members' bills for the adoption of the system were introduced in 1921 and twice in 1923, but did not survive. It was only in Ireland, where special circumstances seemed to merit exceptional treatment that the Society scored a success. Ever since the first Home Rule Bill of 1886 it had been obvious that the Protestant population of north-eastern Ireland was strongly opposed to the idea of a Home Rule parliament in Dublin. Their fears had been further stimulated by the second unsuccessful bill of 1893 but it was not until the election of December 1910 that things developed to crisis point. By then the incumbent Liberal government had lost its independent parliamentary majority and was forced to rely on the votes of the 85 Irish nationalist MPs to survive. As the price of their support they demanded and received a pledge of a third Irish Home Rule Bill. Once again a crisis over the position of the unionist community seemed likely. At this point the president of the PR Society, Lord Courtney, suggested that the adoption of a proportional representation voting system with multi-member constituencies for any Dublin parliament might help to reassure the Unionists (C. O'Leary, 1979). He was invited to lecture on the subject in Dublin and following his visit the Proportional Representation Society of Ireland was formed in April, 1911. Amongst its first members the most significant for the future was undoubtedly Arthur Griffith, the founder of Sinn Féin. Under his influence proportional representation became party policy. Another supporter was James Connolly, the republican labour leader. However, at this stage in their careers neither of them was well known. Until late in 1916 the political initiative in Irish nationalist affairs lay with the Irish Home Rule Party and its parliamentary representatives in London.

When the third Irish Home Rule Bill was introduced in Westminster in 1912 it initially provided for an Irish lower house of 164 members elected by the standard British first-past-the-post election system. But during its parliamentary passage it was amended to allow for the election of one-fifth of the lower house and the entire upper house by the Single Transferable Vote method of PR. This Bill did eventually become law in September 1914, despite militant Unionist and Conservative opposition. But by that time it was overtaken by the climactic events of the First World War. It was agreed between all the main parties that the operation of the Act should be put into cold storage for the duration of the war and that when it was revived, there would be special provision made for Ulster. By 1918 however, the Irish electoral landscape had been transformed. The 1916 Rising and its aftermath had created a vast groundswell of support for the militant nationalism of Sinn Féin. In the general election of December 1918 this party won 73 of the 105 Irish seats at Westminster and the once dominant Home Rule Party had shrunk to a rump of 6. Sinn Féin refused to take its seats in London and instead convened in Dublin as the first Dáil Éireann and set about erecting an alternative Irish administration in place of British government in Ireland. Military conflict between the British administration and their Irish challengers broke out early in 1919 and lasted until a truce in July 1921.

In the middle of this conflict the British government produced what it hoped would be the answer to the Irish problem, namely the division of the island into two political units and the installation of a home rule parliament in each. Under the terms of the Government of Ireland Act of 1920 both the entire lower houses of Northern and southern Ireland were to be elected by the STV method of proportional representation to safeguard the position of their respective Catholic and Protestant minorities.

However, there was another motive behind this conversion to PR. In July 1918 a private member's bill concerning the affairs of Sligo Borough Corporation had become law. Its main purpose had been to increase the corporation's revenue, but it also contained a clause stipulating that future elections for the borough would be conducted under the STV system. The hope was that this would increase the participation of the local Protestant minority in community affairs and dilute the growing strength of Sinn Féin. The first elections under the new system took place shortly after the general election of 1918 and the contrast in results provoked some careful thinking in both Irish nationalist and British government circles. Whereas Sinn Féin carried almost all before it in the general election, in Sligo the largely Protestant Ratepayers' Association came top of the poll and Sinn Fein second. The point was not lost and early in 1919 STV was made the electoral system for all future local government elections in Ireland.

Consequently, the inclusion of STV in the 1920 Government of Ireland Act was consistent with recently established approaches to Irish devolution. This act proposed to set up two home rule parliaments, one in Belfast with jurisdiction over the 6 north-eastern counties, one in Dublin for the remaining 26 counties, and both elected by STV. However, the first large-scale use of the new system did not bear out the partisan calculations of either the Home Rule Party or the British government. In the Northern Ireland local elections of January 1920 nationalists did win some notable victories in the west and south-west of the province and there was also notable minority representation on Belfast city council (Knight and Baxter-Moore, 1972). In the 26 counties however Sinn Féin almost monopolized representation—indeed in many cases it was returned unopposed. The general elections held in May 1921 under the Government of Ireland Act proved even more disappointing. In Northern Ireland the Unionists took 40 of the 52 Commons seats, Sinn Féin and the Home Rule Party 6 each, and in southern Ireland Sinn Féin candidates were returned unopposed in all of the 124 territorial seats. The only contests were for the 4 university seats of Trinity College, Dublin, where the restricted franchise and overwhelmingly Protestant graduate body combined to return 4 independents. This assembly became the second Dáil.

Despite the tumultuous events of this period and the subsequent months, STV was to survive as southern Ireland's electoral system. The Anglo-Irish Treaty of December 1921 had stipulated that there should be a general election as soon as possible in the Free State to test the popular will concerning the settlement. However, with de Valera and his followers already disowning the Treaty in vehement terms and talk of civil war in the air, prospects of a peaceful poll and a free expression of the popular will seemed remote. To avoid an electoral clash between the pro- and anti-Treaty factions of Sinn Féin and the military conflict which seemed likely to follow, in May 1922 Collins and de Valera agreed on a pact whereby the two wings of Sinn Féin would present a joint panel of candidates to the electorate, with supporters and opponents of the Treaty represented in the same proportions as in the second Dáil. Candidates representing other groups were also permitted to stand (M. Gallagher, 1979b). It now seems to have been accepted by everyone without question that proportional representation and specifically the STV variant had become a fixed element of the Irish political landscape.

In January 1922 the provisional government set up under the Treaty to steer southern Ireland to independence had appointed Collins as Chairman of a committee charged with drafting a new constitution. Its draft proposals were published on polling day 16 June. The proposed constitution provided for 153 members to be elected to a lower house by proportional representation, though without specifying which form. It may seem strange that any part of Sinn Féin should be prepared to accept a rather novel and complex

voting system originally foisted upon them by a British administration in an effort to blunt their electoral progress. However, it has
been shown that Griffith was a long-time believer in PR and by then
his personal prestige stood so high that it enabled him to carry the
rest of the nationalist movement with him on this question. Moreover, in December 1921 he had met with a delegation of southern
Unionists and amongst other guarantees of their future under a
Dublin government had assured them that PR would be retained for
Dáil elections. If anything, Griffith's death in August 1922 sanctified
that promise and in any case it was now widely believed that PR was
a strong guarantor of minority rights, both north and south. It is
also true that in the new states created in Europe by the post-war
peace treaties PR was widely regarded as an integral part of any
democratic system (C. O'Leary, 1979) and the newly created Irish
Free State was simply following the trend of the times. The new
constitution formally came into force in December 1922 and further
details were fleshed out by subsequent legislation. The Single Transferable Vote in multi-member constituencies which had been implied
or assumed to be the new electoral system was explicitly adopted by
the Electoral Act of 1923. This specified the method of election and
counting of ballots in some detail. The 1937 constitution went even
further, specifying not only that elections were to be by proportional
representation but that the Single Transferable Vote was the particular form of PR to be used (Bunreacht na h Éireann 16. 2. 5).
Since then this form of voting has become a political characteristic
peculiar to the Irish state. Indeed, for some it has become part of the
nationalist iconography, inseparable from their image of a free and
independent Ireland.

In Northern Ireland the opposite process was at work: as time
passed PR was steadily whittled away. The Ulster Unionists had
been unhappy with it from the first time it was suggested in the
Home Rule debates of 1912, on the grounds that it was 'un-British'
(C. O'Leary, 1979). They accepted its presence in the 1920 Government of Ireland Act in the same grudging fashion with which they
accepted the whole idea of a Belfast parliament. However, while they
quickly revised their opinion of the value of a regional legislature
and soon came to see it as a useful means of exercising control over
their own regional destinies, their dislike of the voting system was
unabated. The 1920 Act forbade any alteration of the parliamentary
electoral system for at least 3 years but the local government franchise was not safeguarded and by 1922 the Unionist administration
had reverted to the standard British first-past-the-post system. Then
in 1929 they also abolished PR for elections to the Northern Ireland

parliament at Stormont. Their motives were quite openly and frankly expressed by the Northern Ireland Premier Sir James Craig. In the elections of 1925 several Labour and Independent Unionist MPs had been returned and this seems to have alarmed the Unionist party. They feared that the electoral system was blurring what they saw as the overwhelming importance of the constitutional cleavage and allowing too many members to be returned on other issues (M. Farrell, 1976). Eventually they feared this could result in the erosion of the pro-partition majority at Stormont (Barritt and Carter, 1972). Consequently the first-past-the-post system was introduced, with 48 single-member territorial constituencies. PR was retained only for the election of the four members from Queen's University Belfast and for the Senate, which was elected by members of the Commons. Aside from the abolition of the university seats and their replacement by 4 territorial constituencies in 1969, this was the basic system used for Northern Ireland elections until the suspension of Stormont and the imposition of direct rule under a British Secretary of State in 1972. Ironically, as part of their search for new political structures in Northern Ireland, the British government subsequently reintroduced STV in all Northern Ireland elections, local, provincial, and European, though not for the Northern Ireland seats at Westminster.

In the Free State, later the Republic, proportional representation has been retained since 1923, though it has not been without its critics. They have tended to concentrate on two points (M. Gallagher, 1987). Some have argued that since the system rarely produces outright comfortable majorities for any one party, it produces uneasy governments depending on the unreliable support of independent or minor party representatives. The alternative solution of an actual coalition between parties is alleged to produce unstable governments formed around policies which have been negotiated between the parties concerned but never put to the elector. Other critics attack the variant of proportional representation used in Ireland, complaining that it induces deputies to build up and consolidate their personal electoral positions by concentrating on local issues and constituency service to the detriment of their broader role as national legislators.

Arguments like these were deployed on the two occasions when efforts were made to replace STV by a British-style electoral system. Such a constitutional change requires a referendum in the Irish Republic. The first referendum was held in June 1959, simultaneously with a presidential election. The Irish voters proved their preference for their known and tested electoral system because, while they elected de Valera, the Fianna Fáil candidate, as president by 56.33% of the vote, they rejected the Fianna Fáil government's attempt to reform the voting system by 51.8% to 48.2%. The second try at abolition came in October 1968 and this too was the result of an initiative by a Fianna Fáil government. This time the majority for retention of PR was even more decisive at 60.8%. Since then there have been periodic grumbles about the drawbacks of the system but no further efforts at abolition.

THE WORKING OF THE SYSTEM

On entering the polling booth the Irish elector is usually faced with a ballot paper that is longer than the British equivalent, largely because multi-member constituencies are used. Each of the main parties will nominate a number of candidates for the seats in contention and so too will the minor parties and independents. Candidates' surnames are arranged in alphabetical order together with address, occupation, and (since 1963) party affiliation; and if the elector wishes to use all the opportunities presented by the system he or she votes by placing a numeral against the name of each candidate, marking it 1, 2, 3, 4, etc. However, there is no compulsion to work down the entire ballot. Voters may simply indicate their first choice, or mark the candidates within a party group, or indeed stop ranking them at any point. To do this, however, is to ignore the full possibilities of the system and curtail the effectiveness of one's vote.

When the ballot boxes from the polling districts in a constituency are gathered at a central point and opened for counting and checking, the first act of the returning officer is to calculate the quota for the constituency. The quota is the threshold of votes which a candidate must equal or surpass to be elected. Originally Thomas Hare had envisaged that an entire country would be one constituency with the quota calculated by dividing the total vote cast by the number of seats in the national parliament. However, the practical details of such an approach overcame its theoretical perfections and the usual practice has been to divide a state into a number of multi-member constituencies and calculate the quota for each constituency.

Southern Ireland has always used the Droop Quota devised in 1869 (Droop, 1869). The formula is:

$$\text{Quota} = \frac{\text{Total number of valid votes}}{\text{Total seats} + 1} + 1$$

The next step is to count the number of first preferences gained by each candidate, and usually at least one has exceeded the quota and is elected on the first count. However, the remaining seats are still to be filled and this is done by transferring votes between candidates. Transfers take place in two ways. First, if a candidate has been elected with more than the required quota, then the surplus votes over and above that quota are redistributed between the remaining candidates. To redistribute this surplus the counting officials re-sort all the votes of the successful candidate and put them into parcels according to the next preferences marked. Candidates who have been given such preferences have a proportionate number of the appropriate parcel of votes transferred to them. The actual number is based on another formula:

$$
\begin{array}{l}
\text{No. of Candidate A's} \\
\text{votes to be transferred} \\
\text{to Candidate B}
\end{array}
=
\frac{
\begin{array}{c}
\text{No. of Canadidate A's} \\
\text{surplus votes}
\end{array}
}{
\begin{array}{c}
\text{No of votes transferable} \\
\text{from Candidate A to all} \\
\text{other candidates}
\end{array}
}
\times
\begin{array}{l}
\text{No. of papers in} \\
\text{Candidate B's parcel} \\
\text{of votes transferable} \\
\text{from Candidate A}
\end{array}
$$

The actual votes to be transferred are physically removed from the top of the parcel of A's ballot papers which have a preference for B marked on them: this means they have been the last added to A's parcel. In this way the elected candidate is left with his quota and the surplus is distributed amongst the other candidates and their totals recounted. If another candidate has now reached the quota, then his surplus is in turn redistributed, although this time it is only the parcel of votes which enabled him to pass the quota which is re-sorted (Chubb, 1982).

It frequently happens during a count that all surpluses have been redistributed and some seats are still unfilled. In these cases the second transfer process comes into play. The candidate with fewest votes is eliminated and his ballot papers redistributed in accordance with the preferences indicated. Sometimes there are preferences for candidates already elected or eliminated, and such papers are discarded as 'non-transferable'. These processes of redistribution and recounting are continued until all the seats in a constituency are filled. However, it quite often happens that at the end of a count there are still one or more seats unfilled, none of the remaining candidates has reached the quota and there are no surpluses left to transfer. In such cases the candidate with most votes is described as 'elected without reaching the quota' (Bogdanor, 1984; Chubb, 1978a, b, 1982a; McVey, 1981).

Some illustration of the workings of the system is provided by the election of June 1981. Figure 2.1 depicts the counts at which candidates were elected. From this it will be seen that 33 (30%) of the elected TDs (the outgoing Ceann Comhairle or Speaker is automati-

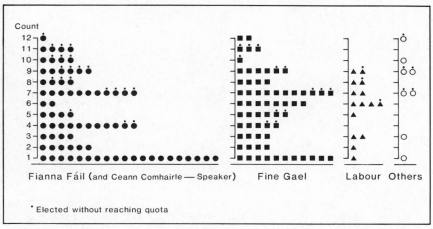

Fianna Fáil (and Ceann Comhairle — Speaker)   Fine Gael   Labour Others

*Elected without reaching quota

FIG. 2.1 General Election 1981: counts at which candidates elected

cally declared re-elected) were returned on the first count and 42 (25.5%) were declared elected without reaching the quota.

The counting in the Kildare constituency in this election shows the details of the system (Table 2.1). This was a 5-seat constituency in which 47,060 valid votes were cast, giving a quota of 7,844. Only one candidate, Paddy Power (Fianna Fáil) passed the quota and was declared elected on the first count. However, when his surplus vote of 1,924 was distributed, 999 went to his party colleague Charlie McCreevy and this, when added to his first preferences, was enough to take him past the quota and see him elected to the second seat. The independent candidate Bracken was then eleminated and his 709 votes redistributed but no one reached the quota at this count. McCreevy's surplus of 208 was then redistributed in the fourth count, but still no one was elected. Frank Stagg of Labour was then eliminated, his votes redistributed, and his party colleague Joe Bermingham elected. Miley, the weakest Fianna Fáil candidate, was eliminated next and his votes shared out but no one was elected on the sixth count; at the seventh count Bermingham's small surplus of 92 was divided out but again nobody quite reached the quota. Lawlor of Fine Gael, the next weakest candidate, was then eliminated and his transfers were enough to elect one of his running mates, Bernard Durkan, on the eighth count. His surplus of 644 was divided between the two remaining candidates, Brady of Fianna Fáil and Dukes of Fine Gael. Neither reached the quota but since Dukes with 7,658 came closer, he was declared elected.

Table 2.1. *Stages in counting of votes: Kildare constituency, June 1981*

	Counts								
	1st	2nd Power's surplus 1,924	3rd Bracken's votes 709	4th McCreevy's surplus 208	5th Stagg's votes 2,975	6th Miley's votes 3,229	7th Bermingham's surplus 92	8th Lawlor's votes 4,964	9th Durkan's surplus 644
Power (Fianna Fáil)	9,768(E)								
McCreevy (Fianna Fáil)	7,053	+999 8,052(E)							
Bermingham (Labour)	5,803	+96 5,899	+123 6,022	+8 6,030	+1,906 7,936(E)				
Durkan (Fine Gael)	5,612	+28 5,640	+53 5,693	+2 5,695	+437 6,132	+58 6,190	+43 6,233	+2,255 8,488(E)	
Dukes (Fine Gael)	4,762	+23 4,785	+52 4,837	+1 4,838	+77 4,915	+94 5,009	+15 5,024	+2,039 7,063	+622 7,685(EQ)
Lawlor (Fine Gael)	4,469	+55 4,524	+56 4,580	+6 4,586	+177 4,763	+180 4,943	+21 4,964(L)	NT 450	
Brady (Fianna Fáil)	3,584	+196 3,780	+134 3,914	+90 4,004	+196 4,200	+2,204 6,404	+13 6,417	+220 6,637	+22 6,659
Stagg (Labour)	2,832	+35 2,867	+105 2,972	+3 2,975	NT 97				
Miley (Fianna Fáil)	2,479	+481 2,960	+86 3,046	+98 3,144	+85 3,229(L)	NT 693			
Bracken (independent)	698	+11 709(L)	NT 100						

E = elected; EQ = elected without reaching quota ; L= eliminated; NT= non-transferable: papers spoiled, showing no further preference, or preference for candidate already elected.

Note: Valid votes, 47,060; seats, 5; quota, 7,844.
Elected: Power (FF, 1st count); McCreevy (FF, 2nd count); Bermingham (Lab., 5th count); Durkan (FG, 8th count); Dukes (FG, 9th count).

Sources: Irish Times, 15 June 81; Browne 1981.

Table 2.2. *Proportionality in the early 1980s* (%)

	Fianna Fáil			Fine Gael			Labour			Others		
	Vote	Seats	Dev'n	Vote	Seats	Dev'n	Vote	Seats	Dev'n	Vote	Seats	Dev'n
1981	45.3	47.0	+1.7	36.5	39.2	+2.7	9.9	9.0	−0.9	8.3	4.8	−3.5
1982a	47.3	48.8	+1.5	37.3	38.0	+0.7	9.1	9.0	−0.1	6.3	4.2	−2.1
1982b	45.2	45.2	0.0	39.2	42.2	+3.0	9.4	9.6	+0.2	6.3	3.0	−3.3

Sources: *Irish Times* 15 June 1981, 22 Feb. 1982, 26 Nov. 1982; author's calculations.

CONSEQUENCES OF VOTING SYSTEM

This unusual electoral system has several consequences for Ireland's political scene. At the national level it produces a fair approximation to what has been termed proportionality, i.e. a close relationship between the proportion of votes a party receives in the country as a whole and the proportion of seats it gains in the national parliament. For many of its advocates this is one of the great virtues of the STV system and it is argued this makes it inherently more democratic than the British first-past-the-post system. In actual fact in Ireland over the period 1923–77 it was found that STV did not produce perfect proportionality. It generally tended to inflate the share of seats going to the two largest parties and to depress slightly the share of Labour and the smaller parties (M. Gallagher, 1975, 1986; C. O'Leary, 1979). This has given rise to the observation that the Irish voting system produces results in terms of the votes–seats relationship which are a compromise between the British system and pure proportional representation, with the latter element dominant (Hogan, 1945).

Generally speaking the results of the general elections in 1981–2 confirmed these generalizations (Table 2.2). Of the three elections, two produced a small surplus of seats over votes for Fianna Fáil and in one (November 1982) there was a perfect match of seats and votes. Of all the parties, Fine Gael did best out of the system, with a surplus of seats over votes in all three contests, though in February 1982 it was only a small bonus. Labour suffered a slight penalty in two elections and a small surplus in one, though of all the parties it came closest to perfect proportionality in all three elections. However as usual it was the smaller parties and independents who suffered most. In all three elections they experienced a deficit of seats as compared to votes, varying from 3.5% in 1981 to 2.1% in February 1982. None the less, there is undoubtedly a closer fit between votes and seats in Irish elections than in British contests (Gudgin and Taylor, 1979) and it has been argued that the distortion which does occur is due to district magnitude and lower preferences (M. Gallagher, 1986).

Under PR-STV outright majorities for a single party are rare and usually small when they do occur. Consequently, minority governments or coalitions are quite frequent: of the 18 Irish governments formed between 1932 and November 1982, only 6 have had outright majorities. On two further occasions the party which went on to form the government had exactly half the seats in the Dáil. There have been 5 minority governments dependent on the support of independents and minor party TDs and 5 coalitions of which 3 have needed the support of more than two parties. However, M. Gallagher (1986) has argued that the number of elections, changes of government, and degree of fractionalization of the party system in Ireland are not unusual by international standards and if anything rather below the average for states using PR systems.

One feature of PR-STV frequently cited by its advocates is that it maximizes voter choice because the elector can choose not merely between parties but also between candidates within parties. The elector is free to rank each individual candidate in each party slate. Some voters of course may simply vote for candidates in the order 1, 2, 3, etc. as listed on the ballot or may even scatter their preferences at random. For others who wish to vote in more considered fashion, a vast array of factors can come into play. Even those who merely wish to vote the party ticket must sort out their preferences in accordance with some criteria. A candidate's age, gender, and personality may be relevant. If there are differences of emphasis on philosophy and policy within party ranks or there have been recent controversies then the candidate's stance on these issues may become important. If kinship and locality are still important in social relations, then a candidate's family background, strength of local connections, and involvement in community affairs can be relevant considerations.

This interplay of factors means that each Irish general election is conducted at three levels. On the national level there is a nationwide campaign co-ordinated from party headquarters in Dublin, preoccupied with national issues such as the economy, education, and security, and involving all the mechanics of national campaigning such as tours and speeches by the leader, press conferences, party political broadcasts, and media interviews. However, in each constituency the party campaigns tend to lay greatest stress on the local issues which then become the basic fare of Irish electioneering. But even within the local party effort in a constituency there are often the quite distinct personal campaigns of each individual candidate on the party ticket, seeking not merely to outpoll the opposition but also to outvote his or her party colleagues. One result is that the election of TDs takes place on the combination of party loyalty and the personal, local appeal of individual candidates. Another is that at each Irish election as many or more seats change hands within parties as across party lines. In the general election of February 1982 21 outgoing TDs who were standing for re-election lost their seats: 11 lost them to party colleagues, while 10 lost out to opponents from other parties. In November of the same year 20 incumbents were defeated, 10 by party colleagues, 10 by contenders from other parties.

A further result of the system is the fact already noted that candidates who do not represent the big parties stand a greater chance of being elected than under the British system. Personality, family background, and local community work can sometimes attract enough lower preferences from supporters of other parties. This helps explain the persistence of independent TDs in the Dáil ever since the founding of the state and the periodic appearance of minor parties of the various sorts already described. Certainly such individuals or groups will sometimes appeal at the ideological level but much more often their breakthrough into national prominence is a result of a long period of local community work and of course, once elected, they have the opportunity to consolidate their position through easier access to ministers, civil servants, and the media.

The three general elections of the early 1980s bear out this point. The general election of June 1981 saw the election to the Dáil of Jim Kemmy, as an Independent Socialist for Limerick East, a constituency which includes almost all the urban areas of Limerick City plus a rural hinterland to the south-east (Smith, 1985). Kemmy gained 8.6% of the first preference votes and was elected on the sixth count on transfers from a variety of sources, though 80.7% came from Labour candidates eliminated at earlier stages (Table 2.3). However, his victory was the culmination of almost ten years of effort outside the major parties. A former member of the Labour Party, he established an independent base in the city and was first elected to the Corporation in 1974, successfully defending his seat in 1979 and 1985. His election to the Dáil was the result of a long process of building up support. He unsuccessfully contested the general election of 1977, gaining 2,333 votes (5.2%), but managed to be elected on the ninth count in June 1981, when he gained 4,190 first preferences (8.6%) and large numbers of transfers from other candidates (Table 2.3). In February 1982 his first preferences rose

Table 2.3. *Sources of transfers to J. Kemmy (independent, Limerick East) in general election, 1981*

First preferences	4,190		
Total transfers	3,786		
Composed of	134	(3.5%)	from Fianna Fáil
	193	(5.1%)	from Fine Gael
	3,055	(80.7%)	from Labour
	404	(10.7%)	from independents

Sources: Browne, 1981; *Irish Times* 15 June 1981; author's calculations.

by a further 5% to 13.7% and he was again returned with large numbers of transfers from other candidates, this time on the tenth count. In April 1982 he founded the Democratic Socialist Party, notable for its conciliatory attitude towards the Unionist community in Northern Ireland. However, the general election of November 1982 demonstrated that while independent or minor party candidates have a better chance of election under the Irish voting system, they are still vulnerable to assaults by their much larger, better-organized and -financed rivals. In Limerick East, Kemmy's share of first preferences dropped by 6.45%, he was eliminated after the eighth count, and his seat went to the Labour Party candidate Frank Prendergast. Of his six DSP colleagues, only one saved a deposit.

This ability of minor party and independent candidates to be elected illustrates another alleged effect of the electoral system. It is argued that it puts a high premium on deputies' constituency work. In order to capture and retain a high proportion of first or later preferences, candidates are under pressure to maintain a higher local profile than competitors. This competition is intensified by the fact that it is not merely between parties but also intra-party since each party puts forward a slate of candidates to win as many of the seats in the multi-member constituencies as possible. It is alleged this has given Irish public representatives a distinctive style and role whereby they are seen not so much as national legislators but as local ombudsmen, acting as intermediaries between the constituency and central government. They are perceived as conduits through whom local grievances and needs are expressed and presented to government and redress is channelled (Chubb, 1963). The details of this relationship between the electoral system, local political influences, and Dáil constituency work and their possible effect on electoral behaviour will be explored in depth in Chapter 5.

A final effect of the electoral system is that parties can campaign as allies, encouraging their supporters to give lower preferences to the candidate of the other party. This of course depends on voters having quite a sophisticated knowledge of the electoral system and

Table 2.4. *Transfer patterns between Fine Gael and Labour, general elections, 1981, 1982* (%)

	FG to Labour	Labour to FG	FG non-transferable	Labour non-transferable
1981	86.8	56.3	0.0	16.3
1982a	69.1	59.5	17.0	13.6
1982b	80.4	59.4	5.5	10.4

Sources: Browne, 1982a; O'Malley, 1983.

being willing to follow party advice. In Ireland the most common alliance has been between Fine Gael and Labour. Indeed, in the past 15 years the relationship between these two parties and the willingness of their supporters to transfer lower preferences to the other party have been important influences on the outcome of Irish elections, though some have argued that they have rarely been decisive at the national level and are only significant at the local level in large 4- or 5-seat constituencies (M. Gallagher, 1979b).

The transfer patterns in the three general elections of 1981–2 varied somewhat (Table 2.4). In June 1981 there were notably high levels of transfers from Fine Gael to Labour and virtually no non-transferable votes for Fine Gael. Labour transfers to Fine Gael held steady at round about the level for 1977 and only 16.3% were non-transferable. In February 1982 however Fine Gael transfers to Labour fell to 69.1%, with 17.0% non-transferable. Labour patterns remained quite stable. Finally, in November 1982 Fine Gael transfers to Labour returned almost to their previous high level at 80.4% and non-transferable votes shrank to 5.5%. Again, Labour transfers were stable at 59.4%, though the level of non-transferable votes dropped slightly to 10.4%.

In the elections of February and November 1982 the constituency of Carlow-Kilkenny illustrates the importance of alliances in closely fought contests (Table 2.5). In February after the eleventh count there was one seat left to be filled, and two candidates in the running, Nolan of Fianna Fáil who was slightly ahead, and Pattison of the Labour Party. Governey of Fine Gael had just been elected and his surplus of 962 votes remained to be distributed. If it had split perfectly equally between the two candidates, Nolan would have taken the seat but in fact 96% of the transfers went to Pattison and were decisive in bringing him past Nolan to take the seat for Labour (Table 2.5a). A broadly similar situation appeared in the November election of the same year. After the tenth count there were still 2 seats left unfilled and three candidates still in the running, Nolan and Gibbons of Fianna Fáil, who were first and second in

Table 2.5. *Transfer of votes at final counts in Carlow-Kilkenny, February and November 1982*

a. 1982a (quota 9,047) Result of 11th count		12th count, distribution of Governey's (FG) surplus of 962
Nolan (FF)	8,207	+ 39 = 8,246
Pattison (Lab.)	8,148	+ 923 = 9,071 (E)
b. 1982b (quota 9,301) Result of 10th count		11th count, distribution of Dowling's (FG) surplus of 1,177
Nolan (FF)	8,847	+ 93 = 8,940 (EQ)
Gibbons (FF)	8,573	+ 95 = 8,668
Pattison (Lab.)	8,568	+ 989 = 9,557 (E)

E = elected; EQ = elected without reaching quota.

Sources: Browne, 1981, 1982a; Trench 1982, with amendments.

terms of votes at this stage, and Pattison for Labour. Dowling, a Fine Gael candidate, had just been elected, and his surplus of 1,177 was now distributed. An even three-way split of his votes would have given the seats to Nolan and Gibbons, but once again differential transfers saved the day for Pattison. He received 84% of Dowling's transfers and this was sufficient to overtake both his opponents and carry him 256 votes past the quota to give him a seat (Table 2.5b). Nolan was deemed elected to the last seat without reaching the quota.

It can be seen that the nature of the voting system can profoundly affect the nature of political life in a state, having an impact on the functions of public representatives, the style and purpose of campaigning, and indeed the actual outcome of an election. But the outcome can also be influenced by the spatial framework of boundaries within which voting takes place.

THE SPATIAL FRAMEWORK: ALLOCATION OF SEATS AND BOUNDARIES

Originally, Thomas Hare had believed that to achieve maximum proportionality, each constituency should have as many seats as possible—indeed the ideal was that the entire country should be one enormous constituency (C. O'Leary, 1979). However, practical considerations have ruled this out. Even for a small country such as the Irish Republic where 408 candidates fought the 1981 election (Busteed, 1982) it could involve an enormous ballot paper and each elector would take a very long time to vote. After the best-known candidates had been chosen, the vast majority of subsequent choices would probably be random, and many voters would probably not even bother to complete the ballot. To avoid these problems the national space must therefore be overlaid with a network of boundaries and constituency areas and parliamentary seats allocated to each constituency. This is a difficult and delicate task, not merely because of the vast amount of information available and the need to choose between a multiplicity of possible solutions (Gudgin and Taylor, 1979), but also because the precise alignment of boundaries and the number of seats allocated to a constituency can determine who wins the seats and even who wins an election and subsequently forms the government. In an STV system as used in Ireland, there has long been a consensus, following Hare, that the greater the number of seats allocated to a constituency, the closer the result will be to proportionality. Conversely, it is argued that the smaller the number of seats in constituencies, the greater the tendency to squeeze out smaller parties and independents, inflate the share of seats going to major parties, and depart from proportionality (M. Gallagher, 1986). It has also been argued as noted earlier that in an STV system the transfer of lower preferences has greater influence on the outcome where there are more seats per constituency (M. Gallagher, 1979*b*).

Ideally, not only should there be large constituencies to give minimum distortion of voter choice but the ground rules employed in delimiting them and allocating seats should be applied uniformly throughout the national territory. Most states have such basic ground rules. In Ireland the constitution of 1937 stated that there should be at least one Dáil deputy for each 30,000 of the population, at most one for each 20,000 (Bunreacht na h Éireann, 1985, 16. 2. 2). In practice, there are two ways in which this ideal of equality can be eroded. One is a change in the population geography of a state, reducing the population in some constituencies, leaving others largely untouched, and adding population to others. The result is known as 'malapportionment', whereby some deputies end up representing more people than others and the political weight of each vote in such constituencies is diluted. Such a situation arose in the Irish Republic during the early 1980s in the Dublin region. Following a revision of boundary and seat allocation in 1979 the constituency of Dublin West had 5 seats, and at the election of June 1981 a ratio of 20,766 people per TD. However, even by the election of November 1982 there had been notable population movements, and the new deputy to population ratio was 1:22,335. Clearly, regular reallo-

Table 2.6. *Constituency numbers and sizes 1923–1980*

Date of Revision	9 seats	8 seats	7 seats	5 seats	4 seats	3 seats	No. of constituencies
1923	1	3	5	9	4	8	30 (153 seats)
1935	—	—	3	8	8	15	34 (138 seats)
1947	—	—	—	9	9	22	40 (147 seats)
1961	—	—	—	9	12	17	38 (144 seats)
1969	—	—	—	2	14	26	42 (144 seats)
1974	—	—	—	6	10	26	42 (148 seats)
1980	—	—	—	15	13	13	41 (166 seats)

Source: Browne, 1982a, with amendments.

cation of boundaries and seats is necessary to keep abreast of population geography and the Irish constitution stipulates that such revisions should take place at least once every twelve years in accordance with the demographic trends revealed by the last census (Bunreacht na h Éireann, 1985, 16. 2. 3, 4). In actual fact the accelerating rate of population change in the country since 1961 has led to increasingly frequent revisions (Coakley, 1980).

Following independence in 1921, two distinct trends appeared in the allocation of seats and boundaries. The first was a persistent tendency to reduce the number of seats per constituency (Table 2.6). From 1923 until 1935 there was considerable variation in the size of constituencies. The first revision of 1935 was quite radical. It reduced the total number of seats by 15 because of the decline in population and abolished all constituencies with more than 7 seats. The number of 3-seaters increased sharply. This set the pattern for the subsequent 30 years. The 1947 revision created 9 new seats, abolished all constituencies with more than five members, boosted the number of 3-seaters to 22 and created 9 constituencies with four members and 9 with five. For the next 30 years 5-seat constituencies would always be the largest and revisions would merely alter the relative numbers off 3-, 4-, and 5-seaters. The total number of seats did change slightly as the total population fluctuated. Thus in 1961 it fell by 3 to 144, remained at that level in 1969, rose by 4 in the 1974 revision, and jumped to 166 in 1980 to allow for the rapid population expansion of the 1970s.

The second trend revealed by the successive revisions is more an allegation backed by strong prima-facie evidence than a firmly established fact. It is the assertion that since the Irish constitution left the revision of constituency areas, boundaries, and seat allocation to ordinary law passed by the government of the day, governments have yielded to the temptation to manipulate these revisions to their partisan advantage. Given the fact that Fianna Fáil has been in office longest and was responsible for all redistributions between 1935 and 1969, it has been the most frequent target of these allegations. The accusations centre on two points. First it is alleged that the party deliberately reduced the 9-, 8-, and 7-seat constituencies and they increased 3- and 4-seaters in the belief that this made it more difficult for their opponents to win seats. Given the formula for the Droop quota noted earlier, then the smaller the number of seats in a constituency, the smaller the quotient when calculating the quota, the larger the threshold of votes a party must pass to win a seat, and the more difficult it becomes for weaker parties to gain seats. To some extent of course both Fianna Fáil and Fine Gael, as the major parties in the system, would benefit from an increase in 3- and 4-seaters (Paddison, 1976). The second allegation however suggests that Fianna Fáil manipulated constituency size in various parts of the country to maximize the impact of their regional pattern of support and minimize that of their chief opponents, Fine Gael and Labour. Traditionally, Fianna Fáil have been strongest in western Ireland, while Fine Gael and Labour have regional concentrations of strength in the east, particularly the Dublin region (Chubb, 1970; Busteed and Mason, 1974). For Fianna Fáil there would be two logical responses to such a support pattern. One would be to allocate to the western counties more deputies than they deserved on a strict application of the normal ratio of deputy to population while at the same time assigning fewer deputies to eastern areas. An examination of the 1969 redistribution in the light of the 1971 Census revealed that the national mean of population per deputy was 20,635. If applied strictly to the 9 north-western counties of the country, they should have had 33 TDs; in fact, they had 36, and a regional mean of 19,241 persons per deputy. Using the same census, Dublin City, County, and the constituency of Dun Laoghaire-Rathdown, with a population of 852,219, deserved 41 seats; in fact they had only 38, and a regional mean of 22,426 persons per seat. Given the geography of support noted earlier, the probabilities are that this pattern gave a few extra seats to Fianna Fáil and deprived Fine Gael and Labour of a few (Busteed, 1975).

The second technique of manipulation would be for Fianna Fáil to ensure that constituency quotas were high in the west, where its own support is strong and other parties would find it difficult to surmount a high quota, and low in the east, where it is weaker and would be assisted by lower quotas. Some variations in the ratio of population to deputies are to be expected in any scheme, but in Ireland the general feeling has been that Fianna Fáil has never striven too officiously to ensure total national conformity, and on one famous occasion the Irish courts found it had indeed gone too far. In 1959 a revision scheme was introduced which at the national level produced 20,100 people per deputy, not a great departure from the constitutional provision of 1 : 20,000. But this concealed variations of possibly partisan significance. For counties Donegal, Galway, Mayo, and Kerry the figure was one TD per 17,758 people while for Dublin City it was one per 22,753. These provisions were challenged in the High Court by a Fine Gael senator and struck down on the grounds that they were an unacceptable departure from the norm laid down in the constitution (C. O'Leary, 1979).

However, this is not to say that the other Irish parties are entirely above suspicion on this issue. There is every reason to believe that they are relatively innocent only because they have lost most elections and thereby lacked the power to push through favourable revisions. On the one occasion in recent years when a non-Fianna Fáil administration was in power and a redistribution fell due, the government was quite blatant about its intentions. The opportunity came with the election of the national coalition of Fine Gael and Labour in February 1973. On the second day of the first sitting of the new Dáil James Tully, the Minister for Local Government, began the process of introducing a bill for constituency revision to be based on the results of the 1971 census of population. When the Bill was eventually produced in November 1973 it was widely interpreted on all sides as an attempt to turn Fianna Fáil's traditional weapon of constituency manipulation against that party and ensure that any advantage in the next election would accrue to the Coalition parties. Certainly the minister himself enthused about his efforts—'I cannot improve on it anyway. I think it is great. Fantastic' (C. O'Leary, 1979)—and the result was widely referred to as a 'Tullymander'.

The 1971 census had revealed a further population increase of 3% over 1966 and in accordance with constitutional provision this resulted in 4 new seats in the Dáil, to give a total of 148. The total number of constituencies remained 42 as before and there were still 26 3-seaters. There were to be 10 4-seat constituencies and 6 5-seaters. However, it was in the allocation of these different-sized constituencies across the national space that partisan considerations were believed to have come into play. As already noted Fine Gael and Labour have traditionally been strongest in the Dublin region and the south-east of the country, whereas Fianna Fáil's greatest strength has always been in western Ireland. Commentators on the Coalition's 1974 boundary revision claimed to find a partisan motive

Table 2.7. *Size of constituencies in Dublin region and western region after redistributions, 1969, 1974*

	5-Seaters		4-Seaters		3-Seaters	
	1969	1974	1969	1974	1969	1974
Dublin region	—	—	8	1	2	13
Western region	—	1	1	8	13	8

Note: Dublin region defined as comprising constituencies in Dublin City and County plus Dun Laoghaire–Rathdown. Western region defined as comprising constituencies in counties Donegal, Sligo, Leitrim, Roscommon, Mayo, Galway, Clare, Limerick, Kerry.

in the allocation of constituencies, particularly in the Dublin region and the far west. In the first place the number of seats allocated to the Dublin region was increased from 38 to 43, though this could be justified on the grounds of population increase. Between 1969 and 1974 this same region had 8 4-seaters and 2 3-seaters. Now there were to be 13 3-seaters and one 4-seater (Table 2.7). It was widely believed that this would present a series of difficult thresholds for Fianna Fáil in what was traditionally its weakest electoral region. In the western counties by contrast the new scheme lowered the electoral thresholds. Between 1969 and 1974 there had been 13 3-seaters and one 4-seater in these constituencies. Under the new scheme there were to be 8 3-seaters, 3 4-seaters and one 5-seater. This, it was believed, would make it easier for Fine Gael, traditionally weak in these regions, to pick up additional seats. It was calculated that if the 1973 general election had been refought on the new boundaries then in Dublin City alone Coalition-held seats would have increased from 14 to 18 and Fianna Fáil seats would have dropped from 13 to 9 without a single voter switching allegiance (Mair and Laver, 1975).

However, while seat allocation and boundary location could be legislated for, public opinion could not. The economic problems which afflicted Ireland in the early and mid-1970s, its heavy-handed treatment of security and civil rights, and a number of self-inflicted wounds referred to earlier combined to produce a massive swing away from the Coalition and in the 1977 general election Fianna Fáil scored a notable victory. In terms of seats the party gained an all-time record majority of 20 over all other parties. Clearly the 'Tullymander' had not worked—in fact, it had backfired, because the 1974 Electoral Amendment Act had located boundaries in such a fashion as to create a large number of marginal seats based on the assumption that public opinion at the next election would divide in the same way as in 1973. In actual fact there was a decisive swing to Fianna Fáil creating a pattern of party support which meant that it captured many of the marginal seats the Coalition had created.

For some time feeling had been growing that there was too much latitude for partisan manipulation of boundaries and that the whole matter should be taken out of the hands of the government of the day. This suggestion had surfaced during the unsuccessful referenda on the electoral system in 1959, and a Committee on the Constitution in 1967 had made a similar recommendation but to no avail. However, the effort at manipulation by the defeated Coalition had been so blatant that opinion had definitely built up in favour of a non-partisan commission. At his first press conference after Fianna Fáil's victory the new Taoiseach Jack Lynch promised future constituency revision would not be a matter for incumbent governments. A three-man boundary commission was set up to propose constituencies for the first direct elections to the European parliament, due in 1979. It consisted of Justice Brian Walsh, a judge of the Supreme Court and President of the Law Commission, as the Chairman, the Secretary of the Department of Environment, and the Clerk of the Senate. Its proposals were accepted by the Dáil without amendment and, possibly encouraged by this experience, the government set up another Commission to advise on Dáil constituency boundaries in October 1979. It consisted of Justice Walsh, the Secretary of the Environment Department once again, the Clerk to the Dáil, and, as secretary, a Principal Officer from the Department of Environment. The Commission reported in April 1980 (*Irish Times*, 28 April 1980) and its recommendations, again without amendment, became law as the Electoral (Amendment) Act, 1980. That was to be the spatial framework within which the three general elections of 1981–2 and the two referenda of 1983 and 1986 were to be conducted (Fig. 5.1*b*).

The Commission was given four elementary guidelines on which to base its work (Dáil Éireann Constituency Commission Report, 1980). First, given the recent remarkable rise in Irish population, there had to be an increase in total membership of the Dáil in accordance with the constitution. It was stipulated that the new Dáil should have between 164 and 168 deputies. Second, the members were to take into account 'geographical considerations'. By this it was explained that when drawing up boundaries the breaching of county borders was to be avoided and the larger seat constituencies were to be allocated to the areas of high population density. Third, it was to take account of other well-established characteristics of constituencies, such as clearly defined natural features, and finally the traditional pattern of 3-, 4-, and 5-seat constituencies was to be retained. Interested parties were free to make submissions to the Commission and 56 of these were received. The majority concentrated on the question of how far the Commission could deviate from the constitutional ratio of one deputy per 20–30,000 of the population, with most assuming that a 5% deviation was reasonable and one even assuming 10%. The Commission concluded that there was no fixed rule for variation but that in every case the test was that used in the Supreme Court decision on the 1961 Electoral (Amendment) Bill, namely whether a departure from the constitutional guideline was of such an extent as to breach its original intention. This same court case was also used for general guidance in the rest of the Commission's decision-making. In particular the court's emphasis on the desirability of following established administrative boundaries such as those of counties, townlands, and electoral divisions and the existence of divisions created by natural features such as rivers, lakes, and mountains was taken as reinforcement of the Commission's own terms of reference.

The Commission seems to have proceeded by looking first at rural areas. It made a provisional allocation of seats to counties on the basis of population. Where this produced constituencies which would deviate significantly from the national average ratio of population to deputy the boundaries clearly had to be adjusted. In several cases counties had to be sub-divided into two or more constituencies. Where this had to be done efforts were made to have the boundaries coincide with some pre-existing administrative division e.g. county electoral area or former Rural District, as suggested by the Commission's terms of reference. This, however, was not always possible. In five cases it had to combine counties and in such places justified its proposals by the fact that this was not the first time that counties had been aggregated to form constituencies. In three cases the Commission had to depart from the criteria laid down and add small parts of one county to another in order to get constituencies of the proper population size. Consequently a small part of county Waterford went to make up Tipperary South; Meath took in part of Westmeath and Roscommon part of Galway. In each case it was stressed that there was some community of interest between the area transferred and the county it joined, such as a previous history of electoral association. In each case the areas transferred were entire administrative units. Thus the area of Galway county included in Roscommon constituency consisted of nine district electoral divisions of the former Glennamaddy Rural District.

When it came to urban areas the Commission seemed to take a rather more relaxed view of the guidelines. It noted the rule that the larger-seat constituencies should be reserved to urban areas but clearly did not feel that this totally ruled out urban 3-seaters. In fact, in both Cork City and Dublin City and region the Commission did confine itself almost entirely to 5- and 4-seat constituencies (Figure 2.2). The only urban 3-seater was Dublin North and there it may well have felt that the very mixed, part suburban, part rural nature of the region amply justified the decision. The Commission also declared that it felt free to ignore county borough boundaries, especially since suburban growth had rendered many obsolete. Consequently, boroughs and neighbouring rural areas were combined in many places e.g. the 5-seat constituency of Dun Laoghaire was made up of Dun Laoghaire Borough plus seven contiguous electoral districts from Dublin County. Overall, there was a national mean ratio of 20,290 persons per deputy; only in five cases was the deviation greater than ±5% (Table 2.8).

This new scheme involved the most radical changes for many years. The Dáil was to contain 166 deputies, the highest total ever. Even more notable was the sharp decrease in the number of 3-seat constituencies to 13, the increase in 4-seaters to 13, and, most notable of all, the creation of 15 5-seaters (Table 2.6). The long-term trend towards increasing the number of seats in the Dublin region was continued but there was also an increase in representation for the western region (Table 2.9) in recognition of the fact that population growth had now diffused from the Dublin region into lower-ranking urban centres such as Galway and Limerick.

The end result is certainly a scheme of seats and boundary allocation which is non-partisan in design and intent with general uniformity of the deputy to population ratio across the country and more equitable allocation of seats to regions. However, it has been suggested that the Commission's work had the unintended effect of muffling the impact of the swing of voter opinion from government to opposition in the 1981 election (Mair, 1982). Briefly this has happened because it allocated most of the 3-seat constituencies to western areas where Fianna Fáil's vote is traditionally strong and stable and thus they could easily hold their seats while allocating 5 5-seaters and 5 4-seaters to the Dublin region thereby lowering the electoral thresholds and enabling the party to hold on to some seats in the face of the swing of voter opinion (Mair, 1986). The only compensation may have lain in the fact that there was now a closer relationship between votes and seats across the country as a whole and any party advantage from the working of the system was accidental rather than intentional.

Table 2.8. *Relation of population size to deputy in constituencies, 1980*

	Population	Average population per TD	Variation from national mean %
Carlow–Kilkenny	107,824	21,565	+6.28
Cavan–Monaghan	104,096	20,819	+2.61
Clare	84,919	21,230	+4.63
Cork East	79,364	19,841	−2.21
Cork North Central	97,475	19,495	−3.92
Cork North-West	57,977	19,326	−4.75
Cork South Central	101,498	20,300	+0.05
Cork South-West	59,804	19,935	−1.75
Donegal North-East	60,701	20,234	−0.28
Donegal South-West	61,240	20,413	+0.61
Dublin Central	101,473	20,295	+0.02
Dublin North	59,125	19,708	−2.87
Dublin North Central	81,789	20,447	+0.78
Dublin North-East	79,258	19,815	−2.34
Dublin North-West	82,645	20,661	+1.84
Dublin South	104,034	20,807	+2.55
Dublin South Central	102,479	20,496	+1.01
Dublin South-East	82,442	20,611	+1.58
Dublin South-West	82,994	20,749	+2.26
Dublin West	103,834	20,767	+2.35
Dun Laoghaire	103,610	20,722	+2.13
Galway East	62,317	20,772	+2.38
Galway West	101,673	20,335	+0.22
Kerry North	60,304	20,101	−0.93
Kerry South	60,052	20,017	−1.35
Kildare	97,185	19,437	−4.20
Laois-Offaly	107,278	21,456	+5.74
Limerick East	98,204	19,641	−3.20
Limerick West	59,203	19,734	−2.74
Longford-Westmeath	84,496	21,124	+4.11
Louth	86,135	21,534	+6.13
Mayo East	59,963	18,988	−6.42
Mayo West	57,056	19,019	−6.27
Meath	96,889	19,378	−4.50
Roscommon	58,037	19,346	−4.65
Sligo-Leitrim	82,454	20,614	+1.59
Tipperary North	58,476	19,492	−3.93
Tipperary South	77,679	19,420	−4.29
Waterford	84,864	21,216	+4.56
Wexford	96,421	19,284	−4.96
Wicklow	83,950	20,988	+3.44
COUNTRY	3,368,217	20,290	—

Table 2.9. *Total of seats awarded to Dublin region and western region in redistributions, 1969, 1974, and 1980*

	Dublin region	Western region
1969	38	43
1974	43	41
1980	48	45

Note: Dublin region and western region as defined for Table 7.

CONCLUSION

The Republic of Ireland's virtually unique electoral system was originally imposed by colonial rulers for decidedly partisan reasons, but despite this unpromising start it has survived almost unaltered since the foundation of the state. Considering the quite radical constitutional changes which marked the first 25 years of Irish independence this is surprising. The explanation is that over the years PR-STV has evolved into a characteristic element of the country's political culture, a development confirmed by the defeat of the two referenda which were aimed at its abolition. This is not to say that it has been without its critics—the mere holding of the referenda would disprove that. Through the years academic political scientists and practising politicians have laid several of the facets of Irish political life at the voting system's door. Amongst the most frequent are multiplicity of political parties, frequent lack of an overall majority for a single party, the need to form coalitions or attract support from independents and minor parties to form a government, and the weakness of a legislature whose members are compelled to concentrate on local grievances to consolidate their voting base, rather than act as national legislators trying to control the executive. In fact, many of these accusations have been exaggerated and some of the features discussed simply reflect the underlying nature of Irish society. One of the most notable features of the Irish voting system is the way in which it maximizes voter choice: an elector can not only choose between parties but also express a preference on every candidate on the ballot paper. Consequently, whatever factors are important in social relations in Irish society will find a fairly true reflection in electoral behaviour. The voting system has not manufactured these features, it has merely articulated them.

In support of the Irish electoral system it can be argued that, given the small number of wasted ballots in general elections and the referenda results of 1959 and 1968, it is both understood and supported by the Irish electorate at large. It can also be argued that it has produced a fairly close relationship between seats and votes in most elections and though single-party majorities are much smaller and more often non-existent than in Great Britain, Irish parliaments have not been shorter lived, governments have not collapsed more frequently, nor has it ever been proved that they were less efficient or competent or more corrupt because of the need to attract support from minor-party or independent deputies. Indeed, by West European standards Irish governments score quite highly in terms of longevity and stability and the Dáil equally well in terms of representativeness and lack of party fractionalization. The imposition of any network of constituency boundaries and the allocation of parliamentary seats inevitably introduces some distortion into patterns of representation, but since 1979 intentional bias has been eliminated by the new non-partisan Constituency Commission.

In recent years the most far-reaching questions about the Irish political system have not come as the result of the workings of the electoral system but are the outcome of profound changes in Irish society as a whole. These must now be examined in detail.

3

Traditional and Modern Influences in Irish Society

INTRODUCTION

Until relatively recently, southern Ireland had an image as a stable and conservative, indeed traditionalist society in which the basic social and religious mores were widely accepted and rarely openly questioned. Doubtless there were always considerable gaps between private practice and public profession and it is certainly true that a small group of literary intellectuals ploughed a lonely path of dissent after independence (Brown, 1981) but on the whole the country was notable for the homogeneity and wide public acceptance of its national ethos.

However, in the late 1950s a process of opening Ireland up to the outside world got under way. Initially this was confined to new thinking on national economic development policy, but this had profound effects on other aspects of national life as well. The process of opening up was reinforced by improvements in travel and tele-communications and the widespread dissemination of knowledge about the activities and values of the outside world. Combined with a growing and increasingly youthful population, the results were a greater awareness of alternative values and behaviour patterns and a questioning of long-accepted ideas and practices. Consequently in the 1970s and especially in the early 1980s the Republic became a scene of conflict between traditional and modern influences and the interplay of these forces provided the environment in which the political parties had to operate. It is therefore essential to understand these forces and their interaction in order to make sense of political behaviour.

TRADITIONAL INFLUENCES

The long and troubled relationship between Ireland and Britain has had a profound effect on the development of the Irish political culture. Given the physical proximity of the two islands it was probably inevitable that they should interact in some way, but interaction went far beyond migration and trade. From 1167 onwards there was an Anglo-Norman or English military presence in Ireland. The fortunes of the medieval English colony in Ireland waxed and waned over the next 400 years. At its maximum in the late thirteenth century the early colony covered almost two-thirds of Ireland; at its minimum two centuries later it was largely confined to a few isolated towns and the 'Pale', the city of Dublin and the region within a radius of thirty miles. However, in the early sixteenth century the Tudor conquest of Ireland got under way and was complete by 1603. For just over three centuries, until 1922, all of Ireland was subject to British rule.

This prolonged contact had far-reaching effects on Irish development at all levels, cultural, economic, and social. In political terms however the impact was greatest after the Act of Union of 1801 abolished the Irish parliament and tied the evolution of Irish political life much more closely to British developments at a crucial formative stage of British history. Consequently, though some of the terminology may differ, many of the institutions of Irish political life and government found their original inspiration in British models which evolved during the nineteenth century when the two islands were governed as one united kingdom (Chubb, 1982). When legislation was required for reform of British political institutions, the Bill for Ireland usually came a little later than that for Great Britain and, while not precisely identical, broadly followed the same lines. The institutional similarities persisted even after independence. The Irish president is a purely ceremonial head of state on the British model rather than an active head of the executive as in the United States. The Irish parliament, after a brief and unsatisfactory experiment with a unicameral system in 1936 and 1937, has always been a bicameral legislature with the real power residing in the lower house, as in the British system. Universal adult suffrage has always been the rule in southern Ireland since independence, and since 1972 everyone aged 18 and over has had the right to vote.

The workings of this system are also closely based upon the British model. As at Westminster, the government is formed by the group which can command a majority of votes in the lower house and the leader of the majority becomes the chief minister of the government, presiding over a Cabinet consisting of the political heads of the most important departments of state. The executive or civil service is regarded as a politically neutral arm of government, with the duty of administering the state in accordance with the view of the government of the day. The judiciary is organized on a rather different basis from the British system, with a High Court and Supreme Court, but here again it operates with a distinctly British ethos as a politically neutral and independent arm of government.

However, standing paradoxically alongside these inheritances from the days of British colonial rule there is a set of values and features which is best described as the nationalist inheritance. It orginates from the struggle to end British rule and establish an independent Irish state. Unlike the United Kingdom, southern Ireland has always had a written constitution. In part this may have been seen as a necessary basic framework of laws and rights in the turbulent early days of the new state, but it may also have been due to a desire to make public the characteristic aims of the first sovereign Irish state after centuries of British rule. The distinctive organization of the Irish judiciary, with a Supreme Court presided over by a Chief Justice as the final court of appeal, reflects the ultimately successful efforts to abolish the right of appeal to the British Privy Council in London and establish a fully independent Irish legal system. However, the greatest impact of the nationalist inheritance is probably felt in the ethos and informal ground-rules of the Irish political system rather than in institutions and organs of government. There is traditionally an element of anti-British sentiment in the Irish political culture. Such negative attitudes towards neighbouring states are a fairly common element in nationalist sentiments, but in the Irish case they are exacerbated by four considerations. First, the 1919–21 War of Independence against British security forces in Ireland inevitably involved some grisly incidents on both sides, and the memory of such events has with time become almost a mythology. Second, there is an ultra-nationalist version of Irish history which sees this conflict as only the final phase of eight hundred years of ceaseless struggle to free the country from foreign British invaders, and such an interpretation has obvious anti-British overtones. Again, the relative proximity of Great Britain means that Ireland's former colonial ruler impinges frequently on the Irish consciousness, a perpetual reminder of past and indeed present relationships. Finally, the contemporary version of anti-British sentiment is fuelled by the continuing British presence in Northern Ireland. For some elements in Irish politics the partition of six counties from the rest of Ireland has always been a violation of Irish territorial integrity. Consequently, the north-eastern corner of the island has been seen as *Hibernia irridenta*, and its reintegration with the rest of the body politic has been a persistent political aspiration. The failure to achieve it has been blamed solely on the continuing British military presence in Northern Ireland.

This anti-British sentiment manifests itself in several ways. Physical symbols of British authority past and present such as monuments and statues become targets for abuse and worse. On occasion the manifestations are more violent, such as the burning down of the British Embassy in February 1972 and the assassination of the British Ambassador in July 1976 and of Lord Mountbatten in August 1979. Elements of anti-British feeling can still be detected in the political rhetoric at election times, especially in Fianna Fáil ranks, and in some parts of the country it can influence voting behaviour. Provisional Sinn Fein is the contemporary political embodiment of this outlook.

The nationalistic interpretation of Irish history as eight centuries of struggle for independence, the experiences of 1916 and 1919–21, and the veneration of the events and personalities of this period have all combined to contribute another element to the nationalist heritage, namely the belief that under certain circumstances political violence is necessary and justified. Those who take this view argue that since it is generally agreed such methods were legitimate in the past to remove British authority from the 26 counties then logically it must be justified when used to eject British authority, where it still exists, from the last six counties of the island.

But the nationalist inheritance can also be seen in some aspects of the Irish political style. Traditionally, the main Irish parties, but particularly Fianna Fáil, have put a heavy emphasis on loyalty to the party and the leadership. Indeed at times attitudes to dissent and discipline have been reminiscent of military rather than political affairs. To some extent these may reflect the circumstances out of which the main parties were generated. Both Fianna Fáil and Fine Gael have their historic roots in Sinn Fein, the political manifestation of that more militant brand of nationalism which carried all before it in southern Ireland after 1916. At various stages between 1919 and 1921 the party suffered harassment, proscription, and the arrest and prosecution of its officers, members, and supporters. In such circumstances a high premium was placed on mutual trust, solidarity, and loyalty amongst members and leaders in the face of British oppression, and these qualities became a valued part of the ethos of Irish political life in the decades after independence.

The experiences of the Civil War reinforced these attitudes. Personnel on both sides once again faced danger and, in the case of republicans, arbitrary arrest, imprisonment, and in some cases execution. Subsequently, both the main parties coalesced not only around attitudes to the Treaty but also around leading personalities who, especially in the case of de Valera in Fianna Fáil, drew on deep wells of loyalty, because of their personal role during the period of 1916–23 and the events and values they came to personify. In time de Valera was to achieve a dominance over his party which inhibited public dissent and may well have discouraged internal party democracy and discussion as well.

The militant nationalism which Sinn Féin came to express after 1916 was the outgrowth of many movements which had been fermenting in the closing years of the nineteenth century and the first years of the twentieth. These developments produced a more robust, self-confident sense of Irish national identity, and one of the most notable features of this development was a revival of interest in Irish Gaelic culture—games, literature, history, and above all, the Irish language. Originally, as organized under the Gaelic League, the intention was that this movement should be apolitical (Lyons, 1979), but with its stress on the need to resist English cultural influences, and its argument that Ireland had a distinctive history and culture, it had obvious political implications. In time some of its adherents developed the argument that political independence was necessary to protect and reinforce this Irish cultural heritage. Even before independence was won, plans were in hand to ensure that in the new Irish state Irish culture would have a high profile. Consequently, after 1921, the Irish language was made the first official language, many of the political institutions of the state were given Irish terminology, Irish culture occupied a significant place in school curricula, and the surviving Irish-speaking districts, mostly in western Ireland, were accorded special treatment in the disbursement of government funds in an effort to stem emigration and preserve the language. Language preservation became, like the reunification of the island, one of the aspirations of the new state (Fanning, 1983).

A further inheritance from the nationalist reaction against British rule concerns Irish attitudes to authority. The sense of reserve towards the British authorities has carried over into modern Ireland in the form of a certain traditional alienation from all central government on the part of the ordinary citizen (Sacks, 1976). There is a latent, cynical belief that government is both distant and venal and that in order to get satisfaction in his dealings with it the ordinary citizen must invoke not merely his statutory rights but also an intermediary who can exert influence on his behalf. In modern times this role has been played by the political representative—councillor, TD, or area board nominee. Such people have come to be regarded as mediators between national government and the citizen or locality and as channels through whom requests and complaints are passed to the central or local government and through whom redress, grants, or assistance in any form will be mediated. The need for such a role may have been greatest in the early days of independent Ireland when the welfare services were skeletal and many payments discretionary. More recently however with the expansion of such services and the extension of access by right the need for intervention by a third party is debatable. However for many electors, especially in rural areas, it is still an article of faith that such personal contacts are necessary and helpful and many local representatives are only too happy to go along with the idea that they still have a vital role of this sort to play.

This tenacious emphasis on the public representative as ombudsman and intermediary is merely one aspect of the great significance of personality and localism in Irish political life. Particularly in rural areas, elected representatives are still expected to be people with strong personal family links in the areas they represent. Indeed, it has been argued that such factors have been the basic reference points in Irish electoral politics from as early as the nineteenth century (Hoppen, 1984) and are only occasionally overwhelmed by great national issues.

One reason for the enduring significance of these factors is that outside the immediate Belfast region Ireland did not experience a classic nineteenth-century industrial revolution. Consequently it escaped the associated features of rural–urban migration which transformed population geography and social relations in Great Britain and the extreme north-east. Even the large-scale emigration of the nineteenth and early twentieth centuries failed to erode the ties of kin and locality, because the family was regarded as an essential vehicle for the holding and passing on of property, especially land, the vital, often only, means of economic survival. One common motive for emigration was the realization that only a small proportion of the family could live off the family land, and the alternative for the others was therefore idleness or emigration.

The ethos of peasant proprietorship also influences Irish political style in other ways. Despite a sharp decline in recent decades, agriculture is still a significant employer of labour in the country and also a large number of people are employed in processing, distributing, and marketing agricultural products and providing services for the agricultural community. In addition, the farming lobby has been described as one of the best organized and effective in the country (Manning, 1979) and the farm vote is still assiduously courted by all three main parties. It is widely believed that the loss of its traditional agricultural support went a long way to explain Fine Gael's heavy defeat in 1977 (Farrell and Manning, 1978). However, the significance of agriculture in Irish politics goes beyond this. Traditionally, the farming life has held a special place in the Irish national psyche, especially in the context of the small family farm. Particularly in traditional Fianna Fáil thinking it has been seen as encapsulating all the ideal social, cultural, and moral virtues of the independent

Irish state, and while circumstances have changed, the ideal lingers in the Irish consciousness.

The Irish Catholic Church has also occupied a large role in the national psyche. Successive census reports reveal a figure of about 95% of respondents claiming to be Catholic. Moreover, it is not a purely nominal faith. Opinion surveys record about 85% of people claiming to attend mass at least once a week, with little significant variation by age, gender, class, or urban as opposed to rural dwelling (Nic Ghiolla Phadraig, 1976). Certainly there is a good deal of popular devotion in southern Ireland. The landscape is studded not merely with Catholic churches, presbyteries, parochial halls, and the property of religious orders, but also with calvaries, Marian grottoes and holy wells, and there are sporadic claims of divine apparitions and miracles at some sites, which then become locations for open-air gatherings.

At the more formal level, the Roman Catholic Church has played a key role in the preservation and development of Irish national sentiment. In no other European nation, with the possible exception of Poland, has there been such a close relationship between people, church, and national identity. The seeds were sown in the Reformation when Britain became Protestant in the early sixteenth century while Ireland remained Catholic. In the circumstances of the time subsequent British efforts to subjugate Ireland and bolster the ruling British Anglican ascendancy there also involved trying to restrict the activities of the Catholic Church and its adherents. In the short term the hope was that they could be denied political power, wealth, and property. Consequently legislation was passed which effectively barred them from political life, restricted their access to education, and hindered the inheritance, purchase, and renting of land. In the long run it was hoped Catholicism would die out and to this end there were laws at various times inhibiting the training and ordination of clergy. Not all of these penal laws were perpetually in force or enforced and the 1829 Emancipation Act abolished the last of them. However, the mere existence of such legislation was symptomatic of widespread official hostility, some of it was occasionally enforced, and the insecurity it produced bonded priests and people together in the face of common apprehension and sometimes actual suffering (Corish, 1985).

At times the Church became an active partner in the development of the national movement, but generally it opposed the more violent tradition of Irish nationalism, and the Irish Republican Brotherhood of the 1860s, the 1916 Rising, and the republicans during the Civil War of 1922–3 all suffered severe censure. However, the more peaceful parliamentary side of the movement often attracted the sympathy, and, at the grass roots, the active support, of the parish priests. Daniel O'Connell's campaign for Catholic emancipation had an obvious relevance for the Church, and the parish and its priest were widely used as the local basis of its organization and funding (Trench, 1984). The same was true of his campaign in the 1840s for the repeal of the Union. In the early 1880s the Land and Labour League drew heavily on Catholic priests as local organizers and supporters, and after 1916 some parish priests were active for Sinn Féin and one, Father Michael O'Flanagan, became a Vice President.

Given this close identity between people and Church it was probably inevitable that many came to see Catholicism as a badge of Irish national identity. It was probably equally inevitable that when Irish nationalism began to organize in formal political fashion that the Church should at least take a supportive, positive attitude. The active involvement of individual clergy at the grass-roots level is the logical local extension of these attitudes but it also reflects the fact that the clergy were recruited from the Irish Catholic population themselves, and thus shared popular attitudes on politics, as on much else. But it is also true that local clergy were far more than merely spiritual leaders and guides in the local Catholic communities. Since they were often the only Catholics with much education and the only ones who were financially independent of both landlords and government, they were often thrust into the role of local community leaders as well. Consequently, it was only logical that they should become locally prominent in nationalist politics and land-reform campaigns and that the already existing structure of parishes should be the basic unit of organization for such activities.

As a result, when Ireland came to independence in 1921, both the religious outlook of the great majority of the Irish people and its track record in Irish national history combined to ensure that the Catholic Church would play a significant role in the public life of the state. From the earliest days it became clear that the ethos of the new Irish state would be profoundly influenced by Catholic values. This tendency was further reinforced by a certain puritanical trend which had been developing in some Irish Catholic circles. This was partly a reaction to the more relaxed social attitudes abroad in western Europe after the First World War. In Catholic Ireland however Catholic puritanism tended to fuse with Irish nationalism and blame any undesirable social changes on ideas introduced via imported English magazines, newspapers, and subsequently films (Brown, 1981).

Consequently, as the 1920s progressed, several pieces of legislation clearly reflected a conservative Catholic viewpoint. As early as 1923 the Catholic hierarchy made clear their opposition to the creation of legal machinery for divorce in the Free State and with some alacrity the Irish government accepted this as the last word on the subject (Fanning, 1983). In 1923 a Censorship of Films Act was passed, and in 1929 a Censorship of Publications Act, which set up a board of five members to review printed matter and ban the import of materials deemed undesirable. Nor did the change of government in 1932 result in any lessening of the Catholic impact on Irish life. On the contrary, on occasion de Valera and Fianna Fáil had seemed at pains to prove their Catholic credentials (Brown, 1981). Perhaps they remembered the hierarchy's condemnation of republicans during the Civil War and wished to prove the Catholic soundness of their new party and avoid at all costs any possibility of hierarchical opposition, a crippling prospect for any party in Irish politics. However, it soon became clear that most of the new Ministers were practising Catholics, some notably devout, and their attendance at Catholic public occasions was regular and highly visible (Whyte, 1980). Any remaining doubts about the party were laid to rest by its legislative record. In 1933 it taxed imported newspapers regarded by some Catholic moralists as a vehicle for corrupting influences. In 1935 it introduced a licensing system for the dance halls which had recently become a marked feature of the Irish rural landscape and had drawn the opprobrium of the Church. In the same year they banned the importation and sale of artificial contraceptive devices.

But it was the constitution of 1937 which put to rest any final doubts about the Catholic soundness of Fianna Fáil. The document was prepared largely by de Valera himself after private consultation with Catholic theologians (Whyte, 1980; Fanning, 1983). The result was a constitution which, while it contained some religious references of a non-denominational nature, also clearly bore the imprint of distinctively Catholic teachings on social and economic relations as understood in the 1920s and 1930s. Article 44 guaranteeing freedom of conscience and worship for all and forbidding religious discrimination recognized the 'special position' of the Roman Catholic Church as 'the guardian of faith professed by the great majority of the citizens', (Bunreacht na h Éireann, 1985, 44. 1. 2). Articles 41, 42, and 43 laid out principles of policy on the family, the position of women, marriage, divorce, and education which closely followed the ideas of the Catholic International Union of Social Studies based at Malines, Belgium (Grogan, 1978). Amongst other things the institution of marriage was guaranteed state protection, and legislation permitting divorce was forbidden, as was the remarriage in Ireland of persons who had obtained a foreign divorce (Bunreacht na h Éireann, 1985, 41. 31, 2, 3). The family was also acknowledged as having the chief responsibility for education of children, especially in religious and moral affairs (Bunreacht na h Éireann, 1985, 42. 1. 2). It has been said that taken separately, these items are not overwhelmingly Catholic and some have been echoed in the constitutions of non-Catholic countries (Grogan, 1978), but taken together they do produce a distinctly Catholic ethos.

Moreover, given the atmosphere in Ireland in the two decades immediately after 1937 and indeed the legislative precedents of the first fifteen years of independence, the interpretation of these principles was almost inevitably conservative. The sensitive subject of health care illustrated the extent and nature of Church influence and reverberated for decades. The Irish health service in the early 1940s was rudimentary and there was widespread latent unhappiness with its workings. This discontent arose from two sources. First there was a growing awareness that the country was not effectively tackling certain chronic problems, particularly tuberculosis and infant mortality. Dissatisfaction was stoked by developments in contemporary Britain, where the Beveridge Report of December 1942 assumed that a comprehensive British national health service would be set up and in 1944 the British wartime coalition government publicly pledged itself to undertake this task (Whyte, 1984). The ideas quicky became a model for other countries, but the impact on southern Ireland was particularly strong, partly because of the historic links and physical proximity of the two countries but also because migration had swollen the Irish community in Britain in the previous few years and modern communications enabled much easier dissemination of news about conditions in Britain.

The result was to stimulate a much more critical attitude towards Irish health care arrangements and in response the Fianna Fáil government introduced a Health Bill in 1947. This proposed the consolidation of all the existing piecemeal health care schemes into a national system covering all children under 16 and all mothers. It was to be free to all, without a means test. The Minister for Health was given powers to take any steps necessary for prevention of infectious diseases and treatment of sufferers, and school health inspections were made compulsory. As in Britain, there was opposition to the scheme from the doctors' professional association, but far more significant politically were the objections of the Catholic hierarchy conveyed privately to the Taoiseach. These centred on the fact that a public body would be providing for the treatment and health education of children and women in gynaecological matters and motherhood. This they argued ran contrary to Catholic teaching and the respective rights of family, Church, medical profession, and voluntary bodies (Whyte, 1984). However, before the matter could develop any further the government was defeated in the general election of February 1948.

The new administration, the first inter-party government (which was to last until 1951) inherited the problem. Its Minister for Health was Dr Noel Browne of Clann na Poblachta, an energetic, impatient radical whose determination to revolutionize the Irish health service was partly inspired by personal and family suffering (Lyons, 1973). As part of his campaign in June 1950 he produced details of a plan for the free medical treatment of expectant mothers and of children up to the age of 16. It became known as the 'Mother and Child' scheme. In many ways it resembled the previous government's bill and it provoked opposition from the same quarters, namely the Irish Medical Association and the Catholic hierarchy. The hierarchy objected to the state taking any responsibility for child health care— this they believed was the right of the parents. They also condemned the intention to provide sex education for children and gynaecological care and advice for mothers on the grounds first that the state had no right to be active in these areas and that the subjects dealt with would include birth control and abortion, topics on which the Catholic Church had definite views but where there was no guarantee that the advice given would be within this framework. The hierarchy also objected to the keeping of records on individual patients on the grounds of invasion of privacy and suggested that the entire scheme was unnecessarily bureaucratic and expensive (Whyte, 1984).

In the subsequent discussions Dr Browne proved unable to satisfy the hierarchy's objections. It also became clear when the matter was discussed in Cabinet in April 1951 that he had no support from his colleagues and he resigned (M. Farrell, 1983). Immediately afterwards he released his entire correspondence with the hierarchy and the whole affair became a matter for intense public debate. The government agreed to replace the sections of the scheme which offended the hierarchy but its majority was already showing signs of fraying at the edges before this damaging debate erupted, and it lost the general election of May 1951.

The whole episode is frequently and correctly cited as a classic Church–state confrontation with the ecclesiastical authorities coming off best. However, in some ways it was merely the tip of the iceberg. Most Irish politicians recognized the extent of Catholic Church influence in the state and adapted their behaviour accordingly. If government proposals were thought to impinge on sensitive matters, civil servants or ministers usually consulted the hierarchy privately. This happened over a social insurance bill produced by the inter-party government in late 1949. On this occasion, the hierarchy had no objections and the scheme would have become law if the government had not lost the 1951 election. The same government was vigorously lobbied by several groups to reform Irish adoption law but the Minister privately consulted the hierarchy who expressed their unhappiness with the idea and he then refused to bring in legislation (Whyte, 1984).

What emerges is a picture of a country where the Catholic Church had played a special role in the historic development of the national consciousness and where the great majority of the population were still strongly Catholic. Given this situation it is therefore hardly surprising that the widely known teachings of the Church should influence the parameters of public debate and the legislation passed by the Oireachtas. The vast majority of politicians recognized and accepted these fundamental facts of Irish political life, either because they were themselves practising Catholics, or because they were political realists. Consequently, some subjects were never raised because they were recognized as beyond the bounds of permitted discussion or legislation. If topics fell in doubtful grey areas there were private discussions with the hierarchy. Consequently, although Catholic Church influence on political affairs was widely assumed, its extent and workings were never revealed until the public debates on the Mother and Child scheme in 1951. These showed that the Catholic Church in Ireland contributed heavily to a political ethos that was in many ways marked by a deeply entrenched traditionalism.

MODERNIZING INFLUENCES

Until the mid-1950s there was no really effective challenge to this strong fabric of very conservative values in Ireland. There was simply no firm and ample base from which alternative ideas could mount an effective challenge. As already pointed out, the political left was chronically weak. The Protestant community was tiny and declined as time passed, eroded by emigration and marriage into Catholic families. Censorship and duties on imported newspapers had effectively checked ideas coming in from abroad. A small group of dissident literary intellectuals did exist, but their influence was minimal.

When the challenge to traditional assumptions and values did come, it came on the economic front. It was not until the 1950s that southern Ireland could really make a proper evaluation of its experiment with economic self-sufficiency. Until then the course of national development had been distorted by a series of events: the aftermath of the War of Independence, the Civil War, the tasks of state building, the world depression, the 'Economic War' with Britain, and the emergency of the Second World War. Only when these events had passed was it possible to review the economic achievements of the new Irish state.

The general reaction as the 1950s unfolded was one of gradually deepening disappointment and discontent. Perhaps one of the most revealing symptoms was the level of emigration. There had long been a tradition of emigration from Ireland and it continued well into the twentieth century. However, beginning in the late 1930s there are indications of a steady increase (Lyons, 1973). This was maintained during the Second World War when the labour-hungry industries of the British wartime economy were the chief attraction. The flow slackened off in the post-war years and the 1951 Census revealed a slight rise in population over 1946, but by the early 1950s there were firm indications that emigration had set in again on an unprecendented scale. The 1956 Census recorded a population decrease and net emigration for 1951–6 of 197,000 people. The population of the Irish republic now stood at 2,898,264, the lowest ever for the 26 counties and even lower than in 1921, the year of independence (Johnson, 1963).

There were various reasons for this steady increase in emigration. One is the enduring fact that simply by being so much larger and more complex, the British and American economies can always offer more numerous and varied employment opportunities than southern Ireland. There is also evidence that from the mid-1930s onward Ireland's standard of living, never on a par with that of her large neighbour, began to lag even further behind (Lyons, 1973). The Irish at home were also much more aware of such contrasts than previously, thanks to the developments in communication and travel already mentioned, and many emigrants continued the tradition of sending money back home, a highly visible proof of the material success possible abroad. The result was that, particularly after 1950 when Britain's welfare state was fully functioning and prosperity began to return to the British economy, more and more people drew invidious contrasts between incomes, opportunities, and welfare services in Britain and Ireland, and took the decision to emigrate. Consequently the 1961 Census recorded yet another record low population and it was estimated that in the period 1956–61 there was a net loss of 212,000 by emigration (Johnson, 1963). For a small country with few valuable minerals or fuels such a loss of human resources was catastrophic.

The demographic crisis was paralleled by a series of economic difficulties. For a short period after 1945 the Irish economy had grown quite rapidly by Irish standards, but against broader West European perspectives it was unimpressive (Lyons, 1973). Then in the early 1950s there was a series of balance-of-payment crises. The second inter-party government responded by cuts in public expenditure which severely hit the level of activity in the construction and allied trades. Curbs on credit hit domestic expenditure and together with the chronic fall in the agricultural workforce, the combined result was a sharp rise in unemployment, and this at a time in Irish development when unemployment pay was low and ceased entirely after an individual had drawn it for six months (B. Walsh, 1979).

The term 'crisis of confidence' usually has a narrowly economic meaning and in that sense it can certainly be applied to the Irish economic outlook in the early and mid-1950s. But it can also be used to describe a certain public mood at all levels in the country at that time. There was a widely diffused conviction that the introverted policies of self-sufficiency which had determined the course of Irish life since 1932 had not produced satisfactory results. It was widely accepted in many Irish communities that the country could not provide a decent living for its population and that when children reached a certain age they would probably have to emigrate (B. Walsh, 1979).

The result of this reappraisal was a decided shift in national economic development policy. The doctrine of self-sufficiency behind tariff barriers was abandoned in favour of a conscious effort to plan Irish economic development in a more coherent, rational manner, and to direct state funds into more productive sectors of the economy and attract foreign-owned industry. The seeds of this policy change had been sown in 1955 when a Capital Investment Advisory Committee had been set up to examine the pattern of Irish public investment. It reported that more investment should be directed towards the generation of greater wealth and output and suggested that there should be a national development programme to co-ordinate it. This programme was drawn up by the recently appointed Secretary of the Department of Finance, T. K. Whitaker, presented to the government in May 1958, and published for public discussion in November of the same year. It formed the basis of the First Programme for Economic Expansion which was launched simultaneously. This was the first of three such plans covering the period 1958–72 (FitzGerald, 1968). Under their guidance the Irish economy was transformed, and a period of unparalleled economic expansion began which with minor fluctuations was to last until the arab-inspired oil-price rises and world recession of the mid-1970s.

The various measures designed to attract foreign firms were consolidated under the aegis of a national development agency, the Industrial Development Authority (IDA) (McMenamin, 1975). This was able to deploy a powerful battery of inducements to attract new investment, but most attractive of all was the minimal tax paid on the profits earned by the new firms. The generosity of the incentives package and the energetic, flexible natue of the IDA led one group of consultants who examined its work to describe it as 'undoubtedly the most effective agency of its kind in the world' (*Irish Times*, 15 Oct. 1982). In the 25 years after 1958, over 1,000 branch plants of foreign-owned manufacturing firms arrived in Ireland, and the IDA assisted almost all of them.

Their arrival affected the Irish economy in several ways. There was a gradual, though not spectacular, increase in manufacturing employment. Taken together with the continued decline in agricultural employment and a notable growth of the services sector, the result was a marked transformation of the employment structure of the country (Wickham, 1986). Many of the new firms were highly capital-intensive and wealth-creating. Their output soon became the chief element in Irish export earnings, and the traditional dominance of agricultural and food products passed away. The ownership patterns in Irish manufacturing industry also changed rapidly until by 1985 over one-third of the Irish employed in manufacturing worked for foreign-owned firms (Wickham, 1986). The most important of the investors were, in order, the United States, United Kingdom, West Germany, and Japan (*Industrial Development in Ireland*, 1980).

The new manufacturing firms and growth of service industries transformed prospects for the Irish labour force. They provided much better working conditions and incomes than traditionally available in Ireland. One notable result was to staunch the flow of emigration. The census of 1966 revealed a small increase in population, the first for 15 years (Johnson, 1963). Subsequent census reports confirmed the trend and by the late 1970s the Irish Republic was experiencing the fastest rate of population growth in Western Europe (Johnson, 1978; Horner and Daultrey, 1980), and in some years was actually gaining population by immigration (Walsh, J., 1979). The decline in the level of emigration inevitably transformed the size and geography of the population. By 1981, the Republic population was 3,443,405 (*Census of Population of Ireland*, 1984) the highest since independence. Traditionally Ireland had been a country of rural dwellers, but during these years there was a decided trend towards urban living. The 1971 Census was the first to record a majority of Irish people (52.3%) living in urban areas (Pringle, 1986) and by the early 1980s over one-third of the total population lived in the Dublin region. With the passage of time the experience of population growth, previously confined to Dublin, Cork, Limerick, and their surrounding areas, was diffused down the urban hierarchy and out into rural areas until by the early 1980s only the remote rural hinterlands of the north-west were still experiencing decline (Horner and Daultrey, 1980).

The structure of the country's population also changed radically. The great majority of Irish emigrants had been relatively young and most had been female. Their increasing tendency to remain in Ireland increased the youthful and female elements in the population. Traditionally there had always been a high rate of celibacy in the country, and the average age of marriage was also high. Now both began to come down. While the average family size also decreased (Coward, 1982), the mere fact that there were more marriages meant that the population became steadily younger (Kennedy, 1986). By the early 1980s Ireland had one of the most youthful populations in Western Europe, 55% were aged under 30 (*Census of Population of Ireland*, 1984), and these younger people were much better educated than earlier generations. These developments inevitably put pressure on the political system to deliver more and new types of output. The rising marriage-rate created a demand for more houses; the high birth-rate had to be met by more health and welfare services and eventually more school places, employment openings, and houses. Along with the process of urbanization and the growing youthfulness of the population, there appeared some of the classic symptoms of urban malaise. Most notably in the Dublin region, but also to some extent in the rest of the country, there were increases in crime, vandalism, and drug abuse (Rottman, 1986). In addition, as the 1980s advanced and the world economic recession worsened, Ireland began to suffer along with the rest of Western Europe. The contraction of agricultural employment and the decline of some traditional Irish industries continued. Service employment held steady or even increased slightly (Wickham, 1986), but some of the industries attracted since 1958 began to falter. Because of the generally adverse economic environment there was very little new inward foreign investment and though the IDA did switch its emphasis to give more encouragement to native Irish industry and smaller firms, the number of new jobs created in some years barely kept pace with losses (*Financial Times*, 8 July 1986). With large numbers each year of young people coming onto the labour market for the first time, the result was a steady rise in unemployment, especially amongst the young (*Guardian*, 17 Feb. 1987). Some long-term relief was promised by signs of decline in the number of marriages and births (Kennedy, 1986) and the renewal of emigration, though in the Irish context this last was widely regarded as a sign of failure. Some observers began to speculate on whether the Irish political system could accommodate the demands and frustrations generated by these developments.

The creation of a more open economy was only one of the changes of the 1950s. The Republic also began to develop a new perspective on the outside world. Traditionally Ireland's foreign affairs had been dominated by the need to work out relations with Britain, her nearest neighbour and former ruler. Even the close links with Irish-American groups and the membership of both the League of Nations and the United Nations had been used first and foremost to publicize complaints about Britain's continued presence in the north-east. Now, however, the parameters of Irish overseas interest were progressively widened. In 1960 the Republic sent a contingent of soldiers to join the United Nations forces in the recently independent Congo. Further units were sent later to Middle East trouble spots and the casualties and publicity involved awakened Irish public opinion to the affairs of a wider world.

A further stimulus came in August 1961 when the Republic made its first application to join the European Economic Community. Entry was to be delayed until 1973, but the interim period, and the debates leading up to the referendum which endorsed entry in May 1972, were a valuable educative experience. When the Republic eventually did join the EEC one of the most notable effects was the reorientation of trade to the point where other EEC members than Britain provided most of the markets for Irish exports (Wickham, 1986). The Anglo-Irish Free Trade Agreement of 1965, with its aim of creating totally unimpeded trade between the two countries within ten years showed how relaxed were the new economic relations between the two states. Ireland also participated in the general world trend towards a lowering of tariff boundaries in the early 1960s, and her entry into the European Monetary System in 1979, involving a break with sterling, showed how the Republic now saw its external relations within a much wider context.

But the wider world in turn impinged on Ireland to a greater extent than ever before, and the effect was to import new ideas and values of an unprecedented volume and range. To some extent this had begun in the 1920s with the arrival of the cinema. While censorship had effectively excluded material deemed blasphemous and vulgar, the American and British films which were shown did portray an outside world previously undreamt of by the Irish who remained in Ireland. An impression was conveyed of the material prosperity of the United States and Britain, and of a wider range of views and behaviour patterns accepted as the norm amongst both adults and young. The news from emigrants and visits between them and their relations reinforced these images. People in Ireland became increasingly aware that the ideas and controls they accepted as norms were not the only possible value systems and lifestyles. For some the effect was to create discontent and a desire for change. These feelings received a considerable boost with the arrival of an Irish television service in 1961. Long before this it was possible to pick up programmes from Britain and Northern Ireland in the border counties and along the east coast where most of the population lived. The Irish Television Service, RTE, run by a state-sponsored body and financed by advertising, was launched on New Year's Eve, 1961. Given the relative inexperience of its staff and the expense of making programmes, it was probably inevitable that a great deal of its material should consist of old films or television programmes purchased from Britain or the USA. Here again new ideas, values, and behaviour patterns were being presented to the Irish public, this time in both sound and vision inside their own homes. Moreover, as the 1960s proceeded, the attitudes of the media themselves changed. This was particularly true in their handling of current affairs. Originally, like their British counterparts, Irish commentators and interviewers had been cautious and deferential in their treatment of public issues and personalities, but as they gained confidence their attitudes changed. Programmes on public issues became more incisive and analytical and interviewers pressed their subjects in a more insistent, searching style (Gageby, 1979). Moreover, in both Britain and Ireland the early 1960s saw the rediscovery of political satire and there was a more daring, mocking mood abroad in some of the media. In Ireland this meant that not only were politicians, literary personalities, and industrialists subjected to quite penetrating questioning, but also clergy, including the bishops. The mere fact that eminent clerics should be questioned and asked to explain and defend their pronouncements was a novel and indeed shocking experience for some viewers (Whyte, 1979). In pursuit of ideas of balance and to enliven programmes, spokesmen for a wide variety of views, not just for the conventional outlook, were invited to participate in discussion programmes. The result was to erode the

mystique of accepted ideas and values and the aura which surrounded their exponents. Knowledge of alternative value systems
and behaviour became widely diffused, discussed, and examined and
somehow became more acceptable.

Partly in response to this change of opinion, some of the restrictions introduced in the early days of the state were modified. By the
1950s the Censorship Board was meeting increased criticism of its
activities: by this time they had placed bans on almost every living
author, including several outstanding Irish writers. However, by
1957 the five members of the Board were relatively liberal in outlook,
their attitudes more relaxed, and their functions evolving into a
preoccupation with the exclusion of pornography. In 1967 the law
under which they operated was modified. Any ban imposed on a
book before 1937 automatically lapsed until specifically reimposed
and any future bans would be lifted after 12 years. Film censorship
was also modified. In 1964 the members of the Appeal Board which
heard appeals from film makers whose work had been banned were
replaced by a panel more liberal in outlook, and the results were
soon to be seen in the increased numbers of successful appeals
(Whyte, 1984).

Rather more far-reaching, however, was the debate on Article 44
of the constitution, recognizing the 'special position' of the Roman
Catholic Church in the life of the state. In 1966 the Taoiseach Sean
Lemass had set up an all-party committee to review the constitution,
a document which by then had lasted almost thirty years without
substantial amendment. When the committee reported at the end of
1967 it pointed out, amongst other things, that clause 44 offended
non-Catholics, gave no recognition to religious groups which had not
been represented in Ireland when the constitution was originally
formulated, and provided a useful propaganda point for those who
wished to argue against Irish unification on the grounds of the
Church's influence in the Republic. None of the Catholic hierarchy
stood over the clause, and the last point about its effect on North–
South relations became increasingly relevant and much stressed
when the Northern Ireland situation came to the fore in the years
after 1968. In 1972 legislation for a referendum on the issue passed
the Dáil with all-party support. The poll was held in December of
that year and on a 51% turnout 84% of electors voted in favour of
striking out the offending section (Whyte, 1984).

On one issue, however, where there was specific Church teaching,
namely birth control, the passage of legislation proved more difficult.
In the 1960s there was evidence that, despite Church teaching and

the 1935 legislation against importation and sale of contraceptives and publicity for their use, a significant number of married couples were practising artificial birth control (Lee, 1979a). This obviously meant that the law was being ignored, though some argued that since the newly developed contraceptive pill acted as a cycle regulator, it did not really flout either Irish law or Catholic teaching. The pill became available on prescription and by 1978 it was estimated that 487,000 Irish women were using it (Whyte, 1984). Clearly, however, it could be argued that this was a breach of both state and Church law in spirit, if not in letter. In 1969 the Irish Family Planning Association had set up their first clinic at which birth-control advice was available to inquirers; since the law forbade the selling of artificial contraceptives, these were available free of charge, though clients could make voluntary donations if they wished. The numbers who came to the clinics suggested that they were meeting a widespread need. There was also evidence that public opinion at large was coming to the conclusion that the law should be changed. The first polls on the issue in the early 1970s had revealed a majority against change, but in time this shrank until eventually majority opinion favoured making legal the sale of contraceptives to married couples at least (Chubb, 1982b). Partly in response to these shifts, in the years 1971–3 efforts were made by independent members of the Oireachtas to introduce bills liberalizing the contraception laws. However, none of the political parties would commit itself wholeheartedly to the idea, the Catholic Church publicly stated its opposition, and all three bills failed (Whyte, 1984).

Late in 1973 a decision of the Supreme Court reopened the debate and changed its parameters. With the support of the Irish Family Planning Association, a Mrs Mary McGee brought an action against that section of the 1935 Criminal Law Amendment Act forbidding the importation of contraceptives. Four of the five judges decided that the section was unconstitutional because it violated the privacy of the family. This decision transformed the situation. A change in the law to accommodate it was now obviously necessary. But even this did not proceed smoothly. In July 1974 the coalition government introduced a bill allowing the importation and sale of contraceptives under licence from the Minister for Justice. These would be sold to married couples through chemists. All the main political parties were divided on the issue. Fine Gael supporters were allowed a free vote, though for tactical reasons Fianna Fáil imposed a whip against the measure. It was defeated by 75 votes to 61, with seven Fine Gael deputies voting against. One of the most sensational features of the episode came when the Minister of Education, Richard Burke, and the Taoiseach, Liam Cosgrave, voted against the bill without any warning to their colleagues.

This meant that the incoming Fianna Fáil government elected in 1977 had to grasp the nettle. Late in 1978 the new Minister for Health, Charles Haughey, introduced a new bill. Contraceptives were to be sold at chemist shops to persons producing a doctor's prescription; doctors were permitted to prescribe only for genuine family planning or for medical reasons. As in the unsuccessful 1974 bill, advertising was to be strictly controlled and contraceptives which were in effect abortifacients were still banned. The measure was described by the Minister as 'an Irish solution to an Irish problem'. It left several questions unanswered. Obviously the prescribing habits of doctors would differ as they would have differing interpretations of what would constitute legitimate medical problems or family-planning needs. Equally, there was no specific ban on the provision of contraceptives to unmarried people. Such awkward practical questions were left unanswered, possibly because it was deemed impossible to frame appropriate legislation though the omissions may have been deliberate.

Just as there were signs of changes in Irish values during this period, so too there were changes within the Catholic Church. Perhaps the most decisive influence for change was the short but revolutionary pontificate of Pope John XXIII (1958–63) and the work of the Second Vatican Council (1962–5) which he launched and which continued after his death. The use of English (or Irish) in the liturgy, priests now facing the faithful when saying mass, the practice of allowing communion to be taken in the hand, the greater role of lower clergy and laity in church government, and the increased participation of lay people in worship were in themselves far-reaching changes. But they had wider effects. Merely by introducing any change at all in a Church which had hitherto given the impression of being infallible and above question was revolutionary in the context of Irish Catholicism. But it was now even permissible to question and evaluate the entire range of Catholic practice and teaching without necessarily suffering guilt or attracting suspicion and opprobrium.

In Ireland the changes were gradual and patchy. Some clerics, such as the redoubtable Archbishop of Dublin Dr John Charles McQuaid, took a distinctly conservative interpretation of the Second Vatican Council's work, but this approach was rare and in any case he retired in 1972. It was impossible to insulate Catholic Ireland entirely from Vatican II, but it has been argued that the extent and nature of its impact were shrewdly and selectively regulated and channelled by the hierarchy under the leadership of the then primate Cardinal Conway (Fisher, 1986). However, this meant that in many ways the authoritarian traditions in the Irish church were preserved since interpretation of the changes was imposed by the hierarchy rather than worked out jointly or individually by the laity. Thus it is argued the Irish Catholic laity have never fully realized the role envisaged for them by Vatican II. Nevertheless there have been some discernible changes. Some of the mystique and aura of infallible authority which had once surrounded all Irish Catholic clergy has faded. This can be seen in, and was partly caused by, their greater willingness to take part in public discussions and interviews where their viewpoints are challenged and criticized. It can also be seen in the marked trend towards less ornamentation in modern Catholic churches—the impression of an aloof, confident, indeed triumphalist institution is no longer present. Attitudes to other denominations have also softened. To some extent this is due to the ecumenical movement which created an increased readiness to meet with other churches and indeed other religions and examine and discuss their views together rather than simply proscribe or dismiss them out of hand. Inter-church relations have also benefited from the growth of a Catholic charismatic movement which, with its emphasis on neo-pentecostal manifestations, finds common ground with parallel movements in the Protestant denominations and thereby crosses traditional barriers. But perhaps the areas where Irish Catholicism most readily took up the teachings of Vatican II was in the sphere of social justice. A strong school of Catholic social teaching emerged which subjected aspects of Irish society to detailed study, pointed to problems of deprivation and unequal life chances, and, in a notable about-turn from the fear of state power in the 1950s called for vigorous government action to ease the plight of the less fortunate in Irish society (Whyte, 1984). Indeed, in the 1970s and early 1980s some of the most trenchant and radical critiques of contemporary Irish society came from sources within the Irish Catholic Church.

The effects of these developments on general public loyalty to the church were difficult to gauge. Successive census reports continued to show about 95% of the population as Catholics. The first scientific social surveys on religion in Ireland revealed a more complex picture. Research in the mid-1970s revealed that about 88% of respondents claimed weekly attendance at mass. By international standards this was an impressively high level, and it did not vary a great deal with gender, age, marital status, or urban or rural background. Yet when the finer details were teased out, there was cause for concern. For example, one-quarter of single people in the 18–30-years age group did not attend, and the figure for 21–25-year-olds was 30%. More disturbing evidence came from declining numbers offering themselves for the religious life, the fact that one in every seven Irish university students brought up as Catholics no longer identified with the faith (Nic Ghiolla Phadraig, 1976), and the knowledge that large numbers of Irish emigrants no longer practised their faith in their adopted countries. There was a widespread belief that many lay Catholics, while continuing to attend mass regularly, had considerable personal reservations on aspects of Church teaching on personal behaviour and followed their own conscience in such matters. Evidence for this could be found in the declining size of the average family in spite of the rise in the marriage-rate and the popularity of the family-planning clinics since their first opening.

Such developments led to speculation that the Irish Republic was on the way to becoming a pluralist state in which Church and state would be separated, no particular Church would have a favoured position, legislation would be framed according to a prevailing moral consensus of the population, and individuals would be free to behave within these parameters according to their own moral principles. One of the earliest to argue for a plural Irish state was the prominent Fine Gael politician, later party leader, Garret FitzGerald (FitzGerald, 1973). Even the Catholic bishops seemed to move slightly in this direction in the early 1970s. In the debate which followed the second unsuccessful attempt to introduce a private member's bill allowing contraception in November 1973, the hierarchy, while roundly condemning the measure, did none the less agree that there were things which the church taught were morally wrong without expecting automatic state legislation against them (Whyte, 1984). This was an important, even historic, statement, because it effectively disowned any special place for Catholic teaching in Irish legislation and implied citizens were free to behave in accordance with their own personal convictions. Significantly, not all the hierarchy were happy with such an outlook and individual bishops periodically aired their disapproval of some of the more broad-minded ideas in circulation and the trend to what they saw as a secular state.

CONCLUSION

By the late 1970s there was a mixture of forces at work in Irish society. There was a deep, underlying, widely diffused traditional Catholicism which by international standards was still strongly entrenched in Irish culture. There was however some doubt as to how deeply it had penetrated the younger and better-educated sections of the population and on some issues of personal, especially sexual, behaviour there seemed to be a gap between profession and practice. Alongside this, the country had experienced some profound economic and social changes in the past 25 years and the Catholic Church itself had altered quite markedly. These developments had brought Ireland closer to the mainstream of West European life and Anglo-American culture, but as with some of the traditional and more modern teachings of the Catholic Church, there was doubt as to how deeply they had penetrated or how well they had been understood. There existed therefore two strands of thought in the country, one which could be broadly categorized as traditionalist and conservative, another as flexible and liberal, with some doubts as to the depth with which both were held and understood. In the country as a whole both citizens and political leaders gave the impression of quite contentedly drifting along and allowing these forces to find their own equilibrium, but the early 1980s were to be a period when their relative strengths would be revealed.

4

Political Events 1977–1983

INTRODUCTION

The period 1977–83 was to witness some notable changes in Irish politics (B. Farrell, 1987a). It was to see an ironic exchange of attitudes between the two main parties. It opened with Fianna Fáil in triumphant mood after a record victory in the 1977 general election and with an immensely popular leader with a national appeal which crossed party boundaries. It ended with the party in defeat and disarray under a new leader who was widely vilified both inside and outside the party.

Conversely, the period opens with Fine Gael having suffered its worst loss of seats and votes since the 1950s, party morale at an unprecedentedly low ebb, and its leader for the past twelve years resigning in the wake of the election defeat. However, by 1981 the party had undergone a remarkable revival, having seen its vote rise in three successive general elections, entering into government after two of those contests and by November 1982, scoring the highest total of seats and votes in its history. In fact, in this last contest Fine Gael came within 6% of the Fianna Fáil vote and was only 5 seats behind.

These developments were part of a wider picture which suggested that changes might be under way in the Irish political system. The Labour Party survived three changes of leader during this period and just managed to hold its own, but the left-wing Workers' Party showed signs of progress in terms of both votes and seats and some commentators talked of a realignment on the left in Irish politics. Underlying all this, however, were signs that traditional forces were still strong.

FIANNA FÁIL

The 1977 general election result was an almost unprecedented triumph for Fianna Fáil and its leader, Jack Lynch. The party had achieved the difficult feat in a democracy of winning a majority of the popular vote, with 50.6%, an achievement only surpassed in 1938. Its total of 84 seats (56.8%) was the highest ever for a single Irish party since the founding of the state.

In explaining the victory, a great deal of credit was attributed to

party leader Jack Lynch. Almost as soon as he went into opposition in 1973 he had set in train a thorough reform of party organization in both head office and constituencies, preparations for an
election were set in hand quite early and when it was finally called
the party was ready with candidates, campaign plans, and a manifesto in place (Farrell and Manning, 1978). During the campaign
itself Lynch emerged as a major asset to the party. He visited all but
three of the 42 constituencies and his appeal was felt right across
party lines. The manifesto 'Action Plan for National Reconstruction'
with its attractive pledges on job creation, abolition of rates on
private houses and road tax on motor cycles and most cars, was very
much the brain-child of Lynch and his close associate Martin
O'Donoghue.

Implementation of the programme was put into O'Donoghue's
hands. He entered the Dáil as a TD for the first time in 1977 and
became the head of a powerful new Department of Economic Planning and Development. Other Lynch associates were also given
economic responsibilities: George Colley became Minister for Finance and Des O'Malley was responsible for Industry, Commerce,
and Energy. Obviously much of the party's fortunes would depend
on being able to fulfil the promise of the manifesto. Initially, things
went quite well: abolition of rates and road tax went through quickly, Ireland's entry into the European Monetary System was successfully negotiated, and there were indications of quickening economic
activity, thanks partly to some improvement in the world economy
and to the stimulus provided by the new government. However, for
this progress to be maintained a number of assumptions had to be
fulfilled and as time passed this seemed increasingly unlikely. The
manifesto had been based on the argument that its cost of £250
million per year could be borne in the first instance by a certain
amount of increased foreign borrowing and a campaign to cut down
imports by persuading home consumers to buy Irish rather than
imported goods. Once these measures had successfully revived the
economy, it was argued, tax revenue would rise and the need for
foreign borrowing would taper off (McDowell, 1981). However, for
this progress to be maintained it was essential that Irish goods
remain competitive in foreign markets and this in turn depended on
average annual wage rises of no more that 5%—anything more and
the entire plan would veer off-course. In fact, the settlements for
1978 and 1979 were almost double the expected level and Ireland's
relative competitiveness began to decline (Arnold, 1984). This meant
that the overall economic buoyancy which had been expected to
carry the manifesto costs in the long run was not appearing and the

high level of foreign borrowing would have to continue. Unemployment also refused to come down and public confidence in the government's competence began to falter.

In its efforts to check wage rises and generate more tax income the government got into a five months' dispute with post and telegraph workers which disrupted services, alienated the powerful public sector unions, and proved a decisive turning point in government popularity (Sinnott, 1987). In addition, the 1979 Budget proposed a 2% levy on farmers' turnover which annoyed the powerful agriculture lobby and played a part in provoking mass demonstrations against the tax system in March 1979. This accumulation of disenchantment finally came to the boil in the local and European elections of June 1979. The party suffered notable loss of both votes and seats at the local level; but, because of their novelty, most attention was focused on the first direct elections to the European parliament. For Fianna Fáil the result was humiliating: it took only 34.7% of votes as against 50.6% in the 1977 general election; even worse, it gained only 5 of the 15 seats as compared to 4 for both Fine Gael and Labour and 2 for independents. Opinion polls that same month confirmed this grim news (Browne, 1981). A subsequent meeting of the parliamentary party officially placed the blame on economic misfortunes, but it was around this time that the first serious rumours about Lynch's leadership began to emerge. Unofficial meetings of some back-benchers revealed a vague unease not only about the leadership, but also the general direction of the party and for the first time Charles Haughey began to be seriously mentioned as a possible successor (Arnold, 1984; Browne, 1981).

Outside events brought the matter to a head. In August 1979 Lord Louis Mountbatten was assassinated in Sligo Bay and eighteen British soldiers were killed in an IRA ambush. Lynch met with the newly elected British Prime Minister, Margaret Thatcher, after the Mountbatten funeral and though precise details of their discussions were not revealed the British Premier described herself as deeply satisfied with the outcome. Some commentators speculated Lynch had given pledges of increased co-operation on security and even perhaps the right of British forces to overfly the Republic's territory in border areas. Such suspicions angered traditional republican elements, including some sections of Fianna Fáil. Their unease was publicly articulated in September 1979 by Sile de Valera, granddaughter of the party's founder, when she spoke at a commemoration ceremony at Fermoy, Co. Cork, and seemed to imply that the party was in danger of losing its republican soul.

The final blow to Lynch's leadership came in the shape of two

by-elections in Cork in November 1979. Fianna Fáil lost both seats
to Fine Gael, suffering a loss of 22.7% of the vote in Cork City. This
was particularly devastating for Lynch, because Cork was his home
territory and it seemed to prove that he had lost his only remaining
value, as a vote-getter. Soundings taken during the next few weeks
revealed a loss of confidence in him in the parliamentary party and
on 5 December 1979 he announced he would step down as party
leader and Taoiseach as soon as a successor was elected. The meeting to elect the new leader was fixed for Friday, 7 December. The
subsequent forty-eight hours was a period of bitter in-fighting unparalleled in the history of any Irish political party. Two contenders
quickly emerged, George Colley, close associate of Lynch and the
choice of the Cabinet, and Charles Haughey the back-bench
favourite. The Haughey campaign over the next two days was tight-
ly organized, energetic, and robust. When the parliamentary party
met for the crucial vote, Haughey won by 44 votes to Colley's 38.
Four days later the Dáil elected him Taoiseach, but only after he
had been subjected to some stinging attacks by the Opposition.

Nor was this the end of the affair within Fianna Fáil. The whole
experience left the party deeply, even bitterly, divided into factions.
While the party establishment, almost the entire Cabinet and most
of the junior ministers had voted for Colley, Haughey's support was
overwhelming amongst the backbenchers, especially those of a traditional outlook representing rural constituencies (Garvin, 1981b).
Moreover, the mere emergence of Haughey as leader revived vivid
memories of the party split over the 1970 arms crisis and the clash
of evidence between him and prominent party members. But additional wounds had been opened by some of the alleged methods of
Haughey's managers in the leadership campaign involving, it was
claimed, rumours, threats, and innuendoes. Further, the new leader's first actions did little to heal the divisions. On the contrary, he
displayed an abrasive tendency to reward his friends and punish his
opponents. When he reorganized the government four people prominent under Lynch were omitted including O'Donoghue, and five
TDs who had formed a pro-Haughey caucus from June 1979 were all
in office by March 1980. George Colley did remain in the Cabinet,
but it became clear this was only because Haughey was not yet sure
enough of his own strength to dismiss him. Confirmation of the
chronic divisions and bitterness within the government came in a
speech by Colley just before Christmas 1979 when he accused pro-
Haughey elements of ruthlessly trying to undermine Lynch throughout 1979 and then using very dubious methods during the recent
leadership contest. Colley concluded from this that the old Fianna

Fáil ground rules stressing loyalty to the party leader had been changed and implied that his loyalty to the new leadership could not be taken for granted either. It was becoming clear that Ireland's chief political party, hitherto a by-word for loyalty and public solidarity, was now deeply and bitterly divided.

It was in this atmosphere of mutual distrust that the new administration settled down to government. Charles Haughey had appealed to a majority of the parliamentary party because he had an image as a decisive Minister of Finance in the late 1960s and a robust nationalist in the early 1970s. Initially, when in a national television broadcast in January 1980 he warned that there was too great a gap between Irish consumption and wealth production, he seemed to be living up to his reputation for decisiveness. To ensure the country lived within its means he suggested government expenditure would have to be curbed and wage-claims restrained. However, Mr Haughey proved something of a disappointment and a puzzle to his supporters. He never followed through from this broadcast: there was no sustained effort to check expenditure, reform taxation, or curb the foreign debt. Even as a nationalist he proved something of a disappointment. There were no obvious signs that co-operation with the British over border security was any less than in Lynch's day. There were two meetings with the British premier, in May and November 1980, and though Haughey claimed the second one was a historic breakthrough in Anglo-Irish relations with the communiqués' references to consultation on 'the totality of relationships between these islands' and 'possible new institutional structures', London soon made it clear that their interpretations of the encounter were somewhat different, and there was no discernible movement on the Northern Ireland question.

The most likely explanation for the government's indecision was the imminence of an election. The 21st Dáil could have lasted until June 1982, but it had become customary to hold elections in a government's fourth year of office: a postponement would have looked like unwillingness to face the electorate. For Mr Haughey victory in an election was essential because it would strengthen his position inside the party and in the country at large by proving his power as a vote-getter. It became increasingly clear that policy in all areas was being tailored to electoral considerations. Imminent rises in postal, telephone, electricity, and transport charges were postponed. The Budget of January 1981 was a neutral affair with studiously vague promises to encourage economic development and embark on a long-term drive to reduce the current deficit, without any details on how this was to be done.

One feature of an Irish election which is normally under the

Taoiseach's control is the date of the poll, but circumstances conspired to deny this to Mr Haughey. It was widely believed he would use the 1981 party *ard-fheis* of 13–15 February to announce the election, but a disastrous fire at an entertainments complex in his constituency with 48 deaths shocked the entire country causing the adjournment of the conference and postponement of an election. The Northern Ireland situation had a similar effect. On 1 March 1981 a hunger-strike was started by republican prisoners in the Maze Prison outside Belfast in support of their claim to be treated as political prisoners. Their ordeal, with its harking back to ancient Irish Celtic customs, the sufferings of the Fenians in British prisons in the late nineteenth century, and the more recent memories of Thomas Ashe in 1917 and Terence MacSwiney in 1920, stoked up considerable emotion in quarters not normally associated with an ultra-nationalist viewpoint. Tension rose even higher when the leader of the hunger-strikers Bobby Sands was elected Westminister MP for Fermanagh-South Tyrone in April 1981 and died on 5 May (Beresford, 1987). It subsequently emerged that in an effort to avoid holding the contest against this fraught background, Mr Haughey had postponed an election on at least two occasions.

The result was that when the election was finally called for 11 June there was a vague feeling that events had passed out of the government's control (B. Farrell, 1987*a*). Moreover, the postponements of the date had thrown the election planning into disarray. These impressions were confirmed by the nature of the Fianna Fáil campaign. There did not seem to be any new policies: even the traditional argument that only they could provide stable government seemed compromised by the widespread knowledge of divisions within the party. Mr Haughey campaigned widely but in a defensive, negative fashion, preferring to attack his opponents' ideas and seeming to yield them the initiative on policy proposals.

The election results of June 1981 were a severe blow to both party and leader. Compared with 1977, Fianna Fáil's share of votes fell from 50.6% to 45.3% and in an enlarged Dáil its share of seats went down from 84 (56.8%) to 78 (47.0%). For a party which had entered the contest as a government with a record majority over all other parties combined, it was a heavy defeat. For a leader who had inherited this record overall majority, turned it into a deficit, and lost office, it was something of a disaster. At this point the unease which some had felt over his policy prevarication since December 1979 began to crystallize into discontent and those who still remembered Mr Haughey's role in the 1970 Arms Trial and the methods by which he had captured the leadership began to regain hope.

His performance in opposition did little to restore his standing.

It seemed characterized by continued indecision and petty point-scoring. He did not announce the composition of his new front bench team until January 1982. When the minority coalition government brought in a summer budget in July 1981 in an effort to reconstruct national finances, Mr Haughey's attacks seemed motivated more by partisan politics than a concern for the good of the national economy. Again when the new Taoiseach, Garret Fitz-Gerald, had his first meeting with the British premier in November 1981, Mr Haughey's assaults on the encounter seemed partisan and ungenerous.

Disenchantment with his leadership was publicly expressed by one backbencher in late December 1981, and there were signs of lack of confidence in some constituencies, but before matters could come to a head the coalition government introduced its severe Budget of January 1982 and suffered an unprecedented defeat on the measure when some left-wing independent TDs voted against it. Another election was called for February 1982.

Superficially, it seemed Fianna Fáil should have been on to a winner in this campaign. It was fighting a government which had suffered the humiliating distinction of being the first in Irish history to lose its Budget. Moreover, the measures in that Budget had been highly unpleasant and should have provided plentiful ammunition for the opposition. In fact, the campaign turned out to be one of the most difficult the party had ever had to wage. The Coalition's message of the need for firm measures to restore economic stability had reached the electorate and found a surprisingly sympathetic response. The rules of Irish politico-economic debate had thereby shifted from the traditional game of parties trying to outbid each other in promises of prosperity. At first Mr Haughey failed to realize this and launched his party's campaign with reassurances that the economic situation was nothing like as grave as the Coalition suggested and any necessary adjustments to the national finances would be painless. However, Martin O'Donoghue, party finance spokesman, disagreed strongly and under severe pressure from him Mr Haughey totally changed tack. The party basically endorsed the view that there was a crisis in the national finances and that expenditure cuts were an essential part of the solution. This U-turn at the outset of the campaign put Fianna Fáil at a disadvantage. It made the party seem indecisive, it involved yielding the initiative on the central economic issue to the Coalition, accepting both their prescription and diagnosis for the national economic situation, and blurring the differences between the two sides. It was also bad for the morale of Fianna Fáil candidates and workers who were caught by surprise and took some time to readjust.

Another obstacle to the party's victory emerged, dubbed the 'Haughey factor'. Since late 1981 successive polls had revealed that in terms of public esteem the Fianna Fáil leader was lagging behind his Fine Gael opposite number; by mid-February 1982 in the heat of the election campaign, the gap was 23%. It was unprecedented for the party to have a leader who trailed so badly in popularity that he was an electoral liability. Even in the middle of the campaign discontent with his leadership surfaced: when local conventions were held to put together slates of Fianna Fáil candidates, several constituency organizations became deeply divided into pro- and anti-Haughey factions. This obviously diverted a great deal of energy and weakened the campaign effort, but it also attracted much unwelcome attention from the media. As if to acknowledge his negative image, the pictures of the party leader which traditionally dominated Fianna Fáil literature shrank noticeably or disappeared entirely.

The result of the February 1982 election was almost the worst possible for the party in that it was neither outright victory nor outright defeat. Its national vote rose by 2.0% to 47.3% and it gained 3 seats to give a total of 81. In a Dáil of 166 this was not enough for an overall majority. With Fine Gael and Labour firmly ranged against him, Mr Haughey's hopes rested with gaining the support of some of the minor party and independent TDs. However, before the Dáil reconvened there came the first outright revolt against the Haughey leadership. Several of his critics had polled well in the election and thus strengthened their hand. For most of the party, however, the experience of campaigning behind a widely unpopular leader had been an unpleasant novelty. The tantalizingly close result provided critics with further ammunition because they were able to argue that with a different leader they might just have been able to achieve an overall majority.

Aware of the feelings against him, Mr Haughey moved swiftly. He brought forward the meeting of the Fianna Fáil parliamentary party from 9 March to 25 February 1982 and, to bring the matter to a head, on Monday 22 February he put a motion for his selection as party candidate for Taoiseach on the agenda. The speed of these moves caught his opponents off guard. They were unable to put together a coherent campaign and not until the day before the party met could they agree on Des O'Malley as their agreed candidate. At the actual meeting their challenge withered in the face of pleas for unity at a time when the parliamentary situation was so finely balanced, Martin O'Donoghue unexpectedly took the same line and it was unanimously agreed to put Mr Haughey forward as the Fianna Fáil candidate for Taoiseach.

However, before he could be sure of the post, Mr Haughey had to gain at least two more votes from outside party ranks. It was decided to support the independent TD Dr John O'Connell for the post of Ceann Comhairle (Speaker) once again, thereby keeping Fianna Fáil party strength intact. It was confidently and correctly expected that the independent Fianna Fáil TD Neil Blaney would continue to support his former colleagues and that the independent socialist Jim Kemmy would ally himself again with Labour and Fine Gael. The three TDs from Sinn Féin the Workers' Party refused to say how they would vote and attention then turned to independent left-wing TD Tony Gregory, ex-teacher and community worker, returned for Dublin Central. He too refused to divulge his intentions.

When the Dáil reconvened on 9 March it was revealed to an astonished house that Deputy Gregory had promised his support to Fianna Fáil in return for a written agreement with Mr Haughey whereby the Fianna Fáil leader promised a £150 million development programme for Gregory's run-down inner-city constituency, providing amongst other things 4,000 new jobs, 3,600 new houses, and increased investment in house-repair and training programmes. The Workers' Party also announced their support for Mr Haughey even though they had not done any deals, and he was elected Taoiseach by 86 votes to 79.

The general reaction to what became known as the 'Gregory Deal' was a mixture of shock and admiration. There were the inevitable accusations of vote-buying from the Opposition, but they rang hollow when it became known that Garret FitzGerald had also tried to obtain Gregory's support (Brennan, 1982). Otherwise, there was a certain mixture of amusement and admiration at Mr Haughey's stroke and his position in the party was sufficiently reinforced to enable him to omit George Colley entirely from the Cabinet and demote O'Malley and O'Donoghue. However, this still only produced 83 votes, exactly half the Dáil strength and barely sufficient to guard against accidents. At this point Mr Haughey attempted what he hoped would be a master-stroke. There was a vacancy for the post of Irish EEC Commissioner and it was offered to Dick Burke, Fine Gael TD for Dublin West. He had occupied it between 1977 and 1981 and was known to be unhappy with FitzGerald's leadership of Fine Gael and his failure to return to the Cabinet in 1981. If he accepted he would have to resign his Dáil seat, thereby reducing Fine Gael strength until a by-election could be held. Moreover, it was a highly marginal seat and the Fianna Fáil candidate would most likely be Eileen Lemass, daughter-in-law of the former Taoiseach and former TD for the constituency. After much indecision, Burke accepted the post and resigned from both the Dáil and the party and a by-election was called for 25 May. Once again the initial reactons were shock and rueful admiration, but Mr Haughey's satisfaction turned to dismay when Fine Gael retained the seat on the strength of massive transfers from minor parties. In the end Mr Haughey got the worst of all worlds. A significant post went to a non-party member, a by-election was lost, Fine Gael's morale received a tremendous boost, and what had initially seemed a political master-stroke back-fired in spectacular style.

Initially it had seemed to observers that the new government might last for about a year (Joyce and Murtagh, 1983) and the administration did its best to reinforce itself by the distribution of public funds, for example, to Knock airport in Co. Mayo in support of an unlikely scheme launched by the administrator of the nearby Pilgrimage Centre, Monsignor James Horan. However, on a series of divisions it survived only narrowly and after the death of a Fianna Fáil backbencher on 15 June it depended on the casting vote of the Ceann Comhairle. Even more nerve-wracking for the government was a series of astonishing misfortunes during the summer which created an image of an accident-prone administration not in control of its own fate. Mr Haughey's constituency election agent and solicitor was accused of voting twice in the recent general election and only acquitted on a technicality; it was revealed that when previously in government Mr Haughey had had a new telephone system installed in Leinster House incorporating the ability to listen in on conversations. There was no evidence to suggest eavesdropping had occurred, but suspicion lingered. In August the Attorney-General had to resign when police arrested a man suspected of murder in his flat and Mr Haughey's handling of the situation appeared clumsy and slow. In September, the Minister for Justice, Sean Doherty, came under suspicion of tampering with police and judicial proceedings. His brother-in-law was accused of assault, but shortly before the trial a key witness, who lived in Northern Ireland, was detained by the RUC. The incident reinforced earlier rumours that Doherty was prone to interfere in such matters for personal and constituency reasons (Joyce and Murtagh, 1983).

To some extent these were pure accidents, but even on the parliamentary scene where the government should have had more control, things began to go astray. The administration had to perform a nice balancing act between controlling expenditure, avoiding unpopular cuts in public services, and delivering on its pact with Tony Gregory. Until July it managed fairly well, but at that point it became clear that public expenditure was running ahead of predictions and significant cuts would be necessary. When they came at the end of July they were handled in a brusque and perfunctory fashion which almost seemed calculated to give maximum offence. A wage increase for public-sector workers negotiated in 1981 was cancelled and a total freeze in all public-sector incomes for the rest of 1982 was announced with no prior consultation. Moreover, the announcement was made by civil servants because ministers were on holiday and the embarrassment was multiplied soon afterwards when a 50% increase in TDs' allowances was unveiled. The situation was made even worse when new health-service charges were equally badly handled, and the government somehow seemed to crown its own misfortunes when it revealed its economic plan 'The Way Forward' on 20 October. This basically underlined the need to scale down the Budget deficit by further wage controls, cuts in public services, and possibly tax increases.

By now the government seemed water-logged and adrift on a sea of accidents, errors, and rumours, scarely surviving in the Dáil and floundering in the opinion polls. Mr Haughey's opponents were encouraged to try their luck again and a long-term back-bench dissident Charlie McCreevy tabled a motion of no confidence in the leader for a party meeting on 6 October. Mr Haughey retorted by announcing that he expected full public support from the national executive, Cabinet, and party and that the vote at the October meeting would be an open roll call with TDs and senators exercising their ballot publicly. This caused a furore since it was interpreted as a heavy hint to party activists, most of whom were pro-Haughey, to put pressure on their TDs. Certainly in the days leading up to the meeting Haughey opponents were subjected to a bombardment of letters and phone calls which, some complained bitterly, verged on threats at times. Once again, however, the dissidents seemed disorganized in that no agreed challenger to Mr Haughey emerged. In contrast, orchestrated messages of support for the leader poured into party headquarters. But it did not all go Mr Haughey's way. The national executive did endorse him, but not unanimously. A majority of the Cabinet fell into line, but both Martin O'Donoghue and Des O'Malley finally resigned rather than conform.

The meeting on 6 October lasted 12 hours. When the roll-call vote was finally taken, the no confidence motion was lost by 58 votes to 22. Mr Haughey had won, but it was a pyrrhic victory. The dissidents, dubbed the 'Club of 22', suspected, possibly correctly, that a secret ballot would have added to their strength. Some wounding attacks had been made. Fianna Fáil was now openly and deeply divided, and led by a man who knew that at least one-quarter of its parliamentary strength had absolutely no confidence in him.

All this was particularly damaging at a time when the parliamentary position was deteriorating. It was well known that the Workers' Party TDs and Tony Gregory were unhappy with government attitudes to public expenditure. Then on 18 October a Fianna Fáil TD died and another entered hospital after a severe heart attack. In the last week of October an opinion poll revealed that for the first time in history Fine Gael and Fianna Fáil were equal in public support, with 36% each. On 3 November Garret FitzGerald, the Fine Gael leader, brought the situation to a head by tabling a Dáil motion of no confidence in the government. It was passed by 82 votes to 80 when the three Workers' Party deputies supported it and Tony Gregory abstained. An election was called for 24 November 1982.

Given the recent poll findings and internal divisions it was clearly going to be a difficult campaign for Fianna Fáil. The difficulties were compounded by the fact that the party had largely accepted the Coalition approach to economic problems, so the economy could not figure as an issue. Mr Haughey, therefore, decided to try and seize the initiative by mounting an aggressive campaign on the themes of trust, credibility, and political stability. His first effort fastened on the question of abortion, an emotive topic, but especially in Catholic Ireland. As early as June 1981 an anti-abortion pressure group had been given promises by both main party leaders that they would introduce a constitutional amendment making legalization of abortion impossible. Just before his government fell Mr Haughey had published a bill containing the proposed amendment and at his first campaign press conference he tried to make it an election issue by pledging to hold a constitutional referendum on the matter before Christmas 1982 and suggesting that the Fine Gael leader could not be trusted to fulfil his earlier pledge. However, FitzGerald quickly defused the issue by accepting the Fianna Fáil wording and promising a referendum by March 1983. Mr Haughey then turned to the traditional 'Green Card', namely nationalistic aspirations, especially as applied to Northern Ireland. He implied that in his frequent visits to the North and his discussions with British ministers, the Fine Gael leader had become too closely identified with British interests. In an effort to put more flesh on these changes he pointed to a meeting between FitzGerald and the Duke of Norfolk, who had once been in British Intelligence, and accused the Fine Gael leader of consorting with a British spy. He also seized on the fact that James Prior, Secretary of State for Northern Ireland, correctly predicted that FitzGerald would revive one of his favourite schemes, namely an all-Ireland court and police system to combat terrorism. This he asserted was evidence of collusion, of British interference in Ireland's internal affairs, and likely to compromise the country's neutrality. In some areas Fianna Fáil literature was circulated implying that Fitz-Gerald was Margaret Thatcher's choice for Taoiseach and that the all-Ireland police force would involve the RUC roaming the fields and streets of the Republic. The campaign ended with a much publicized television debate between the party leaders which was judged a victory for FitzGerald.

Certainly the election was a defeat for Fianna Fáil. Its total vote fell by 2.1% to 45.2% and it lost 6 seats to give a total of 75, only 5 more than Fine Gael. A new coalition government of Fine Gael and Labour was installed with a comfortable overall majority of 6 and a lead of 11 over Fianna Fáil. Mr Haughey was now in the position of being a leader who had inherited a record overall majority and lost it, had led his party into three elections, lost two and barely scraped into power in one. Moreover he lagged up to 15% behind the Fine Gael leader in public esteem and notably behind his own party in popularity (*Irish Independent*, 11 Nov. 1982). The only compensation was that six members of the dissident 'Club of 22' had lost their seats. However, another party crisis built up. During the summer of 1982 rumours had been rife in Dublin that Mr Haughey's govern-ment was tapping the phones of some journalists. The Coalition's new Minister of Justice launched an investigation and soon dis-covered that, alarmed by the accurate reporting of the Fianna Fáil infighting his predecessor, Sean Doherty had indeed authorized the tapping of two journalists' phones and that the positions of the head of the Garda Siochana and his deputy had also been compromised. But it further emerged that there had been a separate, bizarre incident in which the Tánaiste and Minister of Finance, Ray MacSharry, had secretly used a tape recorder supplied by the Garda on Doherty's instructions to record a conversation in which Martin O'Donoghue, suspecting that McSharry's support of Haughey was based on past financial obligations to the leader, had suggested that money might be available to release MacSharry from these ties. The Garda Commis-sioner and his deputy were replaced and the phone taps lifted.

It was a graphic illustration of the Haughey government's methods and attitudes and the depth of mistrust and enmity within Fianna Fáil. Doherty and MacSharry resigned from the front-bench and Doherty later resigned the party whip as well. There was no evidence that Mr Haughey had any knowledge of his colleagues' activities, but as Taoiseach he bore constitutional responsibility for all actions. In addition, both MacSharry and Doherty were his long-time supporters and associates and the two episodes seemed to epitomize the ethos of the governments he had led and the state to which the party had been reduced. There was now a steadily growing groundswell of opinion that he should resign the leadership.

Down to the last week of January 1983 the tide ran strongly against Mr Haughey. Even former supporters came out against him and a majority of the national executive supported resignation. The anti-Haughey side was heartened when several of his close associates failed to win Senate seats. However, his opponents once again fumbled their chances. They failed to agree on a single candidate to replace him and thereby divided their forces: indeed at one point there were no less than four contenders in the field. At the end of January the Haughey counter-attack began, with a vigorous campaign of lobbying activists, TDs, and Senators not known to be definitely against him. The meeting of the parliamentary party scheduled for 2 February was abruptly adjourned to 7 February on the ostensible grounds of the death of a Fianna Fáil TD but it also gave the leader's supporters more time.

When the meeting did finally convene the incoherent and disorganized nature of the dissidents became clear (Browne, 1983a). Much time was spent considering an internal party report on phone tapping and the offer of funds to MacSharry, and disciplining the people concerned. When the motion for Haughey to resign was finally debated it was defeated by 40 votes to 33 and Mr Haughey had survived yet again.

FINE GAEL

For Fine Gael the results and long-term effects of the 1977 general election were almost a mirror image of the Fianna Fáil experience. The party suffered one of the most comprehensive defeats of an Irish political party in modern times: its popular vote dropped back from 35.1% in 1973 to 30.5% and its seats from 54 to 43, the lowest totals since 1957. Four constituencies totally lacked any Fine Gael representation.

Paradoxically this experience launched the party into a new era. The scale of the defeat cleared the ground for drastic changes. Since the mid-1960s there had been two schools of thought in the party. One was traditionalist and cautious in outlook, with an almost amateurish approach to politics and in recent years closely identified with Liam Cosgrave. The other school was generally younger, more open-minded, and professional. Originally inspired by Declan Costello and the 'Just Society' programme, it had lately become identified with Garret FitzGerald. Until 1977 the traditionalist element had been dominant, but the scale of the election defeat under Cosgrave's leadership created an opening for the modernizers.

Within a week of polling day Liam Cosgrave resigned the leadership. Initially it seemed there might be a contest between Garret FitzGerald and Peter Barry who had served in two Cabinet posts in the coalition, but when soundings revealed that FitzGerald's strength was overwhelming (Smith, 1985) Barry withdrew and FitzGerald was unanimously chosen as the new leader on 1 July 1977. The smooth transition was a good start on the party's road to recovery and a sharp contrast to Fianna Fáil's experience when changing leader in 1979.

In strictly party terms the new leader had an impeccable background. His mother was an Ulster Presbyterian with nationalist sympathies. His father was Desmond FitzGerald, poet, intellectual, and Gaelic scholar who was active in the 1916 Rising and the War of Independence. In 1922 he had taken the pro-Treaty side in the civil war, had been a founder member of Cumann na n Gaedheal and between 1922 and 1932 served with distinction as Minister for External Affairs and then in the Defence Department. He had died in 1947.

Garret FitzGerald was born in 1926. A graduate of University College Dublin, he first worked for the Irish state airline Aer Lingus as an economic analyst. This in turn led to a lifelong interest in the Irish economy and to part-time lecturing and journalism. In 1959 he was appointed lecturer in the Political Economy Department of UCD and subsequently set up an economic consultancy which evolved into the Economist Intelligence Unit of Ireland. He also served on a variety of economic advisory bodies and championed Irish entry into the EEC. His background and training produced an outlook which by Irish standards was remarkably open and liberal. Consequently, when he entered politics, first as a Fine Gael senator in 1965 and then as TD for Dublin South-East in 1969 he naturally gravitated to the liberal wing of the party, then led by his friend Declan Costello. Immediately after his election he became frontbench spokesman on education and then in 1972 on finance. He quickly emerged as a leading figure in the party, though there was some awkwardness in his relations with the conservative and suspicious Liam Cosgrave.

However, his ability and stature could not be ignored and in the 1973–7 coalition he served with great distinction as Minister for External Affairs. Although it had been expected he would be appointed to Finance, this proved a fortunate move. His involvement with Irish foreign relations meant he escaped the blame for economic difficulties when the full force of the arab-inspired oil-price rises and the world economic recession hit Ireland. He also avoided blame for some of the government's over-zealous security policies. On the positive side his post provided a unique opportunity to exercise his personal abilities. The Republic had entered the EEC in 1973 and was still finding its feet amongst all the activities and institutions of the community. Under FitzGerald's active and energetic leadership the country played its full part and when the Irish term came round for the Presidency of the Council of Ministers in 1975 he filled the role with distinction. His personal standing at home and abroad increased enormously.

There was however one domestic issue in which he became closely involved and here too his personal background and abilities were remarkably appropriate: Northern Ireland. FitzGerald cared deeply about the northern issue and had been known to say it was the basic reason for his entry into politics (Smith, 1985). In his writings on the subject (FitzGerald, 1973) he displayed a close knowledge of the north and of the unionist position, a product of his mixed family background and his frequent visits and contacts with a wide variety of Ulster politicians. But he also argued that there would have to be a searching reappraisal of the Republic's ethos and institutions if unionists were to be expected to look favourably on a new relationship with the south. He got the opportunity to play a role in the northern situation when the Irish and British governments met with representatives of Ulster political parties at the Sunningdale Conference of December 1973. These intensive negotiations resulted in the setting up of a power-sharing executive drawn from both unionist and nationalist groups and a Council of Ireland, composed of members of both the Northern Ireland and Dublin governments to discuss matters of mutual concern, harmonize policies, and act as a consultative forum. The Council was to prove stillborn and the Executive collapsed in May 1974, but FitzGerald's reputation in both Irish and British eyes was considerably enhanced by the stamina and ingenuity he displayed during the negotiations (Smith, 1985).

He demonstrated all these qualities to the full when he took over as party leader. The first six months of his leadership were taken up with a searching inquest into the recent election débâcle, assisted by privately commissioned opinion polls. It was concluded that the party had no strong overall image, lacked positive appeal for younger people and women, had concentrated too much on security issues in government, and had underestimated the appeal of Fianna Fáil's manifesto. These lessons were to inspire a far-reaching shake-up of Fine Gael that transformed it into a modern political party.

One of the first decisions was to launch a total reorganization of party structure and finances. To boost morale and get the feel of the party, FitzGerald began a nation-wide tour of the constituencies during which he made himself as accessible as possible to all comers. This convinced him that the party needed a new constitution. To a considerable extent Fine Gael, especially in rural areas, retained its traditional, *ad hoc*, personalized attitude towards organization. Local party structures still tended to be organized around the most politically prominent local personality, usually a sitting councillor or TD. These in turn tended to defend their own support bases and opposed efforts to run any other strong candidates in their bailiwicks for fear of risking their own seats. Office-holders often held their posts for years on end, in many cases without the formality of an election. Such a set-up discouraged new members and especially younger people by its air of cliquish dullness verging on corruption. A new party constitution was endorsed by the 1978 *ard-fheis*. It set the entire national organization on a new basis and tried to open it up to new people and ideas. In future all local offices would come up for re-election every year and no one could serve as chairman, secretary, or treasurer for more than three successive years (O'Byrnes, 1986). Some observers thought it had the added advantage of shifting power away from local notables towards party headquarters. Two new posts of constituency organizer and public relations officer were created in each constituency and some of the more traditionalist party members regarded these as spies for head office (O'Leary, 1985c). The reforms undoubtedly created more efficient, lively local branches, but they also roused the ire of some longer-serving members.

However, the organizational reform was extended to party head office itself. This was expanded, reorganized on modern managerialist lines, and moved into new and larger premises in Upper Mount Street, ironically just across the road from Fianna Fáil. A new general secretary was appointed, Peter Prendergast, who had a highly successful record in marketing. It soon became clear that if Fine Gael was to be run as a modern party it would need much more funding. Traditionally it had relied on the annual national collection and sporadic contributions from local party branches and committed individuals. Compared to Fianna Fáil it had operated on a shoestring. Now strenuous efforts were made to extend the sources of income. The national collection was reorganized and constituencies were required to raise funds, pass a proportion on to head office, and set some aside to fight elections. Gradually a list of sympathetic firms and private donors was compiled and the party began to construct a more reliable and predictable income and a record election fighting fund.

But it was perhaps in human resources that the greatest and most rewarding efforts were invested. Regular opinion polls and panel research had revealed that the party had a negative image amongst young people and women and steps were taken to repair the situation. The new leader made special efforts to seek out and encourage younger people on his tour of constituencies, a party Youth Officer was appointed and Young Fine Gael was founded, specifically to attract younger members. It soon became a notable success and evolved into a lively, if sometimes over-enthusiastic and embarrassing ginger group. Also strenuous efforts were made to appeal to the women's vote, which was recognized as increasingly important in Irish society. Partly as a result of greater awareness of women's activities in the USA and Britain, a women's movement had emerged in Ireland in the 1970s. It was a diffuse, many-faceted grouping, but amongst other things it pressed for official recognition both of women's traditional roles as mothers and housewives and of the need for more women in public affairs, including politics. In response to these pressures, Fine Gael policy planners began working on tax reform ideas and more effort was made to recruit women to the party and have them nominated as election candidates. An early and widely publicized success came when the 22-year-old Myra Barry won the Cork East by-election in November 1979.

As the reorganization of the party got under way there began to coalesce around FitzGerald and Prendergast a group of people with proven skills in administration, fund-raising, public relations, advertising, and marketing. At first the group was casual and unstructured but a catalyst was provided by a by-election in Donegal North-East in December 1980 when Fine Gael did less well than expected after their successes in the European and local elections and the Cork by-elections of 1979. Shortly after this disappointment there were several meetings of the group and by early 1981 it was meeting regularly as a strategy committee. In time knowledge of these gatherings became public and the group was variously known as the 'Twelve Apostles', or most memorably the 'National Handlers' (Browne, 1982b). They were to meet regularly until November 1982 though most frequently during the three election campaigns. Their influence was to be felt in party strategy, policy evolution, and campaign management. However, they included some individuals with a masterly grasp of the electoral situation at both national and local level, and at their encouragement the party began its nominating conventions for the next election early in 1980. It was intended that as soon as possible candidates would be in place, getting to know their constituencies and getting themselves known, well ahead of polling day.

The party also set up a communications committee which had some overlap of membership with the strategy committee but had the task of marketing the leader, the party's ideas, and its policies (M. Farrell, 1986). It advised on publicity before and during a campaign and worked on some of the organization details of such things as the leader's national tour, an experiment which had proved successful during the European elections. Early in 1980 a new election committee was set up. It commissioned market research of both the traditional type and what was known as qualitative research whereby groups of people chaired by trained leaders aired their views on selected topics where the party wished to test opinions and reactions. The findings confirmed the significance attached to young people and farmers and revealed a widespread willingness to make sacrifices for the national good. They also disclosed a certain admiration for FitzGerald's compassion and integrity on the one hand, but an image of a sometimes garrulous and bumbling intellectual on the other.

When it came to the June 1981 general election the party produced a manifesto which had absorbed the lessons learnt from 1977, clearly mirrored FitzGerald's concerns, and incorporated lessons from the market research. It advocated a switch from direct to indirect taxation, reducing the standard rate of income tax to 25%, providing generous tax credits, and increasing indirect taxes by 3.5% and health charges by 1.5%. Research had shown widespread popular discontent with direct taxes. It was also felt the 1977 defeat partly reflected farmers' discontent with tax proposals, so it was significant that almost half the revenue raised from the tax measures would be used to assist the agricultural community. Welfare benefits were to be increased and, possibly the most novel and widely publicized idea, it was proposed that £9.60 per week be paid to every spouse not earning an income. It was widely seen as a pitch for the women's vote.

The manifesto helped Fine Gael to seize the initiative from Fianna Fáil and enabled it to present an attractive and coherent programme to the electorate. As the campaign developed it became increasingly clear that a new Fine Gael was at work on the Irish political scene (Busteed, 1982). Gone was the air of genteel amateurism and the virtual disdain for the vulgarities of modern electioneering which had characterized the party in previous contests and left it trailing behind the almost ruthless professionalism of Fianna Fáil. Fitz-Gerald himself undertook a national tour which, in sharp contrast with Liam Cosgrave's limp effort in 1977, was well-organized and highly publicized. Fine Gael was now on a par with Fianna Fáil in all the paraphernalia previously monopolized by that party—slogans, parades, bands, T-shirts, paper hats, stickers, badges, and a campaign song were all deployed (M. Farrell, 1986). It was financed by the war chest accumulated since 1977, and party expenditure soared from £125,000 in 1977 to £600,000 (O'Malley, 1987).

Traditionally, Fianna Fáil had attacked Fine Gael on two issues, Northern Ireland, where it was implied that it lacked nationalist ardour, and its need to join an allegedly unstable coalition with Labour before it could form a government. On the northern issue FitzGerald if anything could trump Fianna Fáil's nationalist card on the grounds of his family background and personal study of the situation over a period of years. On coalition it was true that despite gains in the opinion polls, Fine Gael would still need to join with Labour and it was also true that there were some significant policy differences between the two likely partners, most notably over a wealth tax and the state's role in job creation. Fianna Fáil strongly attacked the instability and indecisiveness which it alleged flowed from all coalitions and presented itself as the only party able to provide stable one-party government. Fine Gael responded by pointing up the well-known divisions within Fianna Fáil itself and the potential instability of that party, but it was not an entirely convincing reply.

The result in June 1981 showed Fine Gael had more than recovered from the débâcle of 1977. The party took 36.5% of the vote, an increase of 6% and its best performance since it fought as Cumann na n Gaedheal in September 1927. It took 65 seats or 39.2% of the total, as compared with 43 (29.1%) in 1977. It had scored an undoubted success, but hardly a triumph. It was still a long way behind Fianna Fáil, a coalition with Labour would be necessary to form a government and even then it would be a minority administration with only 80 TDs in a house of 166: the support of some minor party or independent deputies would be needed.

There was a pause while the Labour Party elected Michael O'Leary its new leader to replace Frank Cluskey who had lost his seat and the two party leaders then began negotiations on a programme for coalition government. After seven days of talks they produced an agreement with a general emphasis on protecting the poorer sections of the community against the adverse effects of any changes in taxation or price increases and shifting some of the tax burden on to financial institutions and the better off. There was also to be a Youth Employment Scheme and a National Development Corporation to encourage growth industries. In the Cabinet Fine Gael was to have eleven Ministers with FitzGerald as Taoiseach and Labour four with O'Leary as Tanaiste. A special Labour conference accepted the agreement by 737 votes to 477.

Attention then shifted to the first meeting of the new Dáil on 30 June which would elect the Taoiseach. The fate of any government would depend on the eight minor party and independent TDs. The two Maze prisoners would obviously not take their seats. When it came to the election of the Taoiseach Mr Haughey was defeated by 83 votes to 79, having polled his party vote plus Neil Blaney; when FitzGerald was proposed he was elected by 81 votes to 78, gaining the full support of Fine Gael and Labour along with Kemmy. All others abstained. FitzGerald then proceeded to present his Cabinet and in so doing reopened some strains within his party (Browne, 1983*b*). From quite early on his liberal outlook and bustling reformist style had irked some of the more traditonalist elements in the party to the point where in late 1980 he had been forced to bring some of their number back to the front bench. In forming his Cabinet however he ignored almost all the traditional ground-rules of seniority and geographical balance, going for youth and ability, and ruffling some feathers in the process. Three long-serving senior TDs did not receive portfolios and the point was driven home by some of the appointments which were made. The Minister of Agriculture, Alan Dukes, was only 36 years old and entered the Cabinet on his first day in the Dáil; the Minister of Foreign Affairs, Professor James Dooge, was not even a TD though later elected to the Senate. The episode revealed a certain characteristic political insensitivity.

Two issues demanded immediate attention by the new government: Northern Ireland and the economy. In the short-term the ongoing hunger-strike for political status by republican prisoners in the Maze prison made the first the more pressing issue. By 30 June 1981 four strikers had already died. The deaths and subsequent massive funerals were stoking tension and riots in Northern Ireland and in July disorders spilled over into the Republic. FitzGerald made energetic but unsuccessful efforts to encourage more flexibility by the British but the strike only ended in late September when relatives of the prisoners began to take them off their fasts and a new, more amenable Secretary of State for Northern Ireland was in place (Beresford, 1987). By then however 10 had died on the hunger-strike and Provisional Sinn Féin had received a considerable boost.

As this immediate crisis eased FitzGerald clearly believed he could begin to expound some of his long-held convictions on the northern issue. In late September he gave a radio interview in which, without prior consultation with colleagues, he declared his belief that if the Republic were ever to attract northern unionists into a united Irish state then it would be necessary to re-examine the whole framework of public life in the country because as it stood at present unionists viewed the south as 'a sectarian state'. He envisaged something like a 'constitutional crusade' to create a more pluralist Republic, able to accommodate the unionist tradition. In early November 1981 Fitz-Gerald had his first meeting as Taoiseach with the British Prime Minister at which they agreed to set up an inter-governmental council to give expression to their countries' 'unique relationship' and committed themselves to co-operation on economic, social, and cultural affairs. In the Dáil Mr Haughey was vehement in his condemnation of both the 'constitutional crusade' and the meeting between the premiers but his strictures seemed out-dated and partisan, especially since he had met twice with Mrs Thatcher. Fitz-Gerald's efforts by contrast appeared fresh and constructive and seemed to mark a further stage in a process whereby Fine Gael was breaking Fianna Fáil's moral monopoly on the 'national question'.

On taking office the new government concluded that their second main problem, the national economy, was much more severe than they had alleged even in the heat of electioneering. They discovered the previous administration had underestimated both the inflation rate and the level of expenditure and concluded that a special corrective budget was necessary. Room for manœuvre was limited given their lack of an overall parliamentary majority and the fact that the coalition programme ruled out the obvious solutions of higher taxes and drastic cuts in expenditure. An emergency budget was introduced on 21 July which, while it raised welfare benefits, also brought forward the imminent rises in public utility charges postponed by their predecessors and increased excise duties. Thanks to the regular support of two independents the government weathered the divisions by 2 or 3 votes. However the rather hectic pace of events after the election was taking its toll on the Fine Gael parliamentary party. Backbenchers in particular felt the Taoiseach was not sharing his thoughts with them and were increasingly alarmed when such matters as the emergency budget of July and the 'constitutional crusade' of September 1981 were produced with no consultation. A meeting of the parliamentary party elicited promises of better communication but the feeling persisted that the Taoiseach lacked a certain basic political common sense.

This was to be illustrated by the manner in which the government tried to tackle the economic problem. In the months after the Budget of July 1981 the administration became even more concerned with the state of the national finances. In particular it was worried by the high level of foreign borrowing. This had been growing since the mid-1970s but had accelerated notably after Fianna Fáil's return to power in 1977 (Browne, 1986; McDowell, 1981). Its programme had been postulated on the assumption that the initial stimulus given to the national economy, based on increased foreign borrowing, would launch the private sector on such a sustained course of expansion that future development would be self-financing and foreign borrowing could be pared down. In fact, the private sector did not respond as hoped, the necessary level of domestic wealth generation did not occur, and, rather than face the harsh and unpopular measures of cutting expenditure, it had been decided to continue foreign borrowing and allow the budget deficit to increase. By 1981 the current budget deficit amounted to 7.4% of GNP, and debt servicing was absorbing 26.2% of total tax income (Browne, 1986).

Fearing that the size of the debt would erode both domestic and foreign confidence in the Irish economy, compromise its creditworthiness, and inhibit future growth, the government determined to embark on a restructuring of the national finances. The Budget introduced in January 1982 had the overall aims of eliminating the current budget deficit within four years and substantially reducing foreign debt. Social welfare benefits were to be increased but there were to be high excise duties on petrol, alcohol, and tobacco, and milk and butter subsidies were reduced. The election pledge to reduce the basic rate of income tax to 25% was withdrawn and there were to be increases and extensions of VAT. The luxury rate rose by 5% to 30%, the standard rate from 15% to 18% and was to apply to children's clothing and footwear for the first time.

In some quarters there was admiration for a government which, even though it lacked an overall majority, was still prepared to preach financial austerity and admit it could not fulfil an election pledge. However, when the Budget went before the Dáil it soon became clear that the coalition was in difficulties. Of the independent TDs, socialist Jim Kemmy had been a regular supporter since June 1981, but the extension of VAT to children's clothing and footwear was unacceptable and he voted against the coalition. The government was defeated by 82 votes to 81 and a general election was called.

The initial reactions within Fine Gael to fighting this election were a mixture of anger and fear. The anger was directed at FitzGerald and Finance Minister John Bruton who, it was argued, should have realized the likely reaction of the socialist Kemmy to the VAT measures, sounded him out beforehand, and amended their Budget accordingly. The point seemed borne out when, shortly after the Dáil was dissolved, the government announced that if it were re-elected, VAT would not be imposed on children's footwear and clothing. The fear and despair at the outset of the contest was provoked by the prospect of having to go before the electorate defending such a harsh Budget. Moreover, it was humiliating to be forced into an election as the result of any Dáil defeat, but defeat on a Budget, the most vital and basic of all government measures, was even more degrading. It was in fact an historic event: the first time since independence that a government had lost a Budget in the Dáil. To cap it all, the party coffers were empty after the last election and there was nothing like the fighting fund of June 1981 available. The only consolation seemed to be that Fianna Fáil would be in exactly the same position.

However, as the campaign got under way it soon became clear that all was by no means lost. The general Fine Gael strategy was to make a virtue out of necessity as far as the Budget was concerned. It was admitted to be severe but it was argued that given the very serious state of the national finances the measures were necessary and long overdue. In accordance with the market research findings noted earlier which had discovered widespread readiness for sacrifice in the national interest, the government was presented as patriotic and high-minded in that it put the long-term national interest first and showed the moral and political courage necessary to set the country's house in order regardless of the short-term electoral consequences for itself. To the surprise and gratification of many in the party, the strategy succeeded and throughout the campaign Fine Gael retained much of the initiative on the economic front. This was symbolized by the way in which after some initial hesitation Fianna Fáil accepted the government analysis of the economic situation, thereby leaving little room for debate on what should have been the coalition's most vulnerable flank. Given the stress on financial rectitude, there were relatively few sweeteners Fine Gael could offer the electorate, but as noted they did withdraw the proposal to put VAT on children's footwear and clothing. They also brought forward items already budgeted for, such as schemes for youth employment and agricultural assistance.

But the party also realized that its most fruitful ploy was to emphasize the quality of its leadership, and imply a contrast with Fianna Fáil. It was during this election campaign that Garret Fitz-Gerald made a remarkable breakthrough in public appeal. By polling day, despite a lack-lustre performance in a televised debate with Mr Haughey, he was up to 20% ahead of his rival in popularity and highly rated for sincerity, integrity, and courage. For the first time in Fine Gael's modern history it was they and not Fianna Fáil who had a leader with national cross-party appeal and they moved quickly to capitalize on this development. Scarcity of funds curtailed the leader's campaign tour but his picture appeared widely in all party broadcasts, posters, and leaflets, with strong emphasis on his personal qualities.

The election result was better for Fine Gael than anyone in the party had dared hope at the outset. Their performance in June 1981 had been hailed as a historic high tide with the implication that no further advance could be expected. However, though the party lost 2 seats for a total of 63, it actually increased its share of first preferences by 0.8% to 37.3%. Clearly it had held the ground gained in 1981 and even advanced a little further. In the hectic days which followed the result there were some rather nominal efforts to reconstruct the coalition government but the initiative had clearly passed to Fianna Fáil who, though lacking an overall majority, with 81 seats were clearly best placed to form a government, so the election of Mr Haughey as Taoiseach on 9 March 1982 was no surprise.

In the immediate post-election period Fine Gael's mood was a mixture of relief and exasperation. The relief was born out of their surprisingly good showing at the polls in such unpromising circumstances. The exasperation was due to the narrowness of the defeat and the feeling that with a little more political awareness on the part of FitzGerald the Budget might have passed and they would still be in office. Initially, events under the new government depressed the party even further. They were taken aback by deputy Gregory's successful deal with Mr Haughey and then cross with their leader when the independent TD revealed that though FitzGerald had attempted negotiations with him he had not been impressed by the Fine Gael leader's vagueness and lack of preparation (Brennan, 1982). The news of Mr Haughey's incredible coup in persuading Dick Burke to accept the post of EEC Commissioner, forcing a by-election in a difficult marginal constituency, depressed morale even further.

Spirits revived however when Fine Gael held the Dublin West seat with a remarkably efficient campaign and hopes soared even further as the government proved itself deeply divided and accident-prone. Preparations for yet another election campaign were set in hand. A Constituency Review Committee had been set up earlier in the year and it worked hard throughout the summer. It visited marginal constituencies, assessed the electoral situation, and recommended the appropriate strategy in terms of which were the best candidates, how many there should be, and how the slate should be balanced and the vote managed in each case. The aim was to avoid some of the bruising nomination battles which could dissipate the energies of local parties and result in overcrowded or unbalanced tickets (O'Byrnes, 1986). Preparations were also set in hand to raise more funds and the strategy committee began to meet regularly once again. By the end of October the death of two Fianna Fáil TDs, the series of scandals and accidents which had hit the government, the known discontent of its erstwhile supporters in the Workers' Party and independent TDs, and a series of opinion polls had convinced FitzGerald it was time for the *coup de grâce*. His motion of 'no confidence' in the government was passed by 82 votes to 80, and another election was called for 24 November.

The subsequent campaign was probably Fine Gael's most success-ful to date. Three areas in particular demonstrated the party's new-found professionalism: constituency nominations, publicity, and the handling of campaign developments. So thorough was the work of the Constituency Review Committee in spotting the best candi-dates and balancing tickets that they have been described as the best team ever put together to fight an Irish election (Browne, 1982*b*). New ground was also broken in terms of publicity and advertising. Quite early on it was decided not just to concentrate on issues, partly because there was a consensus on economic questions, but also to exploit the strength of the FitzGerald image. All the party publicity featured the leader at length, stressing that he led a united team and implying the contrast with Mr Haughey personally and the well-publicized divisions in his party. At least one broadcast pressed the point home in very explicit terms.

The party's handling of the few issues which did arise was usually prompt and skilful. When Mr Haughey tried to raise the abortion issue at the outset and implied Fine Gael could not be trusted on the matter FitzGerald responded within 48 hours by accepting the gov-ernment wording, committed himself to a deadline for legislation, and effectively killed the issue for the rest of the campaign. The most difficult moment came when the British Secretary of State for North-ern Ireland predicted FitzGerald would make a speech proposing all-Ireland courts and police to combat terrorism. As part of his campaign to stoke up nationalistic feelings Mr Haughey had implied collusion between the British and the Fine Gael leader on northern issues and this seemed to bear him out. In fact, FitzGerald had already aired the idea when he gave the BBC's televised Dimbleby lecture in May 1982. The episode rattled the party's strategists but FitzGerald gave the speech to which Prior had referred. The episode may have stiffened the Fianna Fáil vote (Arnold, 1984; O'Malley, 1983) but it is doubtful if it cost Fine Gael any support since the people most influenced by such a nationalistic appeal were probably Fianna Fáil supporters anyway.

When the election results came in it became clear that Fine Gael had scored another historic victory. Their vote had risen for the third successive election to 39.2%, the highest ever. They had won almost every possible marginal seat, to give a total of 70 TDs, just 5 behind Fianna Fáil. Since Labour had taken 16 seats, it was obvious that another coalition was in the offing, this time with a comfortable overall majority. After negotiations and a favourable vote at a special Labour conference the new coalition government took office on 12 December with FitzGerald as Taoiseach and Dick Spring, Labour's new leader, as Tánaiste. However, so striking had been Fine Gael's progress that some of its more euphoric members could be heard suggesting that in the near future the party might be able to form a government on its own.

LABOUR PARTY

For the Labour Party the 1977 election result had not been as devastating as for Fine Gael: its vote fell by 2.7% to 11.6% and it retained 17 of its 19 seats. As in Fine Gael the defeat brought about a change of leader: Brendan Corish, leader since 1960, resigned and there was a contest for the succession between Michael O'Leary and Frank Cluskey. On the second ballot Cluskey won by a single vote.

His period as leader from 1977 to 1981 was not a prosperous one for the party. The close contest for the leadership soured relations between the two contenders and O'Leary was effectively excluded from the inner counsels of the party. Cluskey emerged as a very able parliamentarian but a poor constituency TD and it was noted that his personal vote had been slipping in elections. The party's only electoral success in this period came at the Euro-elections of June 1979 when it gained 14.5% of the vote and 4 seats; however, it made little headway in the local elections held at the same time and it lost a seat in the Cork City by-election of November 1979. The party was also the poorer for the loss of several gifted members during this period either by death (David Thornley), expulsion (Noel Browne), or development of other interests (Conor Cruise O'Brien). Nor were there any great policy developments after 1977. A new programme was accepted in 1980 but it was hardly novel in its advocacy of a

more extensive health service, women's rights, removal of the constitutional ban on divorce, and the setting up of a national network of
state-funded family-planning clinics. Most internal discussion centred on the eternal question of attitudes towards coalition. This was
thrashed out at the annual conference in Killarney in April 1979
when it was agreed to fight the next election as a separate party with
a distinctive programme; if the election failed to produce an overall
majority for any party then the party leader would open negotiations
with other parties about a possible coalition. A special delegate
conference would then decide whether or not to enter a coalition on
the terms negotiated.

This was the stance adopted during the election campaign of June
1981. The party manifesto put strong emphasis on the need for
comprehensive national economic planning and there were proposals
for a wealth tax, capital taxation, more extensive food subsidies, and
a totally free health service. As the campaign developed Labour
voters were officially advised to give their later preferences to Fine
Gael candidates and this inevitably drew attention to the likelihood
of coalition.

The election result was something of a disappointment. The
Labour vote fell yet again, to 9.9%, and it lost 2 seats, to end with
15, but this disguised the fact that in an enlarged Dáil it now had
only 9% of seats as compared to 11.5% in 1977. Unfortunately
Cluskey was one of the casualties and the party had to elect a new
leader, but this was simplified when Michael O'Leary emerged as
the sole candidate and was elected unopposed on 17 June. There
then followed a week of negotiations with the Fine Gael leader and
an agreed programme and division of Cabinet posts emerged. Labour got four Ministries, with O'Leary as Tanaiste and Minister for
Energy. The agreed programme contained pledges to safeguard those
on low incomes against tax charges, a special levy on bank profits,
increased food subsidies, a youth employment scheme, a National
Development Corporation, and a promise of an all-party committee
on marital breakdown. The special delegate conference on 28 June
accepted the programme by 737 votes to 477 after a lively debate. In
general rural delegates, most Labour voters, and eleven of the TDs
were in favour, while the party chairman Michael D. Higgins, the
Administrative Council (National Executive), the youth wing, the
two largest affiliated unions, and the Dublin delegates were against.

During the eight months of its life the ministers of the 1981–2
coalition worked well together, despite being drawn from two different parties. Certainly the Labour ministers were happier under the
liberal-minded FitzGerald than they had been under the authorita-

rian and conservative Liam Cosgrave between 1973 and 1977. They shared a common concern for social reform and the restructuring of the national finances, but some disagreement did emerge over timing and means. Labour felt Fine Gael was going too slowly on the matter of family law reform and also became anxious about some of its partner's ideas for financial reform. In particular the pledge of a 25% basic income-tax rate seemed to threaten the revenue available for social services, and the consequent rises in indirect taxes might hit the lowest earners. Consequently the party was pleased when the pledge was dropped in the 1981 budget. There was also some impatience when the Youth Employment Agency and National Development Corporation seemed slow to get under way. Most of the disquiet about being in coalition during this period was expressed by those elements who had voted against at the special delegate conference. They were partly motivated by the fact that the left-wing Workers' Party was threatening the Labour vote in some areas.

It was hardly surprising therefore that the circumstances of the coalition's fall over a proposal to extend VAT to children's footwear and clothing were deeply embarrassing to a party which claimed to represent working-class interest. Of all the elections of this period, Labour probably found February 1982 the most difficult—at times it seemed to be fighting as two parties. There was sharp public disagreement between the party leader and chairman Michael D. Higgins over the question of whether the party would serve in another coalition. O'Leary declared Labour and Fine Gael were fighting as allies, should exchange lower preferences, and were certain to reform a coalition if they had sufficient seats; Higgins vehemently denied any electoral alliance and denied that another coalition was a foregone conclusion. The dispute continued right up to polling day. In the event the party did less badly than feared. Its 9.1% of first preferences was a decline of 0.8% on June 1981, but it managed to retain its total of 15 seats, with 2 losses and 2 gains, including the return of Cluskey. In view of Fianna Fáil's strength the question of coalition became somewhat academic, but formal contacts were initiated with other parties and it was eventually decided the party would not enter another coalition but would support a minority Fine Gael government.

The period of February to November 1982 was to prove almost as traumatic for Labour as for Fianna Fáil. The differences over coalition had revealed a mutual disenchantment between the party and its leader. To O'Leary the party seemed increasingly unrealistic in its attitudes; to the party he appeared too comfortable in coalition, too ready to compromise on principles, too much at ease with Garret

FitzGerald's liberalism. The issue came to a head in dramatic fashion when the whole question of coalition was debated at the annual conference at Galway in October 1982. An outright anti-coalition motion was defeated but the conference did accept an amendment committing the party to fight the next election on its own programme, open negotiations with other parties, and then to convene a special delegate conference to decide on the coalition issue. O'Leary was irked by the outcome because he preferred the matter to be dealt with by a joint meeting of the Parliamentary Party and the Administrative Council. The extent of his displeasure became clear five days later when he suddenly resigned from the leadership and the party and joined Fine Gael.

This move, unprecedented for an Irish party leader, rocked the Labour Party. It became necessary to elect a new leader for the second time in 16 months. Two candidates emerged, Michael D. Higgins, left-wing party chairman and TD for Galway West, and Dick Spring, TD for Kerry North since June 1981 and at 32 the youngest Labour deputy. Spring was elected by 12 votes to 2 and within three days of his accession the government had fallen and Labour was plunged into a campaign under an untried leader.

Initially the prospect was quite daunting but the change of leader seemed to act as a catharsis and the party settled down to the campaign quite quickly. The party manifesto, significantly entitled 'Where Labour Stands' sketched out a distinctive programme, with calls for a major tax reform; no further extensions of VAT; taxation of farmers, property, and development land; a powerful National Development Corporation; and the maintenance of welfare expenditure in line with the cost of living. On the question of electoral tactics and coalition the new leader successfully walked a tightrope by refusing to give explicit instructions about later transfers. Instead he suggested Labour voters should opt for whatever other candidates seemed closest to Labour's ideas. On coalition he professed an open mind though trenchant criticisms of Charles Haughey did hint at a preference. In this way the new leader managed to avoid a repetition of the open disputes which marred the party's February electioneering. He also proved himself a good campaigner (Kerrigan, 1982). His youth, recent promotion, and record as an international rugby player gave him novelty value and he also came over as sincere, honest, and unpompous. His steadiness seemed to communicate to his party which began to campaign with increased determination and confidence.

The result seemed to justify the change of mood. For the first time since 1969 Labour's vote increased by the admittedly small amount of 0.3% to 9.4%, but it was a psychological boost, and better than anyone had dared hope at the outset. There was also a net gain of one seat for a total of 16, with Michael D. Higgins the sole loss. The next step was the tricky one of deciding whether and with whom Labour should enter into government. Fianna Fáil had already ruled itself out as a partner by repetition of its traditional line that it would rule alone or not at all. Negotiations with Fine Gael began on 26 November. They lasted two weeks and proved intricate, partly because the new leader did not wish to appear as over-eager as his predecessor (Holland, 1983). The resulting 'Joint Programme for Government' contained several items dear to Labour's heart such as a National Development Corporation; new taxes on property and derelict and development land; pledges to expand provision of housing, health, and educational services; and pushing ahead with social reform and dialogue with Britain over Northern Ireland. The proposed coalition was to consist of eleven Fine Gael ministers and four from Labour, with Spring as Tánaiste and Minister for the Environment. In accordance with the Galway conference decision, the proposals were put to a special Labour Party delegate conference at Limerick on Sunday, 12 December, and after lively debate passed by 846 votes to 522. The new Taoiseach and Cabinet were formally elected by the Dáil on 14 December.

MINOR PARTIES AND INDEPENDENTS

During this period the votes for minor party and independent candidates and the number of TDs returned were higher than at any time in the previous 20 years and they played a crucial role in making and breaking two governments.

The 1977 general election had been the first fought by Sinn Féin the Workers' Party since its change of name from Official Sinn Féin at its *ard-fheis* in January of the same year. At its April 1982 conference it became simply the Workers' Party and the change encapsulated its ideological evolution away from physical-force republicanism into a left-wing parliamentary socialist party. However, its electoral progress was slow and it was not until June 1981 that Joe Sherlock won its first seat in Cork East as the result of persistent local effort. Given the delicate parliamentary balance his voting was highly significant. He voted against Charles Haughey for Taoiseach, abstained on Garret FitzGerald and voted against the 1982 coalition budget. Partly thanks to the publicity gained since June 1982, the party vote rose to 2.3% in February 1982 and it gained 2 further seats. This time it supported Charles Haughey's nomination out of displeasure at the January Budget but as the summer wore on it became increasingly disenchanted with the government and in particular its abrupt switch to a wages standstill and cuts in the health service. Consequently it voted for the 'no confidence' motion on 4 November 1982 and helped bring down the government.

In the ensuing election it put up 20 candidates, produced a detailed manifesto, and again increased its vote, to 3.3%. In terms of seats however, it suffered a net loss of one and since the coalition now had a comfortable overall majority, it was rather marginalized in the 24th Dáil. It had clearly gained a parliamentary toe-hold, but its experience of these three elections proved that all 3 seats were vulnerable and its limited progress due more to persistently hard constituency work than its marxist ideology.

In June 1981 and February 1982 there were candidates from, or representing the views of, Provisional Sinn Féin. Its re-entry into the republic's electoral politics after an absence of 25 years was an attempt to capitalize on the emotions roused by the Maze hunger-strike begun in March 1981. By the time of the June election four prisoners had died and feelings were running high even in some areas not normally sympathetic to militant republicanism. When the election was announced, the H-blocks/Armagh Committee, the prisoners' support group dominated by Sinn Féin, announced it would field nine candidates, all currently serving sentences in northern jails and four of them on hunger-strike. A patchy campaign was mounted and few gave it any chance of success (Beresford, 1987) so there was considerable surprise when it polled 2.5% of the vote, an average of 10.2% in the constituencies contested, and actually won 2 seats, in Louth and Cavan-Monaghan, and ran strongly in some other areas. Since they were prisoners and abstentionists neither of the TDs could take his seat but they and their fellow candidates were deemed by some to have cost Fianna Fáil vital votes and seats (Beresford, 1981). When it came to the February 1982 election Provisional Sinn Féin decided to enter the contest in its own right and put up seven candidates. But the hunger-strike had ended in late September 1981 and despite the ten deaths the emotional heat had gone out of the situation. Consequently, the party's seven candidates took only 1% of the vote and it lost both seats gained in 1981. It did not contest the November 1982 election.

Independent TDs were returned in greater numbers in the elections of 1981 and 1982 and played more significant roles than in the past two decades. Neil Blaney was returned as independent Fianna Fáil TD by the electors of Donegal North-East in all three elections and he equally faithfully voted with his former colleagues in Fianna

Fáil throughout the period. The eccentric Sean Dublin Bay Loftus was elected for Dublin North-East in June 1981 only, and though generally pro-Fianna Fáil, was somewhat unpredictable. Dr John O'Connell was in some respects the most successful independent of the period. Originally a Labour Party member he had quarrelled with the party over nominations for Dublin South-Central, resigned, stood as an independent and won at the expense of party leader Frank Cluskey in June 1981. He was elected Ceann Comhairle in June 1981 and February 1982 and was therefore returned automatically as a TD in both elections of 1982. Noel Browne, after many changes of party, emerged from the June 1981 election as the sole TD of the Socialist Labour Party though he soon parted company with them. His vote regularly sustained the 1981–2 Coalition but he did not stand in 1982. Jim Kemmy, the independent socialist returned in June 1981 and February 1982 also regularly supported the Coalition until in January 1982 he found its proposals to extend VAT unacceptable, and his switch of vote was widely regarded as the decision which brought down the government. He founded the Democratic Socialist Party in March 1982 and put up seven candidates in November 1982 but all including Kemmy were defeated. Tony Gregory, elected for Dublin Central in February 1982 played a crucial role in securing the election of Charles Haughey as Taoiseach in return for the extraordinary development package for his inner city constituency referred to as the 'Gregory Deal'. His regular support enabled this minority government to survive the summer and his abstention in the no confidence debate of November 1982 equally helped to bring it down. The fame and credit for his agreement with Charles Haughey were sufficient to re-elect him in November 1982.

CONCLUSION

By the end of 1982 the Irish electoral scene had changed notably from that of 1977. A Fianna Fáil government with a record majority had been turned out of office in June 1981. The party, long regarded as almost the natural party of government in Ireland, had failed to win an outright majority in any of the three general elections of June 1981 to November 1982. Its administration of February to November 1982 had been a minority government, depending on independents and minor parties for survival, and shaky from the outset. Moreover, the party had lost several of its long-standing assets, such as a leader with cross-national appeal, and its reputation for unity and discipline, as well as the monopoly on nationalistic issues and skilful electioneering. Fine Gael, for its part, had revived and effectively challenged its traditional enemy on these very points. It now had a notably popular leader who could speak with authority on Northern Ireland, and a well-organized and well-financed party machine. Labour for its part managed to survive during this period but was strongly challenged for the left of centre vote. On the one hand were the attractions of the more liberal stance of Fine Gael under Garret FitzGerald. On the other was the Workers' Party which did make progress in some urban constituencies and roused apprehension in Labour ranks that it could take over as the parliamentary voice of the Irish left. The spatial patterns of these situations and the factors underlying them will now be examined.

5

Spatial Patterns and Influences in the General Elections of 1981–1982

INTRODUCTION

The three general elections held in the relatively short period of 17 months between June 1981 and November 1982 provide unprecedented opportunities for analysis of the geography of Irish electoral behaviour. In the first place, the short time-period precluded any radical changes in the social and demographic make-up of the country. Second, the electorate did not change too rapidly during this same period. Indeed, for two of the contests, June 1981 and February 1982, the same electoral register was used and even though these registers contained errors from the outset and some electors undoubtedly died or moved house between these two polls, nevertheless the differences in the overall electorate between the two dates were probably minimal. Comparisons were also enormously assisted by constituency boundaries remaining virtually unaltered throughout the period (Fig. 5.1*b*). Finally, there was a census in the Republic in 1981 and although its results were not issued for parliamentary constituencies, careful aggregation of some of the data can yield material which, with some care, may be used for ecological correlations (Appendix). The purpose of the present chapter is to examine the geography of support for the various parties during this period and the factors which contributed to these spatial patterns.

FIANNA FÁIL

Despite the fact that the party failed to win an outright majority in any of the three elections under discussion and only formed a minority government after one of the contests, Fianna Fáil was still the largest single party in the country after each contest. Its share of first preferences averaged 45.9% over the three polls and never fell below 45.2% in any of them. The picture is confirmed if the strength of Fianna Fáil *vis-à-vis* the other parties is considered. Using the three-election mean, it emerged as the largest single party in 33 of the 41 constituencies, and it had over 50% of first preferences in 12 of these (Table 5.1). The results in the individual elections confirm the picture of an impressive bedrock of strength, even in a period when it was not at the height of electoral success. In 1981, when it

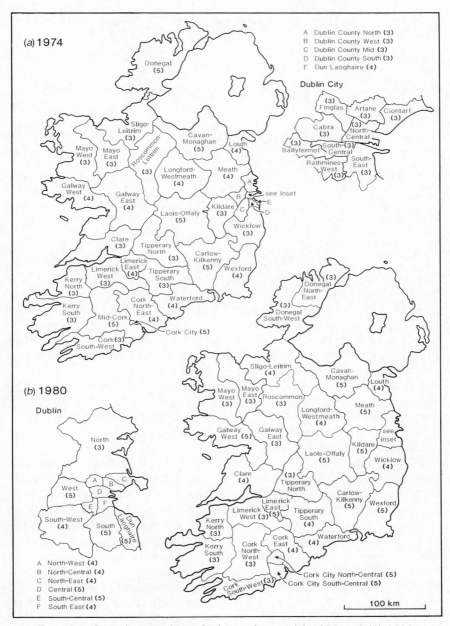

FIG. 5.1 Constituency boundaries and seats (*a*) 1974 and (*b*) 1980

Table 5.1. *Fianna Fáil electoral performance 1981–1982* (no. of constituencies)

	1981	1982*a*	1982*b*	3-election mean
Largest single party	34	34	29	33
Over 50% first preferences	8	14	13	12

Source: Author's calculations.

Table 5.2. *Correlation analysis of Fianna Fáil vote 1981–1982*

Vote 1981 and 1982*a*	+0.9155
Vote 1982*a* and 1982*b*	+0.9208
Vote 1981 and 1982*b*	+0.8544
Mean vote and proportion Irish-speaking 1981	+0.5707
Mean vote 1981–2 and proportion in agricultural employment 1981	+0.6540

Note: All results significant at 0.1% level. Speakman's Rank Correlation used here and in
subsequent correlation analyses.

lost office it was still the strongest party in the country and the
largest single party in 34 constituencies, with over half the vote in 8;
in February 1982 when it formed a minority administration it was
once again the largest party in 34 constituencies with over 50%
in 14; finally, in November 1982, which was regarded as a notable
defeat, it was still the dominant party in 29 constituencies, and the
majority party in 13 of these. The picture is confirmed in terms of
seats, with Fianna Fáil the largest single party in the Dáil after each
election, never winning fewer than 75 seats (45.1%) even at its
lowest point in November 1982. Moreover, it won at least one seat in
every constituency after each election: on no occasion was a constituency left without a Fianna Fáil TD.

The picture, therefore, is of a party with a strong grip on the
political loyalties of the electorate, despite its lack of an overall
majority in these elections. Some impression of the steadiness of its
support was obtained by correlation analysis of the three sets of
results for 1981–2 (Table 5.2). In every case the results were strongly positive with values over +0.85, (significant at the 0.1% level).
But even within this picture of widely spread national strength it is
still possible to discern notable spatial variations in the party's
electoral strength. Examination of the three-election mean reveals
that the core of Fianna Fáil strength is to be found in the west of
Ireland (Fig. 5.2*a*). There lie 11 of the 12 constituencies in which the
party took an average of 50% or more of the first preference votes in
these three elections. They comprise a solid regional block stretching
from Sligo-Leitrim and the Mayo constituencies in the north to

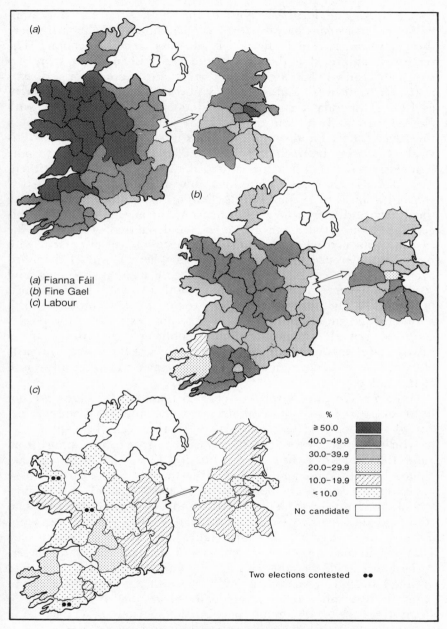

(a) Fianna Fáil
(b) Fine Gael
(c) Labour

%

≥ 50.0

40.0–49.9

30.0–39.9

20.0–29.9

10.0–19.9

< 10.0

No candidate

Two elections contested   ●●

FIG. 5.2 Mean votes for three main parties 1981–1982

Kerry North and Limerick West in the south-west. The only non-western constituency in this category is Dublin North-Central, where the party leader headed the poll in all three general elections. The picture is amplified if those constituencies with a mean score between 40% and 49.9% are added: these comprise a cluster of 5 seats in the far south-west, and a great arc of constituencies which stretches from Tipperary through the midlands up to the border with Northern Ireland and 5 in the Dublin region of which 4 are north of the River Liffey. Finally come the constituencies where the party is weakest, scoring between 30% and 39.9%. Into this category come 9, including Donegal North-East and the 2 neighbouring constituencies of Cork East and Waterford, but the most notable spatial concentration is to be found in the Dublin region, especially south of the Liffey and in the neighbouring constituency of Wicklow. This general picture of strength in the west and relative weakness in the east is confirmed when the individual elections are discussed, with particular reference to the constituencies where Fianna Fáil polled over 50% of first preferences. In each case a notable Fianna Fáil stronghold emerges in the west with an outlier in Dublin North-East; in February 1982 this stronghold extends further into the north midlands and in November 1982 it incorporates most of the border counties. Equally the impression is confirmed that the areas of relative weakness lie in the most easterly area of the county, in parts of Cork County, above all in the Dublin region and especially south of the Liffey.

However, the three elections revealed that these patterns are not fixed and that some notable movement of Fianna Fáil support occurred. Surveying the three contests overall, there were 4 constituencies in which the party experienced a consistent growth in support from June 1981 to November 1982, Limerick East, Cavan-Monaghan, Donegal South-West and Longford-Westmeath. Significantly, these last three are close to the border with Northern Ireland, and supporters of the H-Block/Armagh prisoners and Provisional Sinn Féin had contested the elections of June 1981 and February 1982, but withdrew in November 1982. It seems highly likely that in February 1982 Fianna Fáil was the chief beneficiary of the fact that the hunger-strike had ended, passions had cooled, and the Sinn Féin vote had declined sharply. Equally, in the absence of any Sinn Féin candidates in November their voters had the option of abstention or supporting one of the main parties. There was some decline in turnout in 2 of the 3 constituencies, but there were also increases in Fianna Fáil support in each of them, possibly due to a switch of votes to the traditional party of parliamentary republicanism. In contrast, there were 6 constituencies where the party's support declined consistently in the period under discussion. In Limerick West the accumulated loss was just over 2% and still left the party with 62.2% of the vote in November 1982, its highest support anywhere in the country. Of the remaining 5, Cork South-Central exemplified the steady decline of the Fianna Fáil vote in the region since 1977 and in November 1982 became the first Cork City constituency for 50 years in which Fianna Fáil slipped to second place in a general election. The remaining 4 constituencies (Dublin South, Dublin South-East, Dun Laoghaire, and Wicklow) are all on the south side of the Dublin conurbation or its fringe and demonstrate yet again the inherent weakness of the party in that region.

These spatial variations tended to confirm long-held beliefs that while Fianna Fáil does indeed enjoy support right across the country, the party is particularly associated with the values and social groups characteristic of traditional rural Ireland (Garvin, 1978; Walsh, 1986). To test the validity of this assertion in the early 1980s, two variables describing features of traditional Irish society were drawn from the 1981 Census, Irish-speaking and agricultural employment, and tested against the Fianna Fáil mean vote for 1981–2. The correlation with Irish-speaking was +0.5707, just significant at the 0.1% level, while that for agricultural employment was somewhat stronger at +0.6540 (Table 5.2). Clearly, there is some truth in the assertions of links between the party and the ethos of traditional Ireland and yet the correlations are not particularly strong. This in turn confirms the impression of a party which, whilst retaining its special relationship with rural and Irish-speaking Ireland, has managed to extend its appeal beyond these elements into other groups and regions of Irish society and can still retain this breadth and depth of appeal, even in a series of elections where it failed to win an overall majority of votes or seats.

FINE GAEL

The three general elections of 1981–2 saw popular support for Fine Gael rise to unprecedented heights, with each successive result breaking party records. As already noted, at one point late in 1982 an opinion poll showed Fine Gael and Fianna Fáil to be equal in popularity for the first time in the history of the state.

The party polled a mean vote of 37.7% over the three elections, though it failed to average 50% or above in any constituency. However, 16 constituencies came in the 40–49.9% category. They are to be found in three clusters (Fig. 5.2b). One is in Cork City and

County where it includes every constituency except Cork North-
Central. A second lies in the west midlands and north-west of the
country and includes Cavan-Monaghan, and a third consists of 4
constituencies in the Dublin region of which 3 are to be found
south-east of the Liffey. There were 22 constituencies in the next
category of 30–39.9% of the poll. Most of these are to be found in a
great arc which stretches from Galway West and Clare down
through Limerick and the counties of the south-east and continues
up to the border with Northern Ireland in Louth and Donegal. It
also includes 6 Dublin constituencies, 4 of them north of the Liffey.
Finally, come the 3 constituencies where Fine Gael was weakest,
Dublin Central and the two Kerry constituencies, in one of which,
Kerry North, no Fine Gael TD was returned in any of these three
elections.

Correlations of the results of these three elections (Table 5.3)
produced a picture of a vote which was quite steady. The association between the election results of 1981 and February 1982 was
+0.8855, between February and November 1982, +0.9422, and between 1981 and November 1982, +0.8541 (Table 5.4). With one
exception these correlations, though high and all statistically significant at 0.1%, were not quite as strong as between the Fianna Fáil
results, suggesting that perhaps Fine Gael support is more variable
between elections. In the period under review, however, most of the
overall changes have reflected a rise in support for the party and this
is borne out by reference to the individual election performances
In June 1981, Fine Gael was the largest single party in 7 constituencies (Table 5.3) of which 4 were in the Dublin region and 3 in
counties Cork and Waterford. In February 1982 the party gained
over 50% of the total vote in Dublin South and was the leading
party in 3 other Dublin constituencies, 2 in Cork and one in Donegal
North-East. Finally, in November 1982 it was the largest party
in a dozen constituencies: in 2 of these (Dublin South and Dun
Laoghaire) it polled over 50%; of the remaining 10, 4 were in the
Dublin conurbation, 5 in the Cork-Waterford region, and the other
was Donegal North-East.

Further detail is supplied by an examination of changes over the
three elections. Between June 1981 and November 1982, Fine Gael
experienced a consistent increase in support in 22 constituencies and
a decline in 2. Of the 22 with a consistent increase, 8 were in the
Dublin region and 2 others were nearby Wicklow and Kildare.
Wexford also came into this category, as did South Tipperary and
Limerick West. There were 3 constituencies in Cork City and region
which also saw the party vote rise steadily and the same feature

Table 5.3. *Fine Gael electoral performances 1981–1982* (no. of constituencies)

	1981	1982*a*	1982*b*	3-election mean
Largest single party	7	7	12	8
Over 50% first preferences	—	1	2	—

Table 5.4. *Correlation analysis of Fine Gael vote 1981–1982*

Vote 1981 and 1982*a*	+0.8855[1]
Vote 1982*a* and 1982*b*	+0.9422[1]
Vote 1981 and 1982*b*	+0.8541[1]
Mean vote 1981–2 and proportion in agricultural employment 1981	+0.3638[2]

[1] Significant at 0.1% level.
[2] Significant at 5.0% level.

appeared in 3 border counties and nearby Roscommon and Longford-Westmeath. The only persistent decreases may have been due
to local factors: in Dublin North-West the Workers' Party made
considerable progress in this period at the expense of all three main
parties, eventually capturing a seat at Fine Gael expense in February
1982. In West Mayo the steady slide in the party's vote may have
been due to the presence of a Labour candidate in the 1982 elections
who doubled his vote in November at the expense of both main
parties.

Overall, Fine Gael emerges as a party which made steady progress
in all three elections, even against the difficult background of February 1982. Moreover, especially in November 1982, this progress was
notable throughout the country. However, distinctive regions of
strength and weakness do emerge. The weakest districts are on the
northern side of the Dublin conurbation and the very rural constituencies of the west and far west, especially along the Atlantic coast.
One notable concentration of strength is found on the south side of
the Dublin conurbation and on its western and southern fringes,
including Wicklow. Another area of strength is the Cork region,
particularly in the rural areas but with signs of growing strength in
Cork City itself. Finally, in the north and north-west midlands there
emerged a group of rural constituencies which were increasingly
strong for Fine Gael, though in some this may have been merely a
recovery from a particularly poor showing in the 1977 election.

The overall impression which emerges is of a party whose support
base seems remarkably diverse and unstructured, an impression
confirmed by previous studies at both national and local level (M.

Gallagher, 1976; Garvin, 1977; Parker, 1984). One element which, it has often been argued, is notable in the Fine Gael support base is the farming community (Manning, 1972). However, when the mean vote was tested against agricultural employment, the result of +0.3638 was weak, and just significant at the 5% level. It would seem, therefore, that Fine Gael, like Fianna Fáil, draws support right across the Irish electorate and has some extra support in some sections, but overall its attraction is significantly weaker than its great rival. Beyond this one is left only with speculation about the regional variations in the party's support base. Its concentration of strength on the southern side of the Dublin conurbation and in parts of the north and north-west midlands represents the enduring support it has traditionally enjoyed amongst the urban middle-class and the more prosperous farmers who have appreciated its emphasis on peace, stability, and economical government ever since the early days of the state. Opinion poll analysis has confirmed that the party strengthened its hold on these groups during this period (Sinnott, 1987). Its support in rural Cork may be a historical hangover since south-west Cork was the home territory of Michael Collins, the moving spirit behind much of the military campaign against British forces from 1919 to 1921 and Commander-in-Chief of the pro-Treaty forces in the Civil War. The recent strength in urban Cork may reflect the decline of the Fianna Fáil vote in that city since the removal of local hero Jack Lynch as Fianna Fáil leader in 1979. It may also be due to his replacement as the dominant local political personality by Peter Barry, TD for Cork South-Central and deputy leader of Fine Gael.

LABOUR

For the Labour Party the period from June 1981 until November 1982 was a notably difficult one. After two of the elections the party was in government, after one it returned to opposition; twice it changed its leadership, on one occasion because its leader not merely resigned, but left to join another party. In terms of electoral support, Labour just about held its ground. From 1969 onwards there had been a gradual erosion of both seats and votes (Table 5.5). The loss of votes continued through February 1982, when the party took 9.1% of first preferences, its lowest level since 1957. In terms of seats it fell back to 15 in June 1981, but managed to maintain that level the following February. November 1982 was the first election when the party experienced an increase in both seats and votes, however minimal, since 1965. If the three-election mean is used, Labour took

Table 5.5. *Labour Party electoral record 1957 to November 1982*

	Vote %	Seats	Seats %
1957	9.1	12	8.2
1961	11.6	16	11.1
1965	15.4	22	15.3
1969	17.0	18	12.5
1973	13.7	19	13.2
1977	11.6	17	11.5
1981	9.9	15	9.0
1982a	9.1	15	9.0
1982b	9.4	16	9.6

Sources: C. O'Leary, 1979; Trench, 1983.

an average of 9.5% of the vote and 9.2% of seats during this period. Of all the major Irish parties, Labour's pattern of support is the most markedly regional. Again using the three-election mean, there emerges a concentration of constituencies, mostly in the south-east of the country where the party polled an average 10% and more of first preferences. Most of these lie south and east of a line which runs roughly from Dundalk (Co. Louth) in the north-east to Limerick City in the south-west, though not every constituency in this large region automatically comes into this category (Fig. 5.2c). North and west of this line lie regions of Ireland where Labour support is chronically weak and Labour TDs have been very rare. This pattern is amplified if one considers those constituencies which Labour did not contest in this period. In 5 cases, no Labour candidates were present in any of the three elections. Significantly, 4 of these constituencies are in the north-west, the fifth being Limerick West. This picture of a region of inherent weakness is confirmed if one includes those 3 constituencies where Labour only fought two of the three elections: here again 2, Mayo West and Galway East, are in the north-west.

Further reinforcement is provided by the spatial pattern of TDs returned over this period (Fig. 5.3a). Here again the Dundalk–Limerick line emerges. North and west of this only one constituency returned a Labour deputy in these elections and even this seat (Galway West) was lost in November 1982. Conversely, all the 11 constituencies which had consistent Labour representation throughout this period were south-east of the Dundalk–Limerick line.

However, even within this region there were concentrations of strength and weakness. Labour emerged from this period confirmed as a party with a decidedly minor vote and a notably rural base. The 4 constituencies of greatest Labour strength (over 20% of mean votes and consistent return of TDs in all three elections—Figs. 5.2

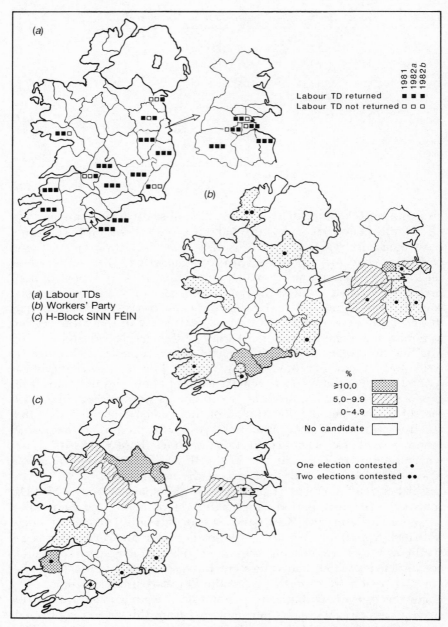

FIG. 5.3 Support for Labour, Workers' Party, and H-Block/Sinn Féin
1981–1982

and 5.3) were predominantly rural (Kerry North and South, Tipperary North and South). There were 14 constituencies in the 10–19.9% category, and all except 2 of these were to be found in the east of the country. In the Dublin conurbation, Labour's strength is concentrated south of the Liffey. Here 4 constituencies came in the 10–19.9% grouping, 2 returned TDs at all three elections and 2 in February and November 1982. North of the Liffey, the party polled over 10% in only 2 constituencies and managed to elect TDs in only one (Dublin Central) and even then only for two elections. There were no very marked changes in Labour support over this period. Of the 33 constituencies contested in all three elections, there was a consistent increase of strength in 9 and a decrease in 9, with no marked spatial concentration in either group. Overall, Labour gave the impression of struggling as ever to hold what support it had against the assaults of the main parties on the one hand and the Workers' Party on the other.

Relatively little detailed knowledge is available about the nature of the party's support base beyond the fact that a significant part of it comes from trade-union members and less skilled urban and rural workers (Manning, 1972; M. Gallagher, 1985; Laver, 1986a, b, c; Sinnott, 1987) with the latter particularly concentrated in the south and south-east where they are employed on the larger commercial farms (Busteed and Mason, 1970). The geographical pattern of voting suggests that these links persist.

MINOR PARTIES

Of the smaller parties in the 1981–2 elections, Sinn Féin the Workers' Party, which became simply the Workers' Party in April 1982, appeared to have the best chance of a long-term future. It made some solid, if modest and patchy, progress during these elections, winning its first Dáil seat in June 1981, 2 more in February 1982, and increasing its vote. The party also gathered some useful publicity during the period of the two minority administrations of June 1981 to November 1982 when the votes of its TDs were crucial. In the November election the total of seats fell from 3 to 2, though further progress was made in terms of votes (Table 5.6a).

However, the party's strength is decidedly regional in distribution. Fewer than half the constituencies in the country were contested during this period and, of the 22 which were fought at some time, only 13 were contested in all three elections (Table 5.6b). The spatial pattern of seats left unfought gives some indication of the party's own perception of its likely areas of strength and weakness. Almost

Table 5.6*a*. *(SF) WP votes and seats 1973–1982*

	Votes %	Seats
1973	1.1	—
1977	1.6	—
1981	1.7	1
1982*a*	2.3	3
1982*b*	3.3	2

Sources: O'Leary, 1979; Trench, 1983.

Table 5.6*b*. *(SF) WP candidatures 1981–1982*

Constituencies contested	
in all 3 elections	13
in 2 elections	1
in 1 election	8
Constituencies not contested 1981–2	19

all the constituencies without a candidate or with only one candidate in this period were predominantly rural in nature and situated in the west or midlands. Of the rural seats which were contested, most had significant urban elements in their population (e.g. Galway West, Louth) or strong local candidates (Donegal South-West), or both (Cork East, Waterford, Wicklow). However, not even the urban constituencies all had candidates in every election: Limerick East and Dublin North were left uncontested in all three elections and Cork South-Central and 4 Dublin constituencies were only contested once. The explanation may lie in a mixture of tactics and milieu. Both Limerick East and Dublin North-Central in 1981 already had, in Jim Kemmy and Noel Browne, left-wing candidates whose outlook on social and economic affairs and Northern Ireland accorded well with Workers' Party policies and it may have been decided to avoid splitting the left-wing vote. Significantly, after Browne stood down before February 1982 the party put up a candidate in November. As for Cork South-Central and the 4 other Dublin seats, they may have been left uncontested because, given the strong middle-class element in their population, the effort would not have been worth the meagre electoral returns.

Using the three-election mean in the constituencies fought in all three elections, it is notable that the party's strongest and most consistent support came from two neighbouring constituencies in the south—Cork East and Waterford—and from Dublin North–West (Fig. 5.3*b*). Supplementary areas of strength were in the Dublin area. Over these three elections the party experienced consistent

Table 5.7. *Workers' Party strength by regions 1981–1982* %

	National vote	Dublin	Leinster (except Dublin)	Munster	Connaught-Ulster
1981	1.7	2.6	1.4	2.2	0.3
1982a	2.3	3.5	1.4	2.9	0.8
1982b	3.3	6.5	1.9	2.9	1.1

Sources: Trench, 1982.

increases in strength in 5 constituencies, 4 in the Dublin region plus Galway West; and a decrease in one, Dublin South-East. The overall impression is of a party strongest in those urban areas which have a significant working-class element in their population and weakest in rural areas. The Dublin region, the most urbanized in the country, is by far the party's greatest stronghold (Table 5.7) and the region in which it has been making the most consistent and impressive progress. However, as already noted, strategic and tactical reasons seem to have influenced its decisions on where to fight, even within its most promising regions.

Two further factors may also influence the level of party support and may actually prove vital in gathering sufficient votes to win a seat outright. One is the availability of a strong local candidate who has worked over a number of years to build up a personal as well as a party vote. In some cases this may involve local authority membership as well. Thus of the four party members who won seats at some stage during this period, three had served on local councils and the fourth (De Rossa) had been active in local community affairs. Of the constituencies where the party experienced a consistent rise in support without as yet winning any seats, Galway West was fought by local councillor Jimmy Brick, and Dublin North-East by the able and active Pat McCartan who remained in contention for a seat until the last count in November 1982 and fell short by only 896 votes.

The second factor concerns the state of the Labour Party in a constituency. An energetic sitting Labour TD seems able to fend off a Workers' Party challenge quite effectively. In Dublin South-West, for example, the Workers' Party only put up a candidate in November 1982 but got a quite respectable 2,365 (6.3%); however, this was at the expense of Fianna Fáil who saw their vote drop by 10.4%, while the Labour vote actually rose by 0.9%. In Dublin South-East Labour's Ruari Quinn proved equally capable of increasing his vote and seeing off the challenge. However, in Galway West, Dublin

South-Central, and Dublin Central where the Labour situation is vulnerable, the Workers' Party has made inroads into the left-wing vote. It would seem therefore that the key to the party's future progress lies in a continuation of recent tactics, namely consistent hard work by local candidates in urban areas with a recognizably working-class element in the population and a vulnerable Labour vote.

Supporters of the republican prisoners in Northern Ireland jails were the only other coherent group to contest more than one election during this period. They fought 9 constituencies in the election of June 1981 as the H-Block/Armagh Prisoners and 7 in the February 1982 contest as Provisional Sinn Féin. No candidates were offered in November 1982, probably because the party had deduced that since the hunger-strike had ended over a year before, the deep-seated passions it aroused had faded away. Over the two elections they did fight, the mean vote for the H–Block/Provisional Sinn Féin candidates was 1.7%, declining from 2.3% in June 1981 to 1% in February 1982. In 1981 two seats were won, but lost the following February.

Candidatures, votes, and seats revealed a definite spatial pattern. There were 5 constituencies fought in both 1981 and 1982; of these, 4 were in border areas, where it was doubtless argued that the electors felt close to the Northern Ireland situation in every sense. Co. Clare was also chosen on both occasions, possibly because of its historic associations with the growth of Irish nationalism. The two-election mean for these 5 contests reveals the strongest support in the 4 constituencies closest to the Northern Ireland border: here the mean vote was 5% or over. In June 1981 there were nine prisoner candidates of whom six were associated with the Provisional IRA or Sinn Féin and three with the Irish National Liberation Army or the Irish Republican Socialist Party. Significantly, however, it was the IRA/Sinn Féin candidates who fought what were regarded as the most promising seats, namely the 3 border constituencies and North Kerry. This deployment accurately reflected the relative strength of political forces in the H–Block/Armagh committee which acted as a support group for the prisoners and sponsored their candidatures. The highest levels of support were indeed found in these areas: 2 seats were won in Cavan–Monaghan and Louth and 4 of the 5 constituencies where they gained over 10% were found here; the fifth, North Kerry, has a strong republican tradition, being the scene of much activity during the War of Independence, the Civil War, and the early 1940s. In all other areas away from the border the vote was 10% or less. The pattern was confirmed in the February 1982 contest. This time there were 7 constituencies contested by Provisional Sinn Féin. Only three of their candidates polled 5% and over, and all these were standing in border areas.

It is clear, therefore, that support for the hunger strikers, Sinn Féin, and probably all varieties of militant republicanism is temporally and spatially specific. It is likely to surface when the Northern Ireland issue has flared up into a particularly virulent phase, and even then the only regions of the country where support is strong will be the border areas closest to Northern Ireland and, to a lesser extent, places such as North Kerry with a tradition of activism.

Significantly, the most enduring independent over these three elections was the strongly republican former Fianna Fáil Cabinet Minister Neil Blaney who represented the border constituency of Donegal North-East and was a strong supporter of the hunger-strikers. A candidate of his Independent Fianna Fáil organization, Paddy Kelly, took 16.2% of the vote in the neighbouring border seat of Donegal South-West in 1981 and came within 724 votes of taking a seat. However, his support faltered appreciably in February 1982, and he did not contest the seat in November. The performance of these two candidates illustrates the fact that, while independent TDs are by definition difficult to categorize, militant republicanism continues to be one source of inspiration. In some respects both these candidates shared many of the views of the H-Block/Sinn Féin candidates just discussed and drew their support from the same sentiments and the same region.

The other source of inspiration for independents has been socialism in various forms. Traditionally, there have been candidates who argued that the existing parties are indistinguishable as conservatives, and the Labour Party mildly reformist rather than seriously socialist. In all three elections, some of the successful independents were of socialist conviction. In June 1981 this applied to two (Noel Browne, Jim Kemmy) and more arguably a third (John O'Connell); Kemmy stood again successfully in February 1982 and was joined by socialist Tony Gregory, but by November only the latter survived. O'Connell as Speaker was returned automatically on both occasions. All four represented urban constituencies.

A further clue to the possible success of independents comes when it is realized that two of those mentioned (Blaney, O'Connell) had been incumbent TDs originally elected as members of major parties when they decided to fight as independents. In each case they quarrelled with their party and were expelled, but they did have the advantage of incumbency when they decided to stand on their own. Another route to the Dáil is revealed by Kemmy, Loftus, and Gregory: all three had been active in local community work and had previously been elected to local councils.

Finally, there are the indefinable independents who fit no classification, have no party affiliations, but gather votes on the basis of tireless local activity. In this period the best example was the indefatigable environmental campaigner Sean Dublin Bay Loftus, elected in June 1981 after five unsuccessful general election campaigns, but defeated in both February and November 1982.

OVERVIEW

These spatial patterns of electoral support over the three elections bear out patterns discerned by other writers (e.g. Garvin, 1977, 1982). Fianna Fáil, whatever its national appeal, remains strongest in the west of Ireland. Even in periods when the party is losing support, it maintains its grip on this historic stronghold and voter movement there was minimal during the period 1981-2 (Mair, 1981). Fine Gael emerges as also having a national appeal, though lacking the overall strength of its great rival. Again it has a historic tendency to be strongest in the east and parts of the north midlands and this emerged in the early 1980s. Equally, Labour's greatest strength is in the east and south-east and the successes of minor parties and independents depend on a mix of local factors, events, and personality.

One feature which does emerge is the consistent gain in support by Fine Gael in parts of eastern and southern Ireland in all three elections. This confirms an impression that, while electoral volatility in the Republic is not as great as in some West European states (Marsh, 1985), there is a certain element of restless movement within the Irish electorate which to date has benefited Fine Gael more than any other party. Moreover, the fact that this movement is most notable in the east and the midlands dovetails with patterns of voter movement discernible since 1948 (Mair, 1982). The explanation, it is suggested, is that these regions contain the largest elements of younger, middle-class, better-educated, and urban-dwelling voters who are less tied to traditional party loyalties and therefore more available to be won over by attractive manifestos (Mair, 1981) and party leaders. In the election of June 1981, as we have seen, the Fine Gael manifesto was particularly aimed at such key groups and succeeded in capturing widespread public attention (Busteed, 1982). The party also set much of the agenda and both moulded and captured the public mood for all three campaigns and the personality of Garret FitzGerald also exerted an increasingly powerful appeal as time went on. Given these geographical patterns of support for the two main parties, it has been suggested that recent changes have, paradoxically, recreated some of the electoral patterns of the 1920s (Garvin, 1982). The implication that there is a persistent co-existence of tradition and change in Irish political behaviour will now be further examined.

KINSHIP

In addition to the links between electoral behaviour, social class, occupation, age, and urban or rural background, kinship and locality have long been regarded as significant influences on Irish electoral behaviour (McCracken, 1958; Whyte, 1966; Chubb, 1970, 1982b; B. Farrell, 1970, 1975, 1985; D. Farrell, 1984; M. Gallagher, 1984).

Kinship remains important in Irish society for several reasons. First, the Irish Republic is small in total area and population and this helps create the air of familiar intimacy which pervades the social ethos. Second, outside the Belfast region, Ireland did not experience the great nineteenth-century industrial and urban revolutions which transformed the size and geography of so many West European populations. Certainly there was endemic emigration after 1845 and for the emigrants to North America and the British dominions the break with previous social relationships was deep and traumatic. For those who settled in urban Britain the break was less complete and as the twentieth century progressed improvements in technology meant the successive waves of migrants could maintain contact with home with greater ease. For those who migrated within Ireland itself, social and family links remained strong. The short distances and improving communication meant contact and visiting were relatively easy. Moreover, the contrasts between the old and new lifestyles were not as violent as those produced by large-scale industrialization and urban growth on the British or American model. Most of the internal migration was to the leading towns and cities of the Republic, chiefly Dublin and its region, but also to Cork and Limerick. Later in the 1960s and 1970s as the pace of economic development quickened, other urban centres also proved attractive. However, by British and West European scales these remained quite small and until recently none developed the symptoms of alienation and rootlessness which came to be such a feature of large-scale urban development elsewhere. Consequently, the break with previous life-styles was less violent than might have been, and there was less strain on social links and relationships.

Table 5.8. *TDs related to previous members of Dáil and Seanad, 1981–1982*

	1981		1982*a*		1982*b*		1981–2	
	no.	%	no.	%	no.	%	no.	%
Fianna Fáil	23	29.5	22	27.2	24	32.0	32	31.4
Fine Gael	13	20.0	12	19.0	17	24.3	17	21.5
Labour	6	40.0	5	33.3	5	31.3	6	30.0
Other	1	12.5	1	14.3	1	20.0	1	8.3
TOTAL	43	25.9	40	24.1	47	28.3	56	26.3

Sources: Browne, 1981, 1982*a*; Trench, 1982; Nealon and Brennan, 1983.

Moreover, as we have seen, the Irish Republic is a devoutly Roman Catholic country, with approximately 90% of the population attending mass at least once per week. Though there are some variations with age, gender, marital status, and social context, the attendance level never falls below 85% for any significant sub-group of the population and temporal studies have not suggested any significant decline in adherence (Chubb, 1982*b*; Nic Ghiolla Phadraig, 1986; Inglis, 1987). It has also been pointed out that Irish Catholicism is notable for its traditionalist and orthodox ethos, which means that those who migrated within Ireland maintained a common store of values and habits with those who remained at home. Catholicism in general is noted for its strong emphasis on the nuclear family as the key element in social structures and relationships and this is certainly true of the Irish Church. Consequently, the importance of family and kinship links is given strong moral and spiritual sanction.

The electoral significance of kinship is clearly seen in the elections of 1981–2. Of the 213 different TDs elected during the three elections, 56, or 26.3%, were related to previous members of the Dáil or Seanad (Table 5.8). There were some slight differences between the parties, with rather more Fianna Fáil and Labour than Fine Gael TDs following relatives into the Dáil. Over the three general elections the proportions if anything increased slightly. In 1981, the overall percentage was 25.9%, dropping to 24.1% in February 1982 and rising to 28.3% for November 1982, possibly because parties had realized how hard fought this last campaign would be and made every effort to nominate candidates who could capitalize on such relationships. For the two main parties their individual patterns followed this general trend quite closely, but in the case of Labour there was a marked drop in the proportion of TDs with such links, from 40% in 1981 to 33.3% in the first election of 1982 and 31.3%

Table 5.9. *Women TDs 1981–1982*

	No. of women elected	No. related to previous TD or senator
22nd Dáil (elected June 1981)	11	7
23rd Dáil (Feb. 1982)	8	5
24th Dáil (Nov. 1982)	14	9
Total women elected 1981–2	15	9

Sources: as for Table 5.8.

in the second. However, since in absolute terms actual numbers showed a decrease of only one, too much should not be read into these figures.

As suggested above, the parties are well aware of the significance of kinship in the Irish political milieu and conscious efforts are often made to nominate candidates with political antecedents. The hope is that electors will recall the record of family service to constituency and party and transfer their allegiance to the new candidate, regarding him as being 'of good stock' (Bax, 1976). A special application of this approach comes when an incumbent TD has died. Strenuous efforts are made to nominate a close relative, preferably a spouse or sibling, in order to capitalize not merely on the family name, but also on a sympathy vote. This can be of particular importance in a by-election. In Irish electoral politics until recently this was the most usual route into the Dáil for women. In all, fifteen female candidates were elected over the period June 1981 to November 1982; of these nine were related to previous TDs or Senators, but a further two came from families with a long tradition of political involvement (Table 5.9). Only four could be regarded as having made their own way into the Dáil without benefit of kinship links. All of these represented Dublin constituencies, suggesting it may be easier to break this traditional habit in urban Ireland. An example of such links was provided by the constituency of Donegal South-West. When the incumbent Fianna Fáil TD Clem Coughlan was killed in February 1983, the party's successful candidate at the subsequent by-election in May was his brother Cathal. When he in turn died in June 1986 his daughter Mary gained the nomination and was elected in 1987.

In several cases there is not merely continuity of kinship links in the Dáil but also geographical continuity in that one family represents a constituency through several generations. In the general elections of 1981–2 there were 40 TDs (18.8%) who sat for the same or a largely identical constituency as their family predecessors

Table 5.10. *TDs related to previous TDs and sitting for same or largely identical constituency*

	1981		1982a		1982b		1981–2	
	no.	%	no.	%	no.	%	no.	%
Fianna Fáil	20	25.6	17	21.0	19	25.3	23	22.5
Fine Gael	11	16.9	9	14.3	11	15.7	11	13.9
Labour	5	33.3	4	26.7	4	25.0	5	25.0
Other	1	12.5	1	14.3	1	20.0	1	8.3
TOTAL	37	22.3	31	18.7	35	21.1	40	18.8

Sources: as for Table 5.8.

(Table 5.10). Again, the figure tended to be consistently higher for Fianna Fáil than for Fine Gael and highest of all for Labour, especially in the first two elections. There was little variation between elections.

A striking example of the dynastic principle at work was provided by the constituency of North Kerry where by 1982 two families had accumulated a total of almost 100 years as TDs. On the Fianna Fáil side Tom McEllistrum (senior) was elected as a republican TD for Kerry in 1923, joined Fianna Fáil in 1926 and from then onwards held a seat in either Kerry or North Kerry until retirement in 1969. His son, also Tom, replaced him in that year and all succeeding elections up to and including November 1982. The Labour Party had been unsuccessful in Kerry until 1943 when Dan Spring, former national and county Gaelic football star, trade-union official, and friend of Kerry IRA member Charlie Kerins (then under arrest for his part in the murder of a Special Branch officer and later executed) succeeded in capturing a seat. He retained it until retiring in 1981 when he was succeeded by his son Dick, subsequently Labour Party leader and Tánaiste in 1982 (O. O'Leary, 1985a).

One sub-group of kinship links highly regarded in the past consists of people with relations who were active during the crucial formative period of the War of Independence and the Civil War, 1919–23. Such links suggest a candidate is 'sound' on nationalistic and constitutional issues, can impress the more traditionalist elements in the electorate and party, and even carry a certain air of excitement and glamour as they stir memories of the exciting days of past glories. The last TD who had actually fought in the War of Independence left the Dáil in 1977, but 25 or 11.7% of all the members returned in 1981–2 came from a family with a record of service during this period. The small numbers involved (Table 5.11) make the war records of Labour and 'other' TDs the most impressive

Table 5.11. *TDs with family record from 1916–1923 period*

	1981		1982*a*		1982*b*		1981–2	
	no.	%	no.	%	no.	%	no.	%
Fianna Fáil	11	14.1	10	12.3	9	12.0	14	13.7
Fine Gael	5	7.7	6	9.5	6	8.6	6	7.6
Labour	3	20.0	1	6.7	—	—	3	15.0
Other	2	25.0	1	14.3	1	.20.0	2	16.7
TOTAL	21	12.7	18	10.8	16	9.6	25	11.7

Sources: as for Table 5.8 plus personal information

in percentage terms, but the most interesting persistent contrast is between Fianna Fáil and Fine Gael. In all three elections there were slightly more Fianna Fáil TDs with a family record of activism, possibly reflecting the more traditionalist nationalistic ethos of that party, but the most striking tribute to the strength of such memories comes from Fine Gael. One of their successful candidates in Dublin North in all three elections was Mrs Nora Owen: she was a grand-niece of the nationalist hero Michael Collins, and the family link was widely publicized by the party and commented on by the media. Nevertheless, there are indications that the significance of such a family background is declining. Throughout the three elections the absolute and relative numbers of TDs with such links declined for all three main parties, presumably because the passage of time renders them less significant in the public memory.

LOCALITY

Locality has always been a powerful reference point in Irish life. In part this is because large numbers of Irish people have always been rural dwellers. As recently as 1961, 49.3% lived in a rural context and 36% were still employed in agriculture; by 1981 the figures were 39.6% and 12% respectively (Horner, 1986). However the influence of rural values persists, even in urban areas, since many town dwellers are themselves migrants from rural backgrounds and many born in urban areas are only one generation off the land. In addition, in some of the more conservative quarters of Irish society the outlook and values of rural Ireland are held up as a national model.

In rural Ireland many people still identify strongly with county and parish. The county, ironically an English administrative device, has found a deep niche in Irish loyalties during the past 100 years in particular. This is partly because it was used from early on by the

Gaelic Athletic Association as the organizational basis of its games and the passionate excitement of the county competitions down through the years, together with their distinctive colours, have helped to establish this originally foreign imposition as a focus of Irish loyalties below the level of nation. The process was reinforced and given an explicitly political dimension when Irish rural local government was reformed in 1898 and many functions hitherto provided by a conglomeration of elected or nominated bodies were consolidated and given to elected county councils and their subordinate bodies. Henceforward the population paid their rates to the county councils and looked to them for an increasing number of services, experiences which helped reinforce the place of the county in the public mind. That sense of identity became more explicitly political through the regular election of councillors. From the outset Irish nationalists looked on the new county councils and their subordinate councils as a means of gaining administrative experience and publicizing the case for home rule, and some lively electoral contests ensued. Within a short time most county councils outside eastern Ulster had strong nationalist representation and in some cases an actual majority. They were also the venue where Sinn Féin gained a few seats before 1914 and a series of notable successes in the local elections of 1920. These institutions of the county therefore played an important subordinate role in the progression to Irish independence and thereby carved out a place for themselves as a political frame of reference for Irish voters.

Below this level the Roman Catholic parishes have played an intimate and enduring role in Irish rural life. In some cases it is claimed they can be traced back to medieval and early Celtic times, but the Reformation and the imposition of the Anglican ascendency created a break with the old system and a new structure of Catholic parishes did not emerge until the nineteenth century. In time each parish had its own church building and resident priest who ministered to the spiritual needs of those who lived within its boundaries. However, once such a useful local spatial framework was established it was used for a great variety of purposes. The Catholic Church took on a significant role in the life of rural and small-town Ireland. Priests were often instrumental in setting up social and sporting clubs and charitable organizations, and the parochial system was naturally used as the spatial basis of organization. When later in the century a national education system emerged a parochial basis was again appropriate. But the parish was also used as the basic unit of other organizations with more explicitly political aims, notably O'Connell's Catholic and Repeal Associations, the Land League,

Table 5.12. *TDs born in or near constituency 1981–1982*

	1981		1982a		1982b		1981–2	
	no.	%	no.	%	no.	%	no.	%
Fianna Fáil	66	84.6	68	84.0	64	85.3	88	86.3
Fine Gael	57	87.7	54	85.7	61	87.1	69	87.3
Labour	10	66.6	11	73.3	14	87.5	16	80.0
Other	6	75.0	7	100.0	4	80.0	9	75.0
TOTAL	139	83.7	140	84.3	143	86.1	182	85.4

Sources: as for Table 5.8.

and the local GAA club. It also became the primary building block of the Irish Volunteers and subsequently Sinn Féin, the IRA, Fianna Fáil, and the rural self-help organization Muintir na Tire, and thereby became the basic local spatial frame of reference for the Irish rural dweller (Nolan, 1986).

The 1981–2 elections showed that such localist feelings are still significant. No less than 182 or 85.4% of all the TDs who served in the Dáil during this period had been born in their constituency or just outside its boundaries (Table 5.12). For those representing Dublin constituencies a birthplace within the city was taken as sufficient. There were no significant variations across the parties or between elections, though until November 1982 the figure tended to be less for Labour—this however may be due to slight variations in small absolute numbers of Labour TDs. Certainly in local party organizations local links are regarded as vital for aspiring candidates and there is strong antipathy towards outsiders who seek party nominations or are occasionally imposed by party headquarters.

The election of November 1982 in County Clare provided a classic example of the fading importance of a national family record and the enduring significance of local links. Sile de Valera, granddaughter of Éamon de Valera the party founder, had been returned as Fianna Fáil TD for Mid County Dublin in 1977. The revision of constituency boundaries in 1979 meant she had to seek another constituency. She was nominated for Dublin South but failed to be elected in both 1981 and February 1982: on both occasions her presence caused deep resentment in the local Fianna Fáil organization. At this point events intervened with the death of Dr Bill Loughnane, Fianna Fáil TD for Clare and a popular medical doctor and student of traditional music. Miss de Valera indicated an interest in the seat. Given her family background, the fact that her grandfather had sat for at least some part of the county for over 40 years, and her

Table 5.13. *TDs with home address in or near constituency 1981–1982*

	1981		1982*a*		1982*b*		1981–2	
	no.	%	no.	%	no.	%	no.	%
Fianna Fáil	75	96.2	78	96.3	74	98.7	88	86.3
Fine Gael	60	92.3	57	90.5	66	94.3	68	87.3
Labour	13	86.7	13	86.7	15	93.8	16	80.0
Other	6	75.0	7	100.0	5	100.0	9	75.0
TOTAL	154	92.8	155	93.4	160	96.4	182	85.4

Sources: as for Table 5.8.

position on the nationalist pro-Haughey wing of the party, no great difficulties were anticipated. She did indeed obtain the nomination for the by-election, but only at the expense of considerable bitterness within the local party, since some members would have preferred a local candidate and specifically Dr Loughnane's son, Billy. The by-election was never held because the government collapsed and Miss de Valera was one of the party's candidates in the general election of November 1982. However, so incensed were the younger Loughnane and his supporters at the presence of this outsider on the slate that Loughnane stood as an independent and proved fatal to de Valera's chances. He gained 5.9% of first preferences and, when eliminated after the fourth count, had 3,641 votes to be redistributed. Of these, 1,365 (37.5%) did not actually go to Fianna Fáil at all; of the 1,778 which did, 1,124 (63.2%) went to another Fianna Fáil candidate, Brendan Daly, who was eventually elected, and only 664 (37.3%) to de Valera, who was defeated. Clearly therefore the de Valera family name was not enough to overcome the local connection, even amongst the Fianna Fáil activists of County Clare.

Another indication of the importance of local links is the fact that over these three elections 85.4% of Dáil members had homes within their constituency (Table 5.13). There was no clear variation between the parties but there was a slight overall tendency for this to become more notable between June 1981 and November 1982. Again this may have been because the parties were anxious to maximize their votes in what they knew would be a series of closely fought contests, but also partly because some TDs who had not had a house in the constituency when first elected, moved in quickly afterwards before the next election. This in itself is a recognition of the importance of such links.

The political parties go to considerable lengths to accommodate local sentiments and this is clearly seen in the patterns of candidate

nominations (M. Gallagher, 1980) and campaigning within constituencies. Candidates are nominated at conventions presided over by
a representative of the national party executive, often an incumbent
TD from another constituency, or a government minister or front-
bench spokesman (Marsh, 1981). Delegates to the convention are
appointed by local party branches, so several hundred people may
be present, with every region in a constituency eager to see their
candidate on the slate. At the same time care must be taken not to
nominate too many candidates or the party's first preference vote
will be dissipated (Katz, 1981). Consequently nominating conventions can be tense and acrimonious affairs as contenders battle for a
place on the ticket. Actual fist fights between factions are not un-
known and sometimes disappointed contenders have stood as independents, as Billy Loughnane did in Clare in November 1982. On
top of these local interests the national party has a need for candidates to represent a balance of age, gender, and ability. To reconcile
these with local criteria the national executive of each major party
has the right to impose additional candidates in a constituency,
though this can sometimes lead to deep resentment at the local level,
as in Dublin South when Sile de Valera was imposed in February
1982.

The ideal end product in a constituency is a slate of candidates
which will maximize the party vote and be geographically 'balanced', in that all the main regions and population centres of the
constituency are represented. Given the vagaries of party infighting
and the occasional imposition of candidates by national headquarters, this is not always attainable. However, several examples are
available from the period under discussion (Fig. 5.4). The Fianna
Fáil slate in Clare for the June 1981 election displayed admirable
geographical balance. Brendan Daly was from the coastal town of
Kilrush in the south-west of the county; Sylvester Barrett was from
Clarecastle very close to Ennis the county town; Dr Bill Loughnane
was resident in Feakle in the north-east, and the only candidate not
elected, McNamara, was from the historic spa town of Lisdoonvarna
in the north-west. Fine Gael proved they too were well able to devise
balanced tickets with the slate of candidates they fielded for Dublin
North in all three elections of 1981–2. Here they had to be careful to
avoid over-nomination since the area was long regarded as strong
Fianna Fáil territory and it was well known that the party leader
Charles Haughey who lived in the constituency was especially keen
to see his party pick up two of the 3 seats. Fine Gael put forward the
same two candidates in each of the three elections, correctly calculating that a larger slate could cause leakage of transfers. With the help

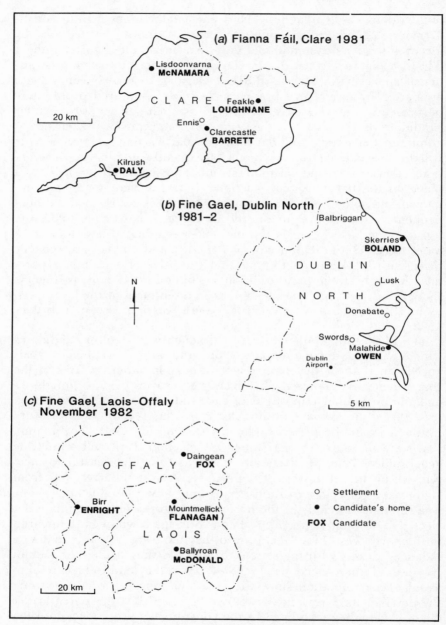

FIG. 5.4 Geographically balanced tickets

of Labour transfers both were elected. They were also assisted by the fact that they were carefully chosen to represent opposite ends of the constituency: John Boland from Skerries in the north-east, and Nora Owen from Malahide in the south-east (Fig. 5.4*b*). Particularly interesting is the recognition that local ties were found to be as significant as ever in a quite urban constituency. A final variation on the same theme occurs when constituencies consist of two counties or parts of counties. Considerable efforts are made to ensure that both are represented on the ticket. Thus in November 1982 Fine Gael nominated four candidates for the constituency of Laois-Offaly: two were from each county and the ticket was also balanced *within* each county (Fig. 5.4*c*).

One of the problems which can arise when a political scene is strongly influenced by kinship and localism is factionalism, the growth of competing groups within parties based on particular personalities and districts. To some extent this can be checked by the need to present a united front in the face of other parties. A common device to defuse such factionalism is the bailiwick system, whereby a party's candidates will agree to divide the constituency between them, each being allowed an exclusive area in which to campaign for first preference votes (Sacks, 1976). The general understanding is that candidates will not trespass on each other's territory when campaigning, and between elections will confine their constituency work to their own bailiwick (Parker, 1983, 1986) otherwise they will be seen as poaching and quite violent intra-party disputes can arise.

The firm conviction that local links can win extra votes lies behind the strenuous efforts to ensure that candidates are local and that party tickets are geographically balanced. Despite the secrecy of the ballot, there is considerable evidence to support this belief. One group of studies has relied heavily on the work of the party observers or 'tallymen' at the official count who watch as ballot papers are initially opened and sorted. They keep notes on the first preferences and thereby compile records of voting patterns in each polling district. Studies of those returns have revealed a 'friends and neighbours' effect whereby candidates receive a larger than usual share of votes in polling districts around places with which they are particularly associated, usually their home but also perhaps their place of work (Sacks, 1970; Parker, 1982). Tallymen's returns are useful but they obviously depend on the sharpsightedness of the observer and co-operation from the counters. Probably more reliable is the official record of transfers. As each Irish voter works down the ballot giving preferences to candidates, local factors can be given full play.

Two examples illustrate their influence. The Meath constituency

Table 5.14. *Differential transfers on the basis of local links*

(a) *Meath, 1982b*, transfer of Conway's (Ashbourne) votes to Fianna Fáil colleagues

Total transferable votes	4,027	
Hilliard (Kilmessan)	1,248	31.0%
Fitzsimons (Navan)	2,305	57.2%
Lynch (Oldcastle)	474	11.8%

(b) *Wicklow, 1982a*, transfer of McManus's (Workers' Party, Bray) votes

Total transferable votes	2,421	
Hussey (FG Bray)	864	35.7%
Timmins (FG Baltinglass)	431	17.8%
Murphy (FF Bray)	716	29.6%
Brennan (FF Carnew)	410	16.8%

Sources: Trench, 1982; Nealon and Brennan, 1983; Browne, 1982a.

in November 1982 returned five TDs. After the fifth count 3 seats had been filled and four candidates were still in the running, all from Fianna Fáil. Sean Conway, the weakest, was eliminated and his 4,217 votes distributed amongst his three party colleagues. Since all were of the same party they should have received an equal share of transfers (Table 5.14*a*). In fact, Fitzsimons and Hilliard between them received 3,553 (88.2%) and Lynch only 474 (11.8%): the most likely explanation lies in the operation of a distance-decay function: Conway's home was in Ashbourne in the south-east of the constituency, Hilliard lived at Kilmessan, and Fitzsimons at Navan, both about 15 miles away, while Lynch's home-town was Oldcastle in the extreme north-west of County Meath. Differential transfers *within* a party on the gounds of localism may not be too surprising: much more striking are transfers *across* party lines, illustrated by the Wicklow constituency in February 1982. After the third count only one of the 4 seats had been filled. The weakest candidate, John McManus of the Workers' Party, was eliminated and his votes distributed amongst the remaining four, two each from Fine Gael and Fianna Fáil. One might expect a fairly even spread of transfers across these four or at least that those belonging to the same party should get similar levels of transfer. In fact, there was marked differentiation within both parties (Table 5.14*b*). Of the 2,421 transferable votes, Hussey of Fine Gael received twice as many as her party colleague Timmins, and Murphy of Fianna Fáil over 300 more than his partner Brennan. The likely explanation lay in the fact that McManus, Hussey, and Murphy shared strong personal links with the Bray area and on that basis the last two received preferential transfers despite their radical philosophical differences with the Workers' Party and their common outlook with their party colleagues.

Local factors can also be seen at work when issues arise which

Table 5.15. *TDs with service on elected local authorities 1981–1982*

	1981		1982a		1982b		1981–2	
	no.	%	no.	%	no.	%	no.	%
Fianna Fáil	62	79.5	64	79.0	61	81.3	81	79.4
Fine Gael	56	86.2	51	81.0	56	80.0	65	82.3
Labour	13	86.7	14	93.3	16	100.0	18	90.0
Other	4	50.0	5	71.4	3	60.0	7	58.3
TOTAL	135	81.3	134	80.7	136	81.9	171	80.3

Sources: as for Table 5.8.

affect particular constituencies and voters respond by abandoning normal electoral habits in favour of the candidate who most effectively champions local interests. One notable example occurred in Waterford in February 1982. In the months before the election the future of the local Clover Meats factory had seemed very uncertain. One of the most vociferous campaigners against closure was Paddy Gallagher of the Workers' Party, a member of Waterford Corporation since 1974 and a trades union activist. An unsuccessful candidate in the 1977 and 1981 general elections, his recent high profile on the issue was largely responsible for his election in February 1982: by November the issue had become less significant and he lost his seat.

One of the most important of local links is a record of service on a local authority: 80.3% of all TDs elected in 1981–2 had served on elected local councils. This high level persisted throughout all three elections (Table 5.15). There were no great contrasts between the two main parties but such links seemed least important for independents and others and most important for Labour—by November 1982 all its TDs had experience as local councillors. There was also some evidence that council membership was less important in the Dublin region. Only 71.7% of all Dublin TDs in 1981–2 had served on a local authority as opposed to 80.3% overall. Some TDs served on more than one council, many were also members of non-elected bodies which provide important services and can therefore be valuable bases for political activity, and many TDs are also members of local sports and recreation clubs.

CLIENTELISM

This high level of membership of elected and nominated bodies is symptomatic of the role which the Irish public representative is widely expected to play. Each representative is regarded as an intermediary between local community and national government, representing the needs of the locality and its people to the government and acting as the channel through which responses come. In this way the politician builds up a network of electors who are under a sense of obligation which it is hoped they will discharge by voting for him at election times. Electors who have been assisted are often referred to as 'clients', the assistance as 'patronage', and this style of politics as 'clientelism' (Komito, 1984). The phenomenon has been studied in depth in two constituencies (Bax, 1976; Sacks, 1976). The reasons for the importance of this feature in Irish political culture have been debated at length (B. Farrell, 1985). It may be one result of the significance of locality and kinship in Irish society as a whole: if locality is still important then it is natural that local public service should be deemed important. Equally, if face-to-face relationships are still important then it is natural they should be carried over into dealings with government. Others have argued that Ireland has an 'intercessory culture' which encourages the use of intermediaries. This is claimed to have originated in the days of the British administration which the mass of the people found alien and distant (Sacks, 1976). Consequently, it was felt that intermediaries were necessary and this role could be filled by surviving Catholic gentry, parish priests, or sympathetic landlords, the only people with the necessary education, status, and confidence. It has also been argued that Catholicism, with its stress on a hierarchical structure of church government and the role of clerics and saints as intercessors with higher authorities, both ecclesiastical and divine, has made the intermediary both familiar and valued (Bax, 1976).

Both explanations are less than satisfactory. British administration in the 26 counties ended in 1921 and as already noted local government ceased to be controlled by Anglican Ascendancy representatives as early as 1898. Nor is the explanation based on the Catholic ethos totally convincing. Other states with a strong Catholic tradition do not have this style of politics, while some which do lack a Catholic-influenced culture.

One possible set of explanations lies in the circumstances surrounding the birth and the first few years of the Irish state. The fact that southern Ireland achieved independence as the result of a violent political revolution affects many aspects of its political culture. It is quite possible that in the early days after 1921 government ministers looked favourably on approaches from people who had shared in the dangers and comradeship of the struggle against the British. The experiences of the Civil War may well have reinforced these attitudes. It has already been seen how for the first ten years of existence the new Irish Free State was governed by the victors in the Civil War. They were preoccupied with building the institutions of the new state and manning them with politically reliable personnel who had been on the 'right' side during the conflict. A similar attitude was displayed by Fianna Fáil when they took office in 1932 and proceeded in turn to favour their supporters. Consequently, by the end of the first two decades of independence it had become habitual for public resources to be distributed in accordance with criteria other then merit or need alone, and it was widely accepted that to redress a grievance contact with a politician was necessary. Finally, it could be argued that Ireland's STV variant of PR plays a significant role in encouraging TDs to become local ombudsmen. Since constituencies are multi-member and each major party nominates more than one candidate then one of the few ways in which candidates from the same party can outbid each other for votes is to provide better constituency service than their colleagues.

Personal contacts with politicians may also have been particularly helpful in the early days of the Irish state because of the narrow range of employment openings and the patchy nature of the welfare system. In rural Ireland until the late 1960s, the range of non-agricultural employment was very narrow. One highly valued set of openings existed in local council employment. Until the early 1940s many such posts were filled by informal agreement between professional officers and elected representatives and it was clearly wise for applicants to ensure that their local TD or councillor knew of their interest in a vacancy. Again, until the 1950s the Irish welfare system was poorly funded and payments often at the discretion of local officials. Here too there was an obvious incentive for an applicant to bring all possible sources of influence to bear and TDs frequently found welfare claims were a significant part of constituency business.

Subsequent legislation put much of this patronage beyond the influence of elected representatives. An Act of 1942 made senior appointments and decisions on expenditure patterns in local government the sole responsibility of professional officers and from the late 1950s onwards the extent and funding of the welfare system were progressively increased and payments made on universal criteria. Nevertheless, officers are still approached by politicians when making appointments, especially to minor or temporary posts which are still filled by politicians either in committee or full council, e.g. rate and rent collectors, postmen, officers of the vocational education and local agricultural services (Bax, 1976).

In the final analysis it is impossible to be sure how effective a politician's representations have been. In some marginal cases they

Table 5.16. *Kerry North:Dick Spring 1981–1982*

| | First preferences | | Results |
	Votes	%	
1981	5,685	16.6	Elected 6th count
1982a	8,552	25.8	Elected 1st count
1982b	9,724	28.9	Elected 1st count

Sources: as for Table 5.8.

may influence a decision and constituents for their part continue to contact public representatives for assistance partly in the knowledge that others do so, partly on the principle that at the very least it can do no harm. It suits the politician to give the impression his influence has been crucial to a successful outcome and some send letters expressing their pleasure at having been able to help. The implication that he has helped is obvious, and so too is the sense of obligation thereby created and the hint that it can be discharged by a preference at the next election. This idea that the politician has helped applicants gain access to resources which are theirs by right has been termed 'invisible patronage' (Sacks, 1976). In actual fact what a politician may be able to do is guide a constituent though the increasing maze of paperwork associated with modern administrative affairs and gain easier access to bureaucrats. The end result is that he builds up a steadily expanding reputation in the community as a good constituency representative with effective influence and this becomes an electoral asset (Komito, 1984).

The discussion to date has focused on the possible impact of patronage on the electoral choice of a relatively small number of voters, but there is evidence that expectations of favoured treatment can exist at constituency and regional level also. It has already been noted how in June 1981 North Kerry elected the Labour TD Dick Spring, but he only took the seat on the sixth and last count with the narrow margin of 144 votes over his Fine Gael opponent. Subsequently he was appointed Minister of State at the Department of Justice, and his electoral position was transformed. In the February 1982 general election he topped the poll and was elected on the first count with 25.8% of first preferences. Recent injury in a car crash may also have pulled in sympathy votes. By November 1982 he was Labour leader and clearly destined to be Tánaiste in any future coalition. The prospect improved his position still further: again he topped the poll, this time with 28.9% of first preferences (Table 5.16). The explanation for his success may have lain in pride at a local boy made good, but it seems equally likely that the electors of North Kerry were drawn to him by the expectation that from his increasingly powerful position he could divert a good deal of patronage to the constituency and by their votes they simultaneously strengthened his base and established a claim on him.

MINISTERIAL APPOINTMENTS

Spring's appointment as a Minister of State in June 1981 is an example of the form of patronage which is directly under the control of every government, namely the allocation of government posts. A variety of factors influence their distribution, including seniority, ability, and the party leaders' need to pay off political debts. However, two further factors are also believed to be relevant, namely geographical balance and electoral geography (B. Farrell, 1987b). There is a general feeling that a broad balance has to be maintained between urban and rural areas, without too much emphasis on Dublin City or any neglect of the cities of Cork, Galway, or Limerick. The Gaeltacht (Irish-speaking) districts have had a Cabinet minister to look after their special interests since 1956 but it is thought important that the west in general should always be represented at the highest level, as well as the major counties. Inevitably, given the relatively small number of posts available, some areas are disappointed and there are local protests each time a government is formed.

The coalition government of June 1981 broke some of these ground rules, with a large number of ministerial posts allocated to the eastern part of the country together with a cluster in the southwest. Significant parts of the central and west midlands were totally unrepresented (Fig. 5.5). The Fianna Fáil government of February 1982 had a rather different geographical bias, with fewer ministers from Dublin, the east, and the south-west and notably more from the midlands and west. The Coalition of November 1982 to some extent reproduced the emphasis of its 1981 predecessor on Dublin, the east, and the south-west, though on this occasion the west was slightly better represented.

But there is always speculation that the spatial allocation of posts is influenced by the geography of electoral support for a government as much as by vague notions of geographical balance across the national space. Thus the emphasis on the Dublin region, the east, and Cork in both coalitions of the early 1980s may reflect the fact already discussed that these were notable regions of strength for Fine Gael and Labour. Equally the greater Fianna Fáil preference for the

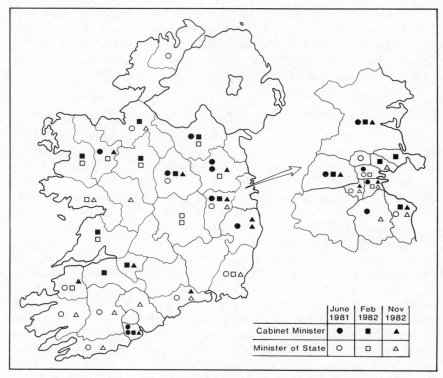

FIG. 5.5 Geography of government formation 1981–1982

north midlands and the west at the expense of Dublin may reflect
the geography of their strength and weakness. The allocation of
portfolios in this fashion will, it is hoped, help confirm voters in their
loyalty. The belief is that the promotion of a TD will in a broad
sense flatter constituency pride. Voters for their party will both bask
in reflected glory and expect that their representatives' extra pull
will now be deployed to the community's material advantage when it
comes to the allocation of public resources. Such considerations are
widely believed to be particularly influential in the appointment of
the junior ministers known as Ministers of State (B. Farrell, 1987b).
Such posts it is suggested are sometimes allocated to TDs who won
marginal seats in the hope that this will consolidate their positions
at the next election. For example, in the 1981 coalition government
Michael Begley, Fine Gael TD for Kerry South was appointed
Minister of State for Trade, Commerce, and Tourism. He was the
only party deputy in either Kerry constituency and his seat seemed

Table 5.17. (a) *Election pledges and announcements May–June 1981*

Category	Number
Industrial development and employment	16
Western development	14
Energy	12
Agriculture	10
Education	8
Communications	6
Facilities	5
Health and welfare	4
Tourism	2
Housing	1
Miscellaneous	1

Source: *Irish Times*, 22 May to 11 June 1981.

vulnerable since his first preference vote had fallen by over 500 compared with the 1977 election and he had only been elected at the fourth count. If his appointment was designed to strengthen his position it succeeded since he was re-elected comfortably in both February and November 1982, his share of first preferences rising from 18.3% through 20.8% to 22.8%.

Public resources cannot be deployed by a Taoiseach or ministers in quite such a blatantly partisan fashion as can government posts but nevertheless there is an extensive literature suggesting that electoral considerations can be an important factor influencing government decisions on resource allocation (Johnston, 1979). The evidence for similar behaviour in the Republic is best described as 'prima facie'. In an attempt at analysis a survey of the *Irish Times* was conducted between 22 May 1981, one day after the announcement of the election, and 11 July, the day before polling. All material on future government intentions was analysed, including details of new facilities recently opened. Some of these announcements may have been purely routine information, such as informing firms and people of grants available but they were included because their timing seemed fortuitous. The material was first categorized into eleven groups (Table 5.17). Industrial development and employment creation made up the most numerous category (16 mentions) possibly because of the recent growth in unemployment. Next came western development, with 14 mentions, probably because, as we have seen, the west of the country has long been a Fianna Fáil heartland: perhaps for similar reasons much attention was paid to western farmers in particular. Energy was the next most important topic, possibly because it is notably expensive in Ireland, but also because there were long-running hopes of commercially viable oil discoveries. Such a find would transform the economic prospects of the country because even a relatively small field would probably be sufficient to meet national requirements and end reliance on expensive British coal and oil imports.

Agricultural matters also loomed quite large, partly because of historic cultural values but also because farming and the related processing industries are still large employers and Irish farmers are an electorally crucial and highly organized pressure group which no party can afford to neglect at election time (Manning, 1979). Education and Communications came next; under 'Facilities' were gathered items such as new telex and telephone services and employment exchanges. The 'Miscellaneous' item could well have been one of the most vital pre-election strokes. A long-running dispute with 11,000 junior civil servants was settled. The agreement included payment of a lump sum on 9 June 1981, two days before polling. It avoided a strike which would have disrupted such electorally sensitive matters as letter and telephone connections, school examinations, and welfare payments. It is also possible to regroup some of these commitments by spatial location. As the 1981 general election campaign progressed Fianna Fáil's private polls revealed that party support in the Cork region was flagging badly. Strenuous efforts were made to repair the situation. Six major commitments and two minor pledges were made involving the city and county area of Cork, (*Irish Times*, 22 May to 11 June 1981) though they were to prove ineffectual:

1. Investment of £3 million in several new industries.
2. Government take-over of 50% Whiddy Island oil storage facilities.
3. Opening of new fish-processing plant in Castletownbere.
4. Promise to straighten road between Bantry and Castletownbere.
5. Whitegate refinery to continue in operation, if necessary through public ownership.
6. Vague indication of new Greek-financed refinery 'somewhere on SW coast'.
7. Research and development section of new national electronics facility to be located at University College, Cork.
8. Plans to go ahead to decentralize an Foras Forbartha to Cork.

One of the customary ploys of TDs and ministers is to announce the allocation or resources or facilities to their constituencies and if possible to be present at their official opening, thereby implying they played a crucial role in the decision to locate the project. During the

1981 general election campaign Des O'Malley, Minister for Industry, Commerce, and Tourism and TD for Limerick East, turned the first sod for the next phase of a development scheme in the National Institute of Higher Education in Limerick, announced that a new £4 million Electronics Test Centre would be located on the campus and that the Department of Education would be contributing 80% of the cost of a new £400,000 schoolroom block and assembly hall for a Limerick Protestant school. The Minister for Posts and Telegraphs, Albert Reynolds, officially opened a new £500,000 post office in Longford town in his constituency of Longford-Westmeath, and Dennis Gallagher, Minister of State in O'Malley's department, announced permission for the setting up of a new factory eventually employing 15 people at Louisburgh in his West Mayo constituency.

FACTIONALISM

So far the discussion has concentrated on the geography of voting behaviour as influenced by historical, socio-economic, demographic, personal, and local considerations, but the structure and tactics of the parties themselves can also influence voter behaviour. Every large political party is a coalition which experiences occasional stresses and strains between its constituent elements and these pressures can influence voter perceptions and choices. As already noted, Fianna Fáil had long been renowned for public unity and had made great electoral play with this image. However, the 1970 Arms Trial had opened serious fissures and with the arrival of Charles Haughey as leader the party embarked on a period of unprecedented public infighting. By November 1982 the two unsuccessful attempts to overthrow the leader had divided the party at all levels into vehement pro- and anti-Haughey groups. Given the Irish electoral system where electors can remain strictly loyal to party while shifting their preferences between candidates, the disputes also affected the behaviour of Fianna Fáil voters who began to align themselves behind either pro- or anti-Haughey candidates on the party slate.

Two examples illustrate the phenomenon. The constituency of Carlow-Kilkenny for the June 1981 election had Jim Gibbons as one of its incumbent Fianna Fáil TDs. He had been involved in the 1970 Arms Crisis as Minister of Defence and was a prosecution witness against Mr Haughey in the subsequent trial. On the accession of the new leader in December 1979 Gibbons had been dismissed from the Cabinet. As disquiet about the Haughey leadership increased Gibbons made his dislike of the leader quite clear and the party organ-

Table 5.18. *The Gibbons–Nolan contests in Carlow–Kilkenny 1981–1982*

Elections and Candidates	Share of FF first preferences %	Final total of votes	Result
1981			
Gibbons	23.3	8,734	defeated
Nolan, T.	27.1	8,904	elected
1982a			
Gibbons	34.2	9,099	elected
Nolan, T.	25.1	8,264	defeated
1982b			
Gibbons	28.3	8,668	defeated
Nolan, M.	28.1	8,940	elected

Sources: as for Table 5.8.

ization in Carlow-Kilkenny became deeply divided. Tom Nolan, another Fianna Fáil TD for the constituency was a Haughey suppor- ter of long standing and had been appointed Minister of State and then a Cabinet member in 1980. The animosity between the two men and the factions they led was reflected in all three electoral contests. The key issue on each occasion was not so much the division of votes and seats between the main parties but the battle within Fianna Fáil between the pro- and anti-Haughey factions. In June 1981 the struggle between Gibbons and Nolan was so close and intense that the count lasted a record 100 hours spread over four days. Nolan eventually triumphed by 170 votes, but battle was resumed in February 1982 and this time Gibbons was victorious, with a remarkable increase in his personal share of Fianna Fáil's first preferences from 23.3% to 34.2% and Nolan suffering a small but significant drop in his personal total (Table 5.18). The third and final contest came in November 1982. Tom Nolan had retired in favour of his son Matthew and, while Gibbons was still in the contest, he was in hospital after two heart attacks. This, together with the fact that the two efforts to unseat Mr Haughey had failed, may explain the decline in his personal vote. At the first count he was only 34 votes ahead of Matthew Nolan and the two battled for a seat throughout all 11 stages of the count, changing position several times, until Nolan emerged the victor by 272 votes.

Collectively, the best example of the impact of factionalism is the fate of the twenty-two Fianna Fáil deputies who publicly voted against Mr Haughey at the parliamentary party meeting of 6 Octo- ber 1982 and became known as 'The Club of 22'. By the election of November 1982 one of its members had retired from politics. Of the remaining twenty-one, fifteen suffered a decline in their personal share of the party vote in their constituency as compared to February 1982, and six showed a gain. Of the fifteen, eleven saw their share decline by more than the 2.1% decrease in the national party vote. Six members of the Club lost their seats, two to Fine Gael, one to Labour and three to pro-Haughey colleagues inside their own party. It would seem therefore that by November 1982 there had been a shift of preferences from anti- to pro-Haughey feelings within those voters who had stayed with Fianna Fáil.

VOTE MANAGEMENT

A final way in which a party's activities can affect its vote is by deliberate tactical manipulation of its support pattern using the STV system. This involves incumbent TDs who are strongly supported trying to spread their votes more evenly between the party's candidates in the hope of capturing more seats: in practical terms they advise some of their habitual voters to switch their first preferences to another party colleague. It can only be successful where local party activists have an intimate knowledge of their voting strength and where that support is both firm and well-disciplined. Wexford constituency in November 1982 demonstrates the successful use of this ploy. In February 1982 Fine Gael had taken 2 of the 5 seats and 3 had gone to Fianna Fáil. Fine Gael strength had amounted to 2.25 times the quota and given the recent history of the constituency the party calculated it could make further advances. In particular they noted the fact that until February 1982 the Corish family had always held a seat for Labour in this constituency, but on the retirement of the Labour TD Brendan Corish in February 1982 his brother had failed to hold the seat, and it had gone to Fianna Fáil. Suspecting that one of the 3 Fianna Fáil seats was vulnerable, Fine Gael proceeded on two fronts. It first decided to breach a long-standing local agreement that it would never seriously challenge a Labour candidate based on the Corish family home base of Wexford Town. In November 1982 its candidate was Avril Doyle, former Wexford mayor from a family long involved in Fine Gael. This it was hoped might pull in some of town's vote which had previously gone to the Corish family but now seemed 'soft'. For their part the incumbent Fine Gael TDs Michael D'Arcy and Ivan Yates agreed to encourage some of their usual supporters to switch their first preferences to Doyle. Both saw notable decreases in their absolute and relative shares of the Fine Gael vote, though the party total rose overall (Table 5.19). However, their sacrifices were worthwhile because they held their seats and Doyle was also elected.

Table 5.19. *Vote management: Fine Gael in Wexford, February and November 1982*

Candidate	Votes 1982a	FG vote %	Candidate	Votes 1982b	FG vote %
D'Arcy	8,787	47.8 (elected)	D'Arcy	7,943	38.1 (elected)
Yates	8,005	43.5 (elected)	Yates	7,166	34.3 (elected)
Hennessy	1,590	8.7 (defeated)	Doyle	5,753	27.6 (elected)
TOTAL	18,382 (37% total vote)			20,862 (41.4% total vote)	

Source: as for Table 5.8.

CONCLUSION

The geography of support for the three main Irish political parties in the early 1980s showed elements of both stability and change. Each party has its traditional strongholds which appear as persistent regions of above average support. The same is true of Provisional Sinn Féin and their associates when they enter the political arena. Areas which supported militant armed republicanism in the 1920s and 1960s re-emerged as H-Block and Sinn Féin strongholds in 1981 and to a lesser extent in February 1982. In every case the basic pattern of support for each party is embroidered by considerations of kinship, locality, patronage, factionalism, and tactics, and the Irish electoral system both allows those factors full play and may even preserve and encourage their importance. Significantly, Labour supporters emerged as the voters who attached most consideration to personal and local factors, confirming a pattern suggested by opinion polls. The findings in this chapter have confirmed observations made elsewhere (Busteed, 1982) that given the nature of Irish society and the electoral system, Irish general elections are multi-dimensional affairs. They consist not just of one national campaign between the various parties, but also of a series of campaigns in each constituency in which the competition is not merely between parties but also between the candidates within each party. In these situations it is probably inevitable that considerations such as family background, local links, constituency service, factionalism, and local tactics come into play.

Nevertheless there are indications of what has been described as an increasing restlessness in the Irish electorate (Marsh, 1985), especially in the parts of the country which have experienced most urbanization and economic change in recent years. Increasing numbers of Irish voters seem prepared to depart from traditional loyalties and consider switching their votes. Some sign of this was apparent in the 1960s with a surge in Labour support and further evidence has accrued since then. Between 1969 and November 1982 no incumbent Irish government had been re-elected and only one election (1977) resulted in a single party administration with an overall majority. Moreover, some elections have seen considerable swings of opinion, most notably to Fianna Fáil in 1977, and to Fine Gael in 1981. Indeed, the steady rise in Fine Gael support was probably one of the most notable features in the period under review. There has also been the reappearance of a persistent vote for independents and new parties have appeared with varying success, including the Workers' Party which made some patchy progress in urban areas, the Democratic Socialist Party founded in 1982, which was much less successful, and the Progressive Democrats founded almost at the end of the period under review in December 1985. The end result was that the Irish political system, like the parties which composed it in the first half of the 1980s, was an uneasy conglomerate of continuity and change. The relative strength of these forces was to be demonstrated in remarkable fashion in two referenda on one of the most sensitive subjects in Ireland, namely marital and sexual behaviour.

6

The Geography of Tradition and Modernity:
Abortion, Contraception, and Divorce

INTRODUCTION

For some time before the early 1980s there had been lengthy, indeed
wearisome, public debates on the various pieces of Irish legislation which enshrined distinctly Roman Catholic teaching on social
values. The debates were first focused on aspects of censorship, but
by the late 1960s there was a considerably more relaxed regime on
this front. By the 1970s discussion was centring on the much more
personal and sensitive issues of sexual mores and behaviour, at first
marriage and the law on divorce, then artificial contraception and
finally abortion. As it happened, each of these questions was brought
to a head, though not in that order, in the early 1980s, two by
referenda, and one by legislation in the Oireachtas, and the opinions
and behaviour of both legislators and voters provided valuable insight into the state of Irish opinion and its spatial patterns at this
time.

   The baseline against which debate on these issues took place was
provided partly by inheritance from the British and partly by the
constitutional evolution of independent Ireland since 1922. On abortion the basic law was the Offences against the Person Act of 1861, a
piece of British legislation which imposed life imprisonment on a
woman who had had an abortion and five years on anyone assisting
her. In all of the discussions which were to take place over the
constitutional amendment of 1983 few people of any significance
were to argue for abortion on demand or even legislation resembling
the British model of 1967. Indeed, the debate was to centre around
how best to reinforce the restrictive legislation rather than dilute it
(Girvin, 1986; Randall, 1986). On contraception the first piece of
relevant legislation had been the Censorship of Publications Act of
1929 which amongst other things made it illegal to publish, sell, or
distribute literature on artificial methods of birth control. A loophole
was closed by the Criminal Law Amendment Act of 1935 which
prohibited the importation or sale of contraceptive devices. This
legislative framework was to be unchallenged until the 1970s. Even
the constitution of 1937 with its endorsement of Catholic viewpoints
on the family and the role of women in society made no reference at

all to abortion or artificial contraception, presumably because existing legislation was judged effective.

However, this same constitution found it necessary to stress the value of the institution of marriage, to pledge the state to its defence, to forbid any legislation allowing dissolution of marriage, and to refuse the right of remarriage to persons divorced abroad. That these clauses were thought necessary may have been a reflection of the very early history of the Free State. Before independence there had been some limited access to divorce for Irish people: they could petition parliament in Westminster for an individual private member's bill. Clearly the expense, publicity, and complexity of the process restricted it to the wealthy, articulate, and well connected but it did mean that in principle divorce was available in Ireland. However, this very subject was to provide the first evidence of the strong influence the Catholic Church would exercise in independent Ireland.

In the very first year of independence enquiries had been made about the likely form of the new Irish Free State's divorce law. When W. T. Cosgrave was approached on the matter in March 1923 he referred the enquirer to Edward Byrne, the Catholic Archbishop of Dublin, who, even before he consulted his fellow clerics, gave a discouraging response (Fanning, 1983). When the government's own Attorney-General put before Cosgrave a tortuous process whereby divorce might be obtained, Cosgrave immediately passed the scheme on to Archbishop Byrne for comment. The clerical reaction was decidedly adverse and the cabinet accepted this as a veto on divorce legislation. The government's ready submission to this clerical ruling was made explicit when it responded in 1925 to three private member's bills seeking divorce which came before the Oireachtas. The administration succeeded in putting through a motion forbidding the subject ever to be raised again in either house, despite vehement opposition from two of the Trinity College TDs and a famous philippic from Senator W. B. Yeats. This effectively ended serious legislative discussion on the matter for half a century. As if to shut the door finally on the question, the 1937 Constitution explicitly stated (Article 41. 3. 2): 'No law shall be enacted providing for the grant of a dissolution of marriage,' and the remarriage of divorced persons within Ireland was also declared invalid. This meant that in future any attempt to legalize divorce would face two hurdles: not only would legislation have to be passed through the Oireachtas, but a referendum would also be necessary.

These were the basic legislative ground-rules on abortion, birth control, and divorce in Ireland until the 1970s, and it is true that on the whole they faithfully reflected the moral and social ethos of the country during the first few decades of independence. During this period several factors converged to make the new Irish state less liberal and more intensely Catholic in its milieu. Partition had removed the bulk of the Protestant population from Dublin jurisdiction, leaving the country 93% Catholic. It was therefore much easier to legislate for Catholic values alone and ignore the susceptibilities of what was now a very small minority. It is also true that several of the personnel in government in those early days were intensely devout Catholics who were more than willing to follow Catholic principles when legislating on social and moral questions. Indeed, some may have believed it their religious duty to do so. For others the impulse was born out of the conviction that Irish national identity and Catholicism were indistinguishable and therefore the more Catholic the new state the more Irish it would be. For some this meant support for legislation against divorce, contraception, pornographic literature, and 'doubtful' films and books. For others the impulse was partly xenophobic because the majority of such literature originated in the United States or Great Britain and by restricting its importation and sale they could express both their nationalistic and Catholic sentiments. Moreover, during these formative years of the Irish state the Catholic hierarchy was deeply concerned at what it believed was a decline in Irish moral standards and was particularly anxious to protect young people against what were seen as the insidious influences conveyed by the new cinemas, foreign newspapers and magazines, and new dances and fashions (Brown, 1981). Hence its sensitivity and severity on all developments which seemed to challenge the traditional Catholic moral outlook. Similar anxieties reinvigorated some of the ultra-conservative Catholic lay pressure groups such as the Catholic Truth Society and the Irish Vigilance Association which, founded in 1899 and 1911 respectively, were particularly vociferous in the 1920s and 1930s.

This remarkably restrictive ethos lasted without widespread challenge until the 1960s. There were periodic complaints from the Protestant Churches and some authors and intellectuals, but their small numbers and limited appeal meant they could be easily ignored and those writers who felt the restrictions most keenly either emigrated or published abroad. It also seems more than likely that mass emigration, by drawing off the younger, more energetic, most discontented elements in the population may have acted as a safety valve. But it is also true that until after the Second World War southern Irish society was remarkably insular and insulated, pre-occupied with state-building and the preservation and expression of political independence and protected by its geographical position, its underdeveloped economy, and its legislative barriers from the full impact of the outside world.

However, as noted earlier, from the late 1950s there were liberalizing forces at work. Emigration, which had been a diversion of pressures for change, now began to generate its own. The Irish living in Great Britain and North America experienced a much more liberal society where, free of legislative and familial constraints, they could exercise much greater personal freedom of choice. Given modern means of communication they were able to convey their reactions back home. Inevitably, ideas from beyond the Irish Sea began to diffuse more widely in southern Ireland. The process was enormously boosted by the arrival of television, the more permissive attitudes of the 1960s, and the opening of the country to foreign investment. The Irish economic progress of the 1960s, though modest by West European standards, was remarkable when measured against previous Irish achievements. It created a sense of confidence and ebullience which went beyond the merely economic sphere (Brown, 1981). For the first time Irish citizens began to realize there were other value systems and life styles. Through the mass media they heard fluent expositions from those who practised them and some were encouraged to experiment. Inevitably many of the traditional restraints on behaviour, opinion, and self-expression began to seem old-fashioned, irksome, or downright ridiculous.

The sense of thaw and movement was encouraged by developments in the Catholic Church after the Second Vatican Council discussed earlier. For Irish Catholics, accustomed to a Church which had long been triumphalist, authoritarian, and conservative in its ethos, nervous of change, and wary in relations with other churches, the outworkings of these teachings were little short of revolutionary (Fisher, 1986). There were inevitable implications for the position of the Church in the public life of the state. Given the enhanced status of lay people *vis à vis* clergy in the new teaching, some began to query the exclusive right of clerics to promulgate Catholic attitudes on life and faith. There was also a growing readiness to discuss rather than merely accept such declarations at face value. The tentative development of relations with Protestants awakened some to fresh thinking on individual rights and duties and relations between Church and state and led some to query the Catholic Church's right to influence the ethos and legislation of the Irish state as it had done so markedly in the past.

There were also changes in the Irish population itself which challenged established laws and values. The growing population, its increasing youthfulness and the numbers and values of returning emigrants generated their own pressures. Alongside the merely structural demographic changes however came evidence of increasing strain on traditional concepts of sexual behaviour and marriage. From the late 1960s onwards there was evidence of a growing rate of marital breakdown, reflected in the larger numbers of people claiming the new deserted wife's allowance, consulting free Legal Advice Centres on marital questions, or claiming maintenance in the courts (Whyte, 1980; Kennedy, 1986). However, there are no comprehensive reliable data on marital disintegration in Ireland and some observers suggest that these indirect measures merely revealed the tip of the iceberg. Other data suggested that cohabitation or at least extra-marital sexual relations were on the increase. The illegitimacy rate rose slowly but steadily from the late 1960s until in 1984 it was estimated that 5,000 children were born out of wedlock, a fivefold increase since 1960. A supplementary, if indirect, measure of changing values is provided by the number of children available for adoption. Almost without exception Irish children up for adoption are illegitimate. In 1960 the number of children adopted in the country had been equal to 50% of the illegitimate births; by the mid-1980s the figure was down to 25% (Kennedy, 1986). Clearly an increasing number of women were deciding to keep their children, indicating a change in personal and public attitudes towards illegitimacy and single parenthood. There were also signs that at least some Irish people were increasingly prepared to abort pregnancies. Again, data are not gathered in Ireland; the only figures available are the numbers of people having abortions in Great Britain who give Irish home addresses. The official figure for 1977 was 2,183; for 1981 was 3,604; by 1984 it was about 4,000 (Kennedy, 1986; *Irish Times*, 28 April 1983) though there have been suggestions that since some patients probably give temporary British addresses the true figure could be much greater (Randall, 1986). Another factor working to change attitudes was the Irish women's movement which began to emerge in the late 1960s. Its various elements campaigned on a wide front, but by North American and West European standards it emerged late, was not well supported and quickly fragmented into single-issue groups. However, one of its more effective projects was support for the clinics which the Irish Family Planning Association began to open in 1969. The numbers of people using them rose steadily, indicating a shift in grass-roots opinion and practice, until in 1978 the Irish Medical Association estimated that 48,000 women were using the contraceptive pill (Beale, 1986).

Partly in response to these developments and partly encouraging them, demands for changes in legislation began to surface. In fact the first proposals for change in these sensitive areas pre-dated most of the more profound social changes. In December 1967 an all-party constitutional review committee had unanimously recommended changes in Article 44 which recognized the 'special position' of the Catholic Church in the Irish Republic. It was argued that this was offensive to non-Catholics and a stumbling block to relations with Northern Ireland. The Catholic Primate declared himself indifferent on the issue and when a referendum to delete Article 44 was held on 7 December 1972, the proposal was carried by 84% of those who voted in a 51% poll. However, the committee also proposed to modify Article 41 to accommodate the views of non-Catholic religious groups on divorce and here the reaction was very different. The Primate publicly opposed the idea as opening the way to serious moral and social deterioration; he also argued that none of the religious minority groups in the country was particularly anxious for divorce facilities. His stance was reinforced by other members of the hierarchy and the idea was dropped (Whyte, 1980).

But there were moves to recognize some of the changes in Irish society. Legislation was passed broadening the legal rights of women in government employment and inheritance and enabling them to sue in their own right. Accession to the EEC in 1973 expedited the process; women were given equal rights in the disposal of the family home and in the workplace. However, some of these changes were superficial in that they were legislative developments imposed as the result of external EEC pressures or judicial decisions. It began to seem that there were broadly two schools of thought in Ireland. The short sharp controversy over the 1967 proposal for constitutional change on divorce proved there was still a deep reservoir of traditionalism, particularly in the highest reaches of the Catholic Church and amongst those who still adhered strictly to its teachings. These sentiments surfaced whenever any efforts were made to alter the traditionalist ethos of the country on what in Ireland are seen as 'moral' issues, i.e. those which touch on aspects of sexual and family relations. But there were also signs that significant numbers of people were drifting loose from traditional attitudes and practices. Doubtless there had always been some divergence between public profession and private practice (Inglis, 1987) but the changes already outlined in patterns of illegitimacy, adoption, use of family planning clinics, and claims for the separated wife's allowance suggested the gap was gradually widening. Successive opinion polls seemed to bear this out. When polls were first taken on divorce, contraception, and denominational education at the start of the

1970s there were quite hefty majorities in favour of the status quo, but by the late 1970s these had been turned into small majorities in favour of change (Chubb, 1982*b*; Girvin, 1986).

Amongst practising politicians there was little hurry to take up the cause of reform given the deeply conservative ethos of the country in the recent past, and memories of the fate of Dr Noel Browne's 'Mother and Child' Bill. There was also probably a fear in each political party that if they were the first to propose change, their opponents would be only too happy to wrong-foot them by taking the opposite viewpoint and branding them as bad Catholics. In the end, it was external circumstances, judicial or political, which forced Irish governments to begin legislating on abortion, contraception, and divorce. It is proposed first to outline the campaigns on these three issues and then to analyse the spatial patterns of opinion.

ABORTION

For a long period there was virtually no public discussion at all about abortion in Ireland: in part this was probably because the vast majority of the population accepted Catholic Church teaching (Randall, 1986). When the subject was raised, it was usually by people arguing against legislative changes on any aspect of sexual behaviour —they took the line that any such changes would be the thin end of a wedge leading eventually to legalization of abortion, a prospect which they suspected would horrify the vast majority of Irish people. An opinion poll in 1977 confirmed their judgement. It revealed that 74% of lay Catholics believed abortion was wrong under any circumstances and another 21% believed it generally wrong; only 5% found it acceptable (Whyte, 1984). Even by 1982 when a process of gradual liberalization had produced majorities, albeit small, for changes in the laws on divorce and contraception, there was still a majority opposed to abortion. A poll in August 1982 revealed that any move to write a specific anti-abortion clause into the constitution would be supported by 47% of voters and opposed by only 36% and there was a small majority—43% for, 41% against—in favour of having such a referendum (*Guardian*, 6 Nov. 1982). The issue came to public prominence in the early 1980s as the result of the activities of two diametrically opposed groups at a crucially significant phase in the Republic's electoral history. The groups concerned were a small section of the women's movement on the one hand and a confederation of traditionalist Catholic groups an the other, and the circumstances were the eighteen months of electoral instability between June 1981 and November 1982 which produced three elections, two minority governments, and one coalition, and therefore politicians who were particularly vulnerable to pressures from lobby groups.

Amongst the various elements involved in the women's movement in Ireland there was probably a majority against abortion on grounds of conviction. There was also for a long time an avoidance of the issue for tactical reasons (Beale, 1986). However, given such a broadly based movement, it was probably inevitable that those individuals and small groups who wished at least to consider the issue should eventually come together. In the mid-1970s an abortion referral centre for students operated in Trinity College, Dublin: in 1978 a Well Woman Centre opened in Dublin, and in February 1980 the Women's Right to Choose Group was launched (Kerrigan, 1983b). In September 1980 the latter group set up the Irish Pregnancy Counselling Centre, offering factual information to women concerned about their pregnancies, including, if requested, information about private abortion clinics in Great Britain. These groups concentrated on internal discussion and some publicizing of their activities and services rather than the organization of grass-roots campaigns or national networks of supporters. Nevertheless the fact that there was a felt need for their abortion referral services was shown by the steady rise in the numbers of Irish addresses given by women having abortions in Great Britain.

It was partly in response to the activities of such groups that the anti-abortion forces began to come together, and when they did so they took an approach to organization which contrasted significantly with their opponents. Groups lobbying in support of conservative interpretations of Catholic moral teaching were by no means new on the Irish political scene and they had scored some notable legislative successes in the 1920s and 1930s. By the 1960s however they had either disappeared or been marginalized in the upsurge of more open-minded discussion. It was in the late 1970s that there were first indications of a counter-attack by traditionalist forces. Two organizations had remained steadfast throughout these years. One was the Irish branch of Opus Dei, an internationally organized Catholic group founded in Spain in 1928 which arrived in Ireland in 1929 (Roche, 1983). Renowned for its emphasis on strict self-discipline and its very conservative morality, it aimed to recruit particularly amongst people influential in the higher echelons of the professions and civil service. Another group of the same outlook was the Knights of St Columbanus, an all-male organization of very conservative lay Catholics, whose activities included lobbying politicians and others in key positions. There were also other organizations which operated at a more restricted, informal level (Kerrigan, 1983*b*) and by 1980 the Responsible Society had been set up as a sort of public front and spokesman for broadly traditionalist Catholic views amongst lay people. There was undoubtedly a great deal of overlapping membership amongst these groups.

The process of fusing these hitherto disparate elements into a cohesive group was probably given a boost by the papal visit to Ireland in 1979. In his addresses the Pope invoked Ireland's historic role as an evangelizer of Dark Age Western Europe and an example of Catholic faithfulness in more recent times. He also suggested that forces were at work tempting Ireland to forsake this historic role and in an address given in Limerick he specifically called for a continuing Irish witness to what he described as the dignity and sacredness of all human life, from conception to death (Beale, 1986). There is little doubt that traditional forces were rallied and inspired both by the experience of the visit and the admonitions he gave. In the following year some members of the British Society for the Protection of the Unborn Child (SPUC) visited Ireland and an Irish branch of the organization was set up.

From the outset SPUC and associated groups proceeded very differently from their opponents. They organized local branches throughout the country, receiving considerable help from many Catholic parish priests who made parish halls and schools available for meetings (Kerrigan, 1983*b*). There were also indications of a drawing together of like-minded groups at the national level. By the end of 1980 a Council of Social Concern had been set up to act as an umbrella organization for all the many groups which shared the traditional Catholic viewpoints on personal morality which they believed were under threat. It was at this point that the proposal for a constitutional amendment specifically banning abortion began to find support. The idea was not totally new. The 1973 Supreme Court decision on the McGee contraception case had opened the way for changes in laws hitherto believed inviolable. Some began to wonder how firm was Irish law on other aspects of sexual and marital affairs and in 1974 it had been suggested that a constitutional amendment would finally take the matter of abortion out of the hands of courts and politicians (Cooney, 1986). The idea had resurfaced at a meeting of the Irish Catholic Doctors Guild and a conference of the World Federation of Doctors Who Respect Human Life held in Dublin in mid-1980, and found considerable support. Early in 1981 a Pro-Life Amendment Campaign (PLAC) was formed to bring together all the varied pressure groups to concentrate on this one issue.

At first the intention was to organize a national petition demanding a referendum on a constitutional amendment, but political circumstances were to present an alternative route. By early 1981 it was widely expected that a general election was in the offing, and all the political parties were in a state of nervous expectancy. Then on 30 March 1981, Maria Stack, a vice-president of Fine Gael, declared that there were medical circumstances in which she believed abortion would be justified. Fianna Fáil seized on the remarks as support for abortion but Garret FitzGerald swiftly repudiated them. One month later, on 27 April, PLAC held a news conference to announce its existence and launch its campaign for a constitutional amendment. In the light of the widely expected general election it was decided to seek out the views of party leaders. FitzGerald firmly committed himself to the amendment, partly out of personal opposition to abortion, partly perhaps to distance Fine Gael as a whole from Maria Stack's opinions and reassure some of the more conservative elements in the party who were showing signs of restlessness at his liberal outlook (Kerrigan, 1983b). Charles Haughey also pledged his party to support an amendment. The Labour leader Frank Cluskey merely promised his party would consider the matter. At this stage in its campaign PLAC was suggesting that the constitutional amendment should read: 'The State recognizes the absolute right to life of every unborn child from conception and accordingly guarantees to respect and protect such right by law' (Kerrigan, 1983b). The Fine Gael and Fianna Fáil election manifestos of June 1981 included a pledge to hold a constitutional referendum to prevent future legalization of abortion. However, it did not become an issue in the 1981 general election, nor was it mentioned in the coalition's Joint Programme, possibly because it was overshadowed by the Northern Ireland hunger strikes and the growing urgency of the economic situation.

To some extent the issue was also overtaken by Garret FitzGerald's announcement of his 'Constitutional Crusade' on 27 September, 1981. This in fact somewhat muddied the waters. It implied for a start that a constitutional amendment on abortion would not be considered in isolation but rather as part of a wide-ranging review of the whole Irish constitution. This of course was a very different situation from a single issue amendment and would probably dissipate the impact of the PLAC campaign. Moreover, FitzGerald's crusade was intended to make the Republic's constitution more acceptable to Northern unionists. This seemed at odds with his commitment earlier in the year to introduce a constitutional amendment being pushed by traditionalist Catholic groups who wished to see their views on abortion enshrined in the constitution. Some bewilderment began to gather plus a certain suspicion of FitzGerald's intentions.

The issue did not catch fire during the life of the first coalition of 1981–2, possibly because of preoccupation with economic affairs and because a great deal of political energy was also consumed by the finely balanced parliamentary situation in the Dáil. The advent of another general election in February 1982 did give PLAC a further opportunity to approach the main political leaders and both renewed their earlier pledges. However, even though Mr Haughey did form an administration in February 1982 and invited PLAC to submit possible wording for a constitutional amendment, he was unable to fulfil his promise of a referendum during that year. In part this was through lack of time, since his minority administration collapsed in October 1982, but his government was preoccupied with its precarious parliamentary situation and the series of accidents and scandals noted earlier. It also depended for its very existence on support from the Workers' Party and Tony Gregory and it was suspected that their support for a referendum bill on this issue was doubtful.

It was not until the dying days of this government that it made any public move on the issue. Just 48 hours before the government fell, and possibly in a move to embarrass FitzGerald and Fine Gael in the general election which now seemed inevitable, Dr Michael Woods, Minister for Health, produced a suggested wording for a referendum: 'The State acknowledges the right to life of the unborn and, with due regard to the right to life of the mother, guarantees in its laws to respect, and as far as is practical by its laws to defend and vindicate that right.' The government also pledged itself to hold a referendum on the issue as soon as possible after the necessary enabling bill had passed the Dáil, and challenged the opposition leader to state his position. FitzGerald responded immediately by saying he found no problems with this wording and in the subsequent election campaign Michael Noonan, Fine Gael spokesman on education, committed the party to introducing the relevant bill in the Dáil and holding the necessary referendum by 31 March 1983. Abortion as an issue between the main parties was effectively defused and it hardly surfaced at all during the campaign (B. Farrell, 1987a). When after their victories Fine Gael and Labour came to negotiate their Joint Programme, there was a definite commitment from the new coalition on the issue. Their programme stated: 'Legislation will be introduced to have adopted by March 31st, 1983, the pro-life amendment published by the outgoing government, which has the backing of the two largest parties in the Dáil. The Parliamentary Labour Party reserves the right to a free vote on this issue.' Clearly events had moved to the point where the issue could no longer be ignored by the coalition parties, as it had been in June 1981. Equally clearly, Labour had reserved its position.

Shortly after the new coalition took office the Attorney-General authorized detailed study of the previous government's proposed amendment. It was concluded that as it stood the proposal was open to too many interpretations, and the Director of Public Prosecutions agreed. By early 1983 there were so many doubts about the matter in the Cabinet that it was decided to publish the Attorney-General's reservations; there would be an amendment but not with the original wording and the commitment to hold the referendum before 31 March 1983 was abandoned. On 24 March the second stage of an enabling bill was adopted by 140 votes to 11, but with no specific wording: this was merely a commitment in principle to hold a referendum. The government finally produced its alternative wording for the final stage of the bill in April. It read: 'Nothing in this constitution shall be invoked to invalidate or to deprive of force or effect any provision of a law on the grounds that it prohibits abortion.' It was a clumsy, dense wording, not easily understood, thanks to its double negative. Moreover, the government's hesitations in the preceding weeks gave the impression it had become half-hearted about the affair, and stoked the doubts which the Pro-Life Campaign and the more traditionalist elements of Fine Gael had about Fitz-Gerald's intentions. So severe were the tensions within Fine Gael over this issue that the parliamentary party accepted the right of eight of its members to vote against their own government's proposed legislation on grounds of conscience. Fianna Fáil on the other hand, sensing a splendid opportunity to embarrass the government on an emotive and sensitive issue, declared its original wording was sound and refused to countenance any alteration.

When the votes were actually taken on Wednesday 27 April 1983 the government's embarrassment and confusion were if anything increased. The first vote was on a motion to accept the new, government-sponsored wording. It was defeated decisively by 87 votes to 65 with 9 abstentions. The Fianna Fáil wording was then voted on and passed by 87 votes to 13 with 58 abstentions and the Bill in its final form was passed by 85 votes to 11. After the votes Garret FitzGerald announced he would advise people to vote 'no' in the referendum but would not actually campaign against the amendment.

THE CAMPAIGN

Voting in the referendum was fixed for Wednesday 7 September 1983, and in the intervening months the various groups involved set about organizing their campaigns. The Pro-Life Campaign as it quickly became known had a number of advantages. Its infrastructure was already in place, with an umbrella grouping, a national organization, local support groups across the country, and the wide range of traditionalist pressure groups and Catholic lay organizations to draw on (Kerrigan, 1983*b*). It was generally buoyed up by the enduring strength of the Catholic ethos and the quasi-nationalist argument that the proposed amendment was an expression and defence of the distinctive Irish cultural ethos. It was also true that the pro-amendment campaign had a simpler message to convey. It was urging a positive vote for something, its viewpoint was relatively clear-cut, could be easily simplified and summarized and could be mounted from a high moral plane that most people could easily comprehend. It could also draw on the physical and psychological revulsion of many people towards the whole subject of abortion. Some of the more fervent Pro-Life elements played up this angle by stressing the physical details of the actual abortion process. Others pressed home their point by arguing that a vote against the Amendment was a vote for abortion and this meant supporting murder of babies. Amongst these elements there was an almost evangelistic fervour in their activities. They were totally convinced of the rightness and righteousness of their cause and campaigned in the conviction that they were striking a blow for the values of traditional Catholic Ireland and helping stem what they saw as an incoming tide of moral permissiveness.

The Catholic hierarchy as such did not actually campaign but they made their views clear and some individual bishops positively urged a 'yes' vote. Their basic guidelines on such matters had been laid down in 1973 following the Supreme Court decision in the McGee contraception case when they condemned artificial contraception but added the significant rider that state law was not bound to follow church rulings and it did not follow that whatever the Catholic Church taught to be morally wrong should be prohibited by legislation (Whyte, 1984). Early in March 1983 the hierarchy issued a statement suggesting that the proposed Fine Gael wording did not finally close the door on future legalization of abortion. This suggested that the Church was coming down against the government and for the Fianna Fáil approach. As the campaign got under way this impression was reinforced and it has been sug-

gested that this suddenly higher profile was stimulated by fear that
the amendment might be lost (Girvin, 1986). At the grass-roots
level, many Catholic parish clergy gave assistance and encouragement to pro-amendment activities. Parish halls and schools were
loaned for meetings, some individual priests were active in a discreet
fashion, and there were inevitable references from the pulpit which,
while they varied in their directness and fervour, had a clear pro-
amendment thrust. Partly in response to protests from opponents to
the amendment, the hierarchy issued a further statement on 22
August 1983. It reiterated the principle of 1973, recognized the right
of each elector to vote according to conscience, and acknowledged it
did not necessarily follow that everyone against the amendment was
in favour of abortion. But it also stated that the amendment was
regarded as a safeguard to the rights of both mother and unborn
child and would be an appropriate fulfilment of the papal wish
expressed at Limerick for a witness before the world. However, for
two members of the hierarchy this was not enough. Dr Dermot
Ryan, Archbishop of Dublin, issued a pastoral letter to be read at all
Masses in Dublin on the Sunday before polling day. Omitting any
reference to rights of conscience, he argued that the poll concerned
an issue of life and death and a vote for the amendment was a vote
against the future possibility of killing unborn children. Dr Kevin
McNamara, Bishop of Kerry and later to succeed Dr Ryan in
Dublin, addressed a pro-life rally and also took up the subject in a
sermon after celebrating Mass at the end of the Irish Medical
Association's annual conference. He asserted that to pass the amendment was not to legalize the views of one Church into the constitution and he also attacked those, including some Protestant clerics,
who he claimed were arguing for abortion in certain situations. This,
he argued, was the thin end of the wedge.

On the party political front Fianna Fáil naturally stood by the
proposed amendment because it utilized its original wording and
it could therefore enjoy the appearance of consistency. It did not
campaign as a party, though many individual members were active
in the pro-amendment cause. Moreover, given the fact that the
wording was Fianna Fáil's, the traditionalist ethos in which the
party operated, and the carefully worded nature of all its statements
on the subject, the vast majority of people were well able to interpret
the barely coded signals of encouragement to vote for the amendment. In general, Fianna Fáil had little to do but sit back and enjoy
the prospect of its opponents' confusion, embarrassment, and internal wranglings as they aligned themselves behind an unpopular
cause and got on the wrong side of the Catholic Church.

From the outset the campaign against the amendment was hindered by a number of obstacles. Some of these were tactical. In urging a 'no' vote it appeared inherently negative and unconstructive. The case against was not so easy to simplify and popularize as the case for the amendment. The original wording was easily understood while the alternative, though shorter, was a rather involved, legalistic formulation. In addition, the anti-amendment case was vulnerable to easy distortion and abusive misrepresentation. Crudely put, those against the amendment could be easily branded as in favour of abortion and the murder of unborn children. Moreover, opponents of the amendment had the feeling of being somewhat on their own from the outset. The Catholic Church's support for the amendment was not surprising, nor was the position of the more traditionalist elements in the main parties. However, the conscious decision of most of the liberal elements in these parties to keep their heads down and not campaign actively was a blow. It robbed the anti-amendment viewpoint of some of its most able and experienced speakers and campaigners. Theoretically the campaign against should have benefited from the assistance of some sections of the women's movement. However, as already suggested, its informal, unstructured, and rather haphazard organization, whilst ideal for exchange of information, discussion, and mutual support, was quite inappropriate as the infrastructure of a nation-wide political campaign. Moreover there were signs of internal dissension over tactics (Randall, 1986). The contrast with the pro-life forces could hardly have been greater. Consequently, the 'no' campaign was patchy in both temporal and spatial terms, lacking both overall co-ordination at the topmost level and a national network of support groups at the grass roots. Campaigns tended to be put together whenever there were sufficient numbers of like-minded people with the necessary concern and resources.

The non-Catholic Churches in the Republic were consistently against the amendment from the outset. Given their conservative theological ethos, they were against abortion as such but opposed the amendment on the grounds that it would write yet another piece of specifically Catholic teaching into the constitution. This they believed would render it even more sectarian and the campaign itself would deeply divide southern society. They also pointed out that if passed, the amendment would erect a further barrier to relations with the Protestant community in Northern Ireland and give ammunition to those hard-line unionist elements who claimed that public life in the republic was dominated by a Catholic Church which denied basic human rights to minority groups.

Elements of the medical and legal professions argued against the amendment but some of their colleagues were equally vociferous in favour. Even the Irish Farmer's Association was divided on the issue (Inglis, 1987). However, given the well-known relative balance of opinions in the country there was little doubt that the amendment would pass. The only question concerned the size of the majority.

CONTRACEPTION: THE FAMILY PLANNING (AMENDMENT) ACT, 1985

In May 1983 the Coalition government launched the New Ireland Forum, with the aim of exploring possible peaceful solutions to the Northern Ireland problem. It held 13 public sessions and 28 private sittings, but most attention focused on a delegation from the Irish Catholic Episcopal Conference. Initially the Conference had only put forward a written submission which had conveyed the view that in a 32-county Ireland the Catholic Church would still expect to be the dominant influence in the national ethos, regardless of the Protestant minority. It subsequently emerged that there had been some misunderstanding and the Conference professed itself quite happy to send a delegation for a public session on 9 February 1984.

From the viewpoint of social reform in the republic the key issue was the hierarchy's view of Church–state relations. Here the clerical answers were somewhat contradictory. On the one hand the Conference spokesman Dr Cahal Daly vigorously rejected the notion that they sought a Catholic-dominated confessional state—'We have not sought and do not seek a Catholic state for a Catholic people'—and assured the Forum that the Catholic Church would stoutly defend Protestant rights in any 32-county republic (*New Ireland Forum*, 1984). The only right the Conference claimed was freedom for the Church to proclaim the gospel and, like any other group, to pass comment on what they thought would be the likely social and moral consequences of any proposed legislation. They denied any claim to arbitrate on which legislation should be passed—such matters they declared must be left to electors and legislators guided by their own conscience.

There was much favourable comment on these declarations as laying out clearly the separation of the Catholic Church from the Irish state and thus by implication avoiding a repetition of the bitterness and clerical activism of the recent Pro-Life Amendment debate. However, subsequent exchanges between the Conference delegation and Forum members revealed significant qualifications of this stance. In the light of their claim that they would champion the continuation of northern Protestant rights in a new all-Ireland republic the delegation was asked why Protestants in the existing 26-county republic were denied rights such as divorce and free choice of contraceptive methods—no direct answer was forthcoming beyond general comments on the dangers of divorce for society as a whole. Again, when one questioner pointed out that any move to alter the constitutional ban on divorce would involve first a referendum to strike out the existing prohibition and then legislation for divorce, and suggested that clerical comment would be most appropriate on the pastoral consequences of the second stage, this idea was neither directly accepted nor rejected (*New Ireland Forum*, 1984).

There were soon definite signs of a divergence between the general principles outlined at the Forum and actual practice. Early in 1984 the Archbishopric of Dublin, the most populous and wealthy diocese in the country, fell vacant. There was a widespread feeling that the appointment made to this key post would give an important signal of the future tone of Church–state relations. The translation of the Bishop of Kerry, Dr Kevin McNamara, to the vacancy in November 1984 was widely interpreted as part of a wider Vatican strategy of conservative appointments (O. O'Leary, 1984). The new Archbishop was well known for his traditional interpretations of Church teachings on sexual and marital matters and his open sympathies with the 1983 pro-amendment campaign were widely recalled.

However, despite the result of the Pro-Life Amendment Campaign and this new episcopal appointment there was a widespread feeling that something would have to be done about the law on contraception. From the moment when first introduced Charles Haughey's Health (Family Planning) Act of 1979 had been widely regarded as unworkable and possibly unconstitutional. It had tried to restrict the sale of contraceptives to persons aged 18 and over on the production of a doctor's prescription specifying their use for medical or family-planning purposes. Mr Haughey himself had described it as 'an Irish solution to an Irish problem'. Since the McGee judgement of 1973 had declared contraception to be the private affair of the people involved, it is quite possible that the act was unconstitutional. On the practical level, it was wide open to abuse. Nowhere did the act expressly forbid the sale of contraceptives to unmarried people; individual doctors varied in their interpretation of family-planning and medical purposes; contraceptives were increasingly imported from Northern Ireland or made freely available in the growing number of centres set up by the women's movement. In some places devout Catholic doctors refused to prescribe under any circumstances and some chemists refused to stock them. It was against this untidy legal background that the coalition government announced its intention to bring in new legislation early in 1985.

The Family Planning (Amendment) Bill introduced by Minister of Health Barry Desmond was in fulfilment of an item in the coalition's Joint Programme, but it may also have been intended to rescue the Taoiseach's rather battered image as a social reformer. It proposed four amendments, but the most significant simply permitted the sale of contraceptives to all over 18 years old. Scarcely had the bill been published than vehement reactions came from two Catholic prelates. The new Archbishop of Dublin issued a statement the same day as the bill's contents became public knowledge, warning that if it were passed Ireland would go the same way as other countries which, he argued, had experienced a steady growth in premarital sex, teenage pregnancies, illegitimacy, abortions, and venereal disease. As for Catholic legislators, Dr McNamara warned that in making their decisions on how to vote they could not treat the teachings of their Church as on a par with other opinions on the matter. He returned to his theme shortly before the Dáil was to vote, when he queried how any legislator could support a measure which he alleged young people would interpret as giving encouragement and legal sanction to breach of divine law. He also reminded politicians that they would be weighed in the balance when God came to adjudicate on the final day of judgement.

Even more outspoken was the Bishop of Limerick, Dr Jeremiah Newman. In a Lenten Pastoral he asserted that all professing Catholics in political life had a duty to follow the guidance provided by their Church rather than their own judgement in areas where the affairs of Church and state overlapped (O. O'Leary, 1985b). The hierarchy as a whole offered only one formal joint contribution to the debate in a statement made by its spokesman Rt. Revd Joseph Cassidy, Bishop of Clonfert. This was much more moderate in tone: it reiterated the stance taken in the 1973 debate on contraception and at the Forum by claiming the Church's right to air her views and disowned the notion that she automatically expected legislation to conform to Catholic teaching. But it was the forceful contributions of Dr McNamara and Dr Newman which made the most impact on the public mind and gave the impression that this was another confrontation between the Catholic Church and the Irish state. This idea was reinforced by the Minister of Health, who at times seemed to relish the prospect of confronting the Church. On the other side, some groups of conservative lay Catholics took the opportunity to begin energetically campaigning against the bill. They lobbied TDs by phone, letter, and personal contact and there were complaints from some legislators that on occasion the pressure was extended to their families and verged on intimidation.

Since the bill was a piece of government business both coalition parties applied a three-line whip. Some of their TDs quickly objected that the legislation ran counter to their beliefs as Catholics and requested permission to vote as conscience dictated. Fianna Fáil decided to vote against even though the party leader had admitted the previous year that there were deficiencies in his 1979 Act (Cooney, 1986). It seems quite likely that the party was unable to resist the chance to inflict yet another defeat on the government and again enjoy the prospect of the coalition embroiled in a dispute with the Catholic Church.

The Family Planning (Amendment) Bill was introduced into the Dáil on 13 February, 1985. On the same day the primate, Cardinal O'Fiaich, reminded the country that no change in state law could change the Catholic teaching that the use of contraceptives was morally unacceptable. He also voiced alarm at their possible abuse by the young and unmarried, though he did declare that the final decision was up to the legislators. The most important vote came on Wednesday 20 February 1985 when the second stage of the bill was taken. Those opposed to it largely reproduced the clerical arguments that it would lead to a general moral decline though some also asserted that public opinion opposed any change. Supporters claimed that on the contrary there was broad support, even within Fianna Fáil ranks; others argued the existing law was unworkable and widely flouted. They denied the allegations that there would be a massive increase in sexual immorality and asserted the right of the legislature to determine the matter, irrespective of the views of any Church. Perhaps the most notable speech came from Desmond O'Malley, the former Fianna Fáil Minister who had lost his party's whip in 1985 when he publicly disagreed with Mr Haughey's attitude to the report of the New Ireland Forum. He argued that the Dáil had to prove itself free to legislate on such matters regardless of Catholic Church teaching, because only then could the 26 counties aspire to the ideal of a secular republic. He declared he would stand by this concept of the republic and would not oppose the bill.

When it came to a vote, the second stage of the bill was passed by 83 votes to 80. The opposition came from Fianna Fáil, the independent Neil Blaney, and three members of Fine Gael and one Labour TD on grounds of conscience. Mr O'Malley was not present for the vote, one Labour TD abstained. The 83 supporters consisted of the bulk of the Fine Gael and Labour parties, together with the independent Tony Gregory and the two members of the Workers' Party.

In party terms the event was to have notable repercussions. All five of the government backbenchers who refused to vote for the bill automatically lost the party whip, though four were later readmitted. However, the former Labour TD Sean Treacy of South Tipperary sat out the rest of the 24th Dáil as an independent. The most far-reaching result concerned O'Malley. By the end of February 1985 he had been expelled from membership of Fianna Fáil and during December 1985 and January 1986 he went on to form a new party, the Progressive Democrats. He was joined by three other members of Fianna Fáil and one from Fine Gael and together they constituted the most powerful new grouping on the Irish political scene for almost 40 years. But possibly even more significant was the impact of the episode on Church–state relations. Certainly the statements of Cardinal O'Fiaich and the official spokesman Bishop Cassidy had kept quite closely to the lines marked out by the Episcopal Conference delegation to the Forum. However, a far greater impact had been made on the public mind by the thunderous denunciations of Archbishop McNamara and Bishop Newman. These had given the impression of another dramatic Church and state confrontation, with the result widely interpreted as a win for the state over the Church thereby evening the score after the anti-abortion debate. This in turn led to a widely diffused conviction that there would be another round in the contest, this time probably over divorce.

DIVORCE

It has already been shown that the question of divorce had been raised at a very early stage in the Irish Free State's existence and W. T. Cosgrave's eagerness to accept the Catholic hierarchy's opinions on the matter and his foreclosure of any further discussion set the tone for official attitudes. The 1937 Constitution with its Article 41 explicitly banning any legislation on the question merely formalized the situation.

The first serious proposal for change came in the report of the All-Party Committee on the Constitution in December 1967 when they suggested alterations to certain sections which could be offensive to other religious groups. The suggestion to remove Article 44 with its reference to the 'special position' of the Catholic Church was accepted without demur and endorsed by referendum in 1972, but there was a very different reception to the idea that Article 41 should be amended to accommodate the teaching on divorce of other religious groups. The primate of the day, Cardinal William Conway, quickly expressed opposition on the grounds that dissolution of a valid marriage ran counter to God's will, and to allow divorce would be the beginning of all sorts of legislation leading to great social evils. It was also suggested that the religious minorities were not themselves eager for changes in the law (Whyte, 1984). The suggestion was not pursued.

This was the last serious attempt to raise the subject at official level for almost 20 years. However, as social and economic changes got under way it became an increasingly frequent subject for discussion at an informal level. By the early 1980s there were only a limited number of options open to those seeking formal dissolution of a marriage in Ireland. They included divorcing abroad, church annulment, state annulment, or judicial separation. All were expensive options, and the last three were lengthy and did not give the automatic right to remarry. It soon became clear that increasing numbers of people were simply separating and establishing new relationships without reference to either Church or state. The figure of 70,000 people in broken marriages was often cited and there was a steady increase in applications for the deserted wife's allowance and maintenance orders (Beale, 1986).

The Labour Party had included the right to divorce in its November 1982 election manifesto and the Coalition's programme contained the pledge of an Oireachtas Committee on marital questions to report by the end of 1983. In fact this All-Party Committee first met in September 1983 and did not report until 2 April 1985. It surveyed the current state of Irish marriage laws and recommended a new Family Tribunal to deal with marital cases. On the question of divorce there was something of an anti-climax. It merely endorsed the idea of a constitutional referendum without giving any opinion on what it thought the result should be or any suggestions as to the grounds on which divorce should be granted. It was widely believed it had avoided these questions in order to present a unanimous report since there was speculation that almost all the Fianna Fáil representatives would have opposed specific support for divorce and the debate would have degenerated into partisan controversy (O. O'Leary, 1985d). The sense of anti-climax was compounded by lack of clear direction in government policy. The government declined to commit itself until after the Oireachtas had debated the report in September 1985. The delay may have been due to preoccupation with economic troubles, its declining support in the opinion polls, a poor performance in the June local elections, or the run-up to the Anglo-Irish Agreement in November, but the result was an impression of indecision and hesitation.

Others were more certain about their course. As early as March 1985 the four Catholic archbishops had issued a bulky pastoral

'Love is for Life' which was read from all pulpits on three successive Sundays and distributed to one million homes. It strongly reiterated that marriage was an indissoluble life-long commitment and the remarriage of divorcees invalid under Church law. Shortly before the Seanad debated the Committee report the Tánaiste Peter Barry welcomed the episcopal conference contribution at the New Ireland Forum wherein they had defended every Church's right to expound its views on current issues and conversely the legislator's right to legislate in accordance with conscience and the national interest. Almost as if in response to this there was a sharp public altercation between Bishop Newman of Limerick and the Minister of Agriculture, Mr Deasy, in which the minister robustly defended the legislator's independence, and the bishop vehemently argued that Catholics in public life could not treat Church teaching as merely one more opinion to be considered equally with others. The Archbishop of Dublin later weighed in on the same lines when he declared his total opposition to the introduction of divorce.

There were increasing signs of impatience at the government's lack of movement on the issue. In November 1985 independent senators tabled a motion calling for a referendum on the issue. It was defeated by 20 votes to 14, but several government senators indicated their desire for legislative change. Fianna Fáil speakers made no direct commitment, but regretted that the discussion had centred on divorce rather than reinforcement of family life. Further signs of loss of patience came when Michael O'Leary, former Labour leader and now a Fine Gael TD tabled a bill for a divorce referendum and another outlining grounds for divorce. Both fell on 5 November 1985: aside from two desultory efforts by the Workers' Party in February 1983 and May 1984, they were the first serious attempts to deal with the question in 50 years. The Labour Party also tabled legislation, but did not press it to a vote. These attempts did have one concrete result: Garret FitzGerald publicly expressed personal support for a referendum on the issue.

The Report of the Committee on Marriage Breakdown was finally debated by the Dáil between 14 November 1985 and 24 January 1986, and by prior agreement there was no vote taken. Overall, most Fine Gael speakers supported a referendum to remove the divorce ban, though some were hesitant and Paddy Cooney, Minister of Education, made his opposition to divorce clear. All Labour speakers supported both a referendum and divorce legislation. Most, though not quite all, Fianna Fáil contributors were opposed to any change. In December 1985 Garret FitzGerald announced his intention to begin consultations with the Churches on the issue, but this was not enough to stem the growing sense of impatience and the desire for a final decision. The Labour Party publicly committed itself to bringing the issue before the Dáil and on 18 February 1986 tabled its own proposals for a referendum and legislation. When it came to the debate and vote eight days later Fianna Fáil abstained. The bills were defeated by 54 votes to 33. The 33 consisted of the fifteen Labour Party TDs, all four of the newly formed Progressive Democrats, the two Workers' Party deputies, and Tony Gregory. In addition, since there was no whip on the Fine Gael Party, eleven of their TDs voted for the proposals.

There might well have been more Fine Gael support, but Fitz-Gerald had just announced that plans for consultation with the Churches were well in hand and he hoped to frame definite legislative proposals after Easter. The sense of progress was reinforced when on the same day as the vote on Labour's proposals, the Catholic Press and Information Centre put out a statement on behalf of the bishops. This basically reiterated once again the position taken at the Forum, namely that the Church merely claimed the right to point out the moral consequences of any proposed legislation, that matters of law were for legislators and electors to decide, and that the Church neither claimed nor desired a veto on divorce. To some it seemed to indicate a more relaxed, less confrontational approach than over the abortion amendment.

Consultations between the Taoiseach and the various Churches took place in late March and early April 1986. The Protestant and Jewish communities generally stressed the value of family life and marriage and their appreciation of the Oireachtas Committee's ideas on reinforcing them, but there was also recognition that some marriages did fracture beyond repair and that divorce facilities should be provided. Before they met with FitzGerald on 7 April the Catholic bishops issued a further statement underlining their view that marriage was an indissoluble sacrament and permitting divorce would destabilize Irish society as a whole. They did not accept that absence of divorce laws created a barrier in relations with Protestant groups or Northern Ireland. In their discussions with the Taoiseach it appears the bishops were not asked their opinion on whether there should be a referendum on the question and did not offer it.

After these consultations there was a pause while the government drafted its proposals. It was now encouraged to move with some speed by favourable trends in opinion polls on divorce and by rumours that a second papal visit to Ireland was planned for August 1986. If true, it would clearly be diplomatic to have disposed of a divorce referendum before then. The government's proposals were finally published on 23 April. They fell into two parts. The Tenth Amendment to the Constitution Bill provided for a referendum on whether to strike the divorce prohibition from the constitution: this was to be held on 26 June 1986. The Coalition also published details of the legislation which would follow if the referendum were passed. There would be a new Family Court to hear all divorce applications in an informal, non-contentious atmosphere. A couple seeking divorce would first have to obtain a separation agreement. The court could then grant divorce provided the marriage had been an irretrievable failure for a period of five years and if satisfactory arrangements had been made for maintenance, the family home, and any offspring. One widespread reaction to the proposals was relief that after two decades there were now some concrete proposals before the public and a definite date by which the question would be settled one way or the other. It was generally believed that the great majority of coalition TDs would support the measure, though there were queries over one or two deputies. It was also expected that the Progressive Democrats, Workers' Party, and Tony Gregory would be in favour. Outside the Dáil elements as diverse as Provisional Sinn Fein and the Church of Ireland also expressed support.

Considerable attention focused on the Fianna Fáil stance. At a special parliamentary party meeting on 25 May the great majority of speakers were against the proposals, but the party issued a statement in which it announced that in order to avoid a divisive partisan debate Fianna Fáil would not be taking a specific stance on the referendum or the legislation, though individual members would be free to campaign as they saw fit. However, the statement ended with a reaffirmation of support for marriage and the family as crucial elements in Irish society, and this led many to wonder if the party was not once again giving a coded signal to its followers to vote and campaign against and discomfit the coalition once more.

There were no such ambiguities about the position of the Catholic Church. Bishop Cassidy declared that while the Church would underline what it believed would be the consequences of divorce for Irish society, including the fact that one partner could now obtain a divorce without the consent of a spouse, it would not be taking an active part in the campaign and would leave its adherents to vote according to conscience. On 26 April the four archbishops issued a statement on behalf of the whole hierarchy in which they welcomed some aspects of the legislation particularly the idea of a Family Court and acknowledged that marital breakdown was an increasing problem in Ireland. However, they denied that divorce was the solution. On the general level they argued that the proposed legislation would abolish the concept that every marriage in the Republic was indissoluble and in proposing marital failure as grounds for divorce the government was introducing a criterion liable to very liberal interpretation. The statement ended with calls for fair and honest debate on the issue and prayer for guidance on how to vote. The hierarchy elaborated on their stance in the second week of May, just as the Dáil opened its debate on the government proposals. One million copies of a leaflet, 'The Church, the Family and Divorce', were distributed, one for every home in the country. It declared that every valid marriage was sacramental in nature and could not be dissolved by state law. It also argued that divorce was irrelevant to relations with the Protestant Churches and Northern Ireland, had disastrous effects on children, and once introduced gradually built up a socially damaging momentum of its own. The Archbiship of Dublin on 16 May instructed the priests of his diocese to begin preaching on the indissolubility of marriage each Sunday until the referendum was over.

But it soon became clear that as in the anti-abortion campaign, the chief burden of the struggle against divorce would be carried by a confederation of conservative lay Catholic groups. Indeed, the experience of the 1983 referendum played a key role in laying the foundations of the anti-divorce movement: it bequeathed experience, confidence born of victory, and some of the infrastructure for another campaign (O'Reilly, 1986). Late in 1983 and early in 1984 various elements which had been involved in the anti-abortion amendment campaign began to come together in anticipation of a referendum on divorce and they formed the Family Solidarity movement. This in turn set about developing contacts with all those groups and individuals who had been active in 1983, and in June 1984 they held a low-profile national conference before going public in August and taking up an accommodation address in Fitzwilliam Street, Dublin. Their aim was threefold. First, they intended to create a framework to be in place in the event of a divorce referendum. This was partly a reaction against the birth control legislation which they believed had slipped through before opponents could properly organize. Second, they wished to bring co-ordination and direction to the otherwise diverse bundle of pressure groups against divorce. Finally, they wanted to put financial and intellectual stiffening into the anti-divorce case by publicizing their arguments in newspaper and magazine articles, pamphlets, and interviews.

When the government's proposals were debated in the Dáil in the third week of May some of the more conservative deputies attacked them with the specifically Catholic argument that marriage was an indissoluble sacrament. The most lengthy attack, however, came from the Fianna Fáil spokesman Dr Michael Woods who mounted a full-scale assault with arguments strikingly reminiscent of Family Solidarity. Mr Haughey's contributions consisted of brief interjections and a lengthy statement released later in which he expressed concern about the stability of the Irish family which he saw as a great buttress of the social order, queried whether divorce would contribute to the good of Irish society, and called for a calm, non-divisive campaign. The deputy leader Brian Lenihan was notably more conciliatory than Dr Woods when he wound up, stressing that Fianna Fáil would not be involved in the actual campaign. His low-key approach may have been designed to counter the widespread impression created by his colleague that the party was coming out officially against the proposals. As expected, the Progressive Democrats, Workers' Party, and Tony Gregory all indicated their support and, with Fianna Fail abstaining, the government's proposal passed all stages without a division. They also passed the Senate unamended and the date fixed for the referendum was 26 June 1986.

This time Fine Gael organized a formal campaign for the referendum. Supervised by deputy leader Peter Barry it included six public meetings to be addressed by the Taoiseach and vigorous activity by young Fine Gael who distributed 250,000 leaflets and mobilized a significant proportion of their 6,000 members to reach what was believed to be the vital but apathetic youth vote. Labour launched its campaign on 5 June with 500,000 leaflets, posters, and instructions to every local branch to urge the 'yes' vote. The Workers' Party launched their campaign on the same day. Each of the five main parties gave a broadcast on the topic.

The Irish Congress of Trades Unions weighed in strongly on the 'yes' side recalling that they had supported divorce legislation since 1982. The Divorce Action Group, a loose confederation of organizations supporting a 'yes' vote, launched their campaign on 3 June. They declared they had support groups in every constituency and expected to contact all electors in the larger urban areas but were hampered by lack of funds. Other groups weighed in on the 'yes' side during the course of the campaign, including the Council for the Status of Women, Gingerbread (the association for one-parent families), the Protestant Churches, the Labour Party Lawyers' Group, the Association of Labour Teachers, the Free Legal Advice Centres Organization, and a variety of voluntary bodies concerned with aspects of family law. Some *ad hoc* groupings put together for this campaign appeared, such as Lawyers for the Tenth Amendment, a collection of 250 barristers, a group of rock stars and entertainers, and an informal assembly of sixty-six personalities well known in the field of acting, painting, and journalism.

Their arguments in support of the legislation fell into several categories. For some, access to divorce was a basic civil right, while others argued that in view of the increase in marital breakdown it was a practical necessity. Some took the line that the majority whose marriages were stable should be charitable towards the less fortunate. Others appealed to the Wolfe Tone and Thomas Davis tradition of secular republicanism and argued this meant the distinctively Catholic ban on divorce should go. A political appeal was also made by those who argued that a failure to pass the amendment would offend Protestent concepts of freedom, worsen relations with Northern Ireland, and provide ammunition for unionists opposed to Irish unity and the Anglo-Irish accord of November 1985. Running through several of these lines of argument there was often the implication sometimes explicitly stated, that repeal of the ban would be a step towards modernizing Ireland and bringing it into line with the rest of Western Europe.

On the anti-amendment side the burden of the campaign was carried by Family Solidarity and the like-minded groups associated with it. These included the remains of the Pro-Life Amendment Campaign which initially merged with Family Solidarity, the Irish section of the Society for the Protection of the Unborn Child and the Responsible Society, the Council of Social Concern, and to an extent not fully known, the Knights of St Columbanus and Opus Dei (O'Reilly, 1986). Here again, *ad hoc* groupings were spawned in the course of the campaign, including a group of deserted and separated wives known as Women Against Divorce, Lawyers Against the Amendment, Youth Awareness, and the Family Rights Council, consisting of Parent Concern, the Family Rights Association, and the Irish Housewives Union. The majority of these groupings were solidly Catholic, but they left the explicitly spiritual and moral arguments against divorce to the clergy. From the outset Family Solidarity and their associates concentrated on how they alleged divorce would affect rights of succession, property, and support for spouse and children. It was argued that the increase in divorced persons and dependent children would mean a much greater burden on the exchequer and the taxpayer, and figures of an extra £1 million per week were mentioned. It was also argued that in the event of divorce the 'first family' (as it quickly became known) would be subordinate in all aspects of law to any subsequent family formed by a divorced person. In particular it was argued that the first family would find their succession rights to property, goods, and state pension compromised and their situation reduced to one of poverty, dependence on state welfare, and virtual second-class citizenship. But it was probably on the question of land inheritance that the anti-divorce campaigners touched the most sensitive chord. They argued that the need for a satisfactory financial settlement before a divorce was granted could lead to the subdivision or outright sale of family land and farm buildings and subdivision of the proceeds. In rural Ireland where land and the expectation of inheriting it have had such historic, economic, and political overtones, it is difficult to imagine a more frightening, emotive, and effective line of argument.

But the anti-divorce groups also tapped another, possibly even deeper vein of sentiment, one rarely articulated but powerful none the less. Underlying many of the predictions about likely increases in marital breakdown and desertion with a spouse being left to cope with children alone was an assumption that it would be the husband who deserted and left the wife to cope with the family on an inadequate maintenance settlement (O. O'Leary, 1986). Discussion along this line often hinted at a well of distrust towards men and a certain frustrated resentment at the traditional roles of mother and housewife which Irish women were expected to fill. In such cases a vote against divorce was actually seen as a blow for women's rights, a guarantee against desertion and poverty and for those already deserted a stroke against the errant husband, who was thereby denied the satisfaction of legitimizing his desertion and any new union and partner he might since have acquired.

Although these lay Catholic groups were the infantry of the anti-divorce campaign and carried most of the burden, there was no doubt where the Catholic Church stood on the issue. Aside from the hierarchy's statements and literature early in the campaign Archbishop McNamara gave a lengthy interview in which, whilst expressing respect for the traditions of other churches and the conscience of Catholic voters and legislators, he strongly asserted the Church's right to speak on legislation likely to touch on the spiritual or moral spheres of life (O'Toole, 1986). Specifically on divorce, he declared again the Church teaching that marriage was permanent, but that the proposed legislation now automatically redefined all marriages as dissoluble. He argued that to change this section of the constitution would call in question all its declarations on the importance of the Irish family and would so alter the ethos of Irish life that divorce would become accepted as normal and stable, long-lasting marriages be less likely. In a much-quoted comment he argued that divorce would generate a social and moral fallout as lethal as the effects from the recent accident at the Chernobyl nuclear power station in the USSR. Other individual clergy took a similar stance in interviews, articles, and sermons with particular stress on the indissolubility of marriage in the eyes of God. In the second week of June 1986 the Catholic bishops met in a three-day conference to review the situation, and issued a statement. This reiterated earlier arguments on the permanence of marriage and the social damage they believed would flow from divorce. At a subsequent press conference Bishop Cassidy suggested the five-year breakdown period in the proposed legislation could be subsequently diluted to 12 months. Under questioning he agreed Catholics could vote for the amendment without committing sin provided they had reached their decision in prayerful fashion, though in a subsequent statement he seemed to dilute this right of independent judgement.

As polling day grew closer, increasing numbers of Catholic churchmen at all levels made public statements or preached sermons on marriage. Dr McNamara called for prayer to save Irish marriages and family life from what he described as the 'great evil' of divorce and all priests preaching on the referendum were asked by the hierarchy to base their comments on the statement of 11 June. There were many such sermons. They varied in approach from those which kept quite closely to the episcopal guidelines including allowance for the rights of conscience to others who omitted this dimension and elaborated with varying intensity on the likely personal and social consequences of divorce. But despite some lurid prophecies about the consequences if the amendment and divorce legislation were passed, the campaign as a whole lacked that extra edge of rancour and bitterness which had crept into the abortion amendment campaign.

Running through many of the arguments mounted by the conservative lay Catholic groups was a strand of thought that could be described as religious nationalism. It implied that not merely was Catholicism a vital ingredient in the Irish national identity but that to be truly Irish one had to be Catholic and traditionalist Catholic at that. No doubt partly inspired by the papal address at Limerick in 1979 this outlook saw Catholic Ireland as standing for distinctive principles on the sanctity of family life in Europe regardless of the laws and behaviour of other European countries and indeed as a Christian witness to such states. It was a combination of two of the most powerful human sentiments, religion and nationalism.

So successful were the anti-divorce campaigners that there were soon signs that they were gaining support. A series of opinion polls revealed that while the support for constitutional change had been quite high early in 1986, by early June it had dropped back, and the number of 'don't knows' had increased substantially (*Irish Times*, 16 June 1986). To counter this trend the government issued a 15-page document a few days before polling in which it sought to allay fears on succession and property rights and access to welfare services after divorce. However, the document was of little help to the government case because of its length and the complexity of the issues involved. But it was politically significant as an admission that the anti-divorce campaigners had captured the initiative and the debate was being conducted on ground of their choosing. The government's increasing anxiety about the result could also be detected in the tone and content of some of the arguments late in the campaign. There were warnings that a referendum defeat would close the divorce question for the foreseeable future (*Irish Times*, 17 June 1986), complaints about the Church's role and condemnation of what were termed the 'scare tactics' of the anti-divorce groups (*Irish Times*, 24 June 1986). As polling day came closer and opinion polls revealed the majority for change slipping away (*Irish Times*, 25 June 1986) an air of desperation crept into pro-amendment statements, with morale-boosting assertions that it was still possible to win (*Irish Times*, 24 June 1986) and all would depend on the turnout.

However, the explicitly pro-divorce groups were not the only problem for the government, because it soon became clear that, as in the abortion referendum, there were elements within its own ranks who had doubts. The most senior was the Minister for Education and TD for Longford-Westmeath, Paddy Cooney, who quite early on welcomed a referendum with the hope it would be defeated. Fine Gael parliamentary policy was to allow members freedom to express their views but not to campaign openly against the government's own proposals. Cooney stretched this liberty to its utmost limits early in the campaign when he addressed an anti-divorce meeting in Longford town and reiterated his views on several occasions, but he refrained from further participation in the later stages of the campaign. Two Ministers of State also declared they would be voting 'no' but did not actively campaign. Of the rest of the party, several members took an active role in arguing for the proposals but there were some suggestions that whatever the official line, there were elements who had severe doubts either on divorce itself or on the political wisdom of the legislation. There were also allegations that overall the party's contribution to the campaign was half-hearted and lacked enthusiasm (*Irish Times*, 27 June 1986). The smaller parties were on the whole more united and committed on the issue.

Labour with a few exceptions supported the proposals energetically and both the Workers' Party and the newly formed Progressive Democrats were highly visible in support. Provisional Sinn Féin also declared itself in favour. But it was the Fianna Fáil stance which drew most comment. Officially the party remained neutral throughout the campaign and there was little doubt that in political terms this was the best position. It avoided the criticism and internal stress which would have followed taking up a definite stance. Support for the proposals would have yielded the initiative to the government giving it a significant victory, upset the more conservative element of the party support base, and drawn the ire of the Church. Outright opposition would have publicly identified the party as conservative and also would have looked like playing politics with a serious social issue. Neutrality thus seemed the best policy: whatever the result it could be accepted as the will of the people and if the proposals were defeated the coalition would have damaged itself and Fianna Fáil would be relatively stronger but without attracting blame.

However, as the campaign progressed there was a growing impression that while the party was officially neutral it was once again, as in 1983, sending out coded signals to members and supporters to campaign and vote against the coalition. The stance was well described as 'neutral but not non-aligned' (*Irish Times*, 5 June 1986). It was known from quite early on that some of the party's TDs were in favour of the proposals, but only two publicly expressed their opinions (*Irish Times*, 16 June 1986) and no really significant party personality campaigned actively for divorce. Instead, it was noticeable that whenever party members made public statements they stressed their doubts about aspects of the legislation and aired fears about the future stability of Irish society. Such comments were widely read as advice to vote 'no'. Some notable party members were active against divorce—Senator Des Hanafin was actually chairman of the Anti-Divorce Campaign and Jim Tunney, chairman of the parliamentary party, addressed an anti-divorce meeting. At a local level and especially in the rural areas, the campaign was widely seen as a Fianna Fáil-versus-Fine Gael contest with Fianna Fáil supplying a good deal of the advice, canvassers, and polling-day workers and transport for the anti-divorce campaign (*Irish Times*, 24 June 1986). The final opinion poll published the day before the referendum vote revealed that the Fianna Fáil faithful had got the message. Of all the political parties, only amongst Fianna Fáil supporters was there a majority (61%) against the proposals (*Irish Times*, 25 June 1986).

TDS' VOTING BEHAVIOUR

The Dáil divisions during the passage of these measures revealed significant groupings of conservative and liberal deputies, and it is proposed to examine these divisions in detail. It is known that there were some differences of opinion within Fianna Fáil, especially on the divorce issue (*Irish Times*, 26 April 1986) but the tradition of public unity allied to party discipline and the opportunities to score off the government ensured that any reservations were never publicly aired and all the party's deputies voted or abstained *en bloc* in every division. The focus of discussion will therefore be on the voting behaviour of Fine Gael, Labour, Workers' Party, and independent deputies. Material from six votes will be analysed:

1. *24 March 1983*
   (a) on a Workers' Party amendment to refer the question of a constitutional referendum on abortion to an all-party committee: defeated 140 votes to 11;
   (b) on the principle of having a constitutional referendum on abortion: agreed 140 votes to 11.

2. *27 April 1983* when three significant votes were taken
   (a) on whether to adopt new government-sponsored wording to be put to the electorate in an abortion referendum: defeated 87 votes to 65;
   (b) on whether to accept the Fianna Fáil wording: agreed 87 votes to 13;
   (c) on whether to proceed with the referendum: agreed 85 votes to 11.

3. *26 February 1986* on whether to proceed with the second stage of a Labour Party bill on divorce: defeated 54 votes to 33.

Particular attention will be focused on the groups of 'conservatives' and 'liberals' who emerged in votes on these issues. 'Liberals' are defined as those who tended to oppose the idea of any referendum on abortion, supported the revised government wording, opposed the Fianna Fáil version and supported the Labour Party divorce bill. On this basis a definite core of twenty-six TDs of various origins emerges. Of these eleven are notably consistent in their behaviour, voting for the Workers' Party amendment and against a referendum in March 1983. Nine voted against the new government wording for the abortion referendum and all eleven against the 'Fianna Fáil' version, when they were joined by two members of Fine Gael. The same eleven voted against the abortion referendum on principle. It is quite possible that party discipline may have inhibited the voting behaviour of some members of Fine Gael, as well as Fianna Fáil, but a clear impression of the extent of liberal views within the party came with the votes on the second stage of the Labour Party Divorce Bill on 26 February. The eleven TDs already referred to were joined by four members of the new Progressive Democrats, who had broken away from Fianna Fáil, and also by eleven members of Fine Gael.

This gives a total of twenty-six 'liberal' deputies. Analysis revealed certain significant features about this group. First, all except four represented urban constituencies and of those four, three represented areas with a considerable urban element in their population—Bermingham (Labour) in Kildare, McGahon (Fine Gael) in Louth , and Molloy (Progressive Democrat) in Galway West. The average age of these deputies in 1983 (when 4 of the most significant votes were taken) was 43 years and 6 months, and in the same year their average length of Dáil service was 6 years. All save five had served or were serving on elected local authorities.

The more 'conservative' deputies were identified by reference to the vote of 24 March 1983 on the Workers' Party amendment proposing the referral back of the abortion question. This particularly revealed the conservative elements in the Labour Party. The series of divisions of 27 April 1983 revealed the extent of the conservative element within Fine Gael, though again some Labour TDs emerged as strong conservatives, along with several deputies who had lost party whips on various issues since November 1982. A footnote to the proceedings was added by the first vote on the Family Planning (Amendment) Bill of 20 February 1985. It was passed 83 votes to 80. The votes against consisted of Fianna Fáil, one independent, and one Labour TD (Sean Treacy) who lost the party whip over the issue and sat out the remainder of the 24th Dáil as an independent.

These votes provided a total of eighteen 'conservative' deputies. Analysis revealed that two-thirds represented rural constituencies, though it should be noted that two of these sat for a constituency with a considerable urban element—Liam Kavanagh (Labour) and Godfrey Timmins (Fine Gael) for Wicklow. Their average age in 1983 was 50 years and 6 months and average length of Dáil service 10 years and 2 months. All save two had a record of service in elected local authorities. Clearly, therefore, the conservative deputies are from more rural backgrounds, are older, and have served longer in the Dáil. In both groups the overwhelming majority had seen service as local councillors.

As noted earlier, several of these votes revealed deep differences

Table 6.1. *Analysis of Labour deputies voting on Workers' Party amendment, 24 March 1983*

	Rural/urban constituency	Age 1983	Dáil service (years)	Elected member of LA
(*a*) *conservatives, against amendment*				
Kavanagh	R(u)	48	14	Yes
McLoughlin	R	37	1	Yes
Moynihan	R	66	1	Yes
Pattison	R	47	22	Yes
Prendergast	U(r)	50	1	Yes
Ryan	R	56	10	Yes
Treacy	R	60	22	Yes
Average		52	10.1	
(*b*) *liberals, for amendment*				
Bermingham	R(u)	64	10	Yes
Cluskey	U	50	17	Yes
Desmond, B.	U	48	14	Yes
Desmond, E.	U	51	10	Yes
O'Sullivan	U	48	2	Yes
Quinn	U	37	5	Yes
Spring	R	33	2	Yes
Taylor	U	52	2	Yes
Average		47.9	7.75	

U = largely urban; R = largely rural; (u) = significant urban element; (r) = significantly rural element.

within the Labour and Fine Gael parties. For Labour the 2 votes on 24 March 1983 on the Workers' Party amendment (to refer back the question of a constitutional amendment on abortion to an all-party committee) were particularly revealing (Table 6.1). Seven Labour deputies voted against while eight were in favour, thereby neatly dividing the party into conservative and liberal groups respectively. Almost all the conservatives sat for rural areas and tended to be older (mean age 52 years) and to have been longer in the Dáil (mean term 10 years, 2 months). Six of the eight liberals sat for urban constituencies, their mean age was lower (47 years, 10 months) and they had less Dáil experience (7 years, 9 months).

A fairly similar set of contrasts emerged between the conservative and liberal elements in Fine Gael. The key votes considered are the divisions of 27 April 1983 on whether to accept the new government wording on the Fianna Fáil version for the abortion referendum. Eight Fine Gael TDs had been given permission to vote against the whip's advice on grounds of conscience: they abstained when it came to the vote on the government proposal and voted for the Fianna Fáil version. They are considered to be the conservatives (Table 6.2*a*).

Table 6.2. *Analysis of Fine Gael deputies voting on wording for abortion referendum,
27 April 1983, and divorce bill, 26 February 1986*

	Rural/urban constituency	Age 1983	Dáil service (years)	Elected member of LA
(a) *conservatives, for Fianna Fáil wording 27 April 1983*				
Begley	R	51	14	Yes
Cosgrave, L.	U	27	2	No
Cosgrave, M.	U	45	6	Yes
Doyle	U	47	1	Yes
Flanagan	R	63	40	Yes
Glenn	U	56	1	Yes
O'Donnell	U	57	22	No
Timmins	R	56	15	Yes
Average		50.25	12.5	
(b) *liberals, for divorce bill, second stage, 26 Feb. 1986*				
Barns	U	47	1	No
Bruton	U	30	1	Yes
Coveney	R(u)	48	2	Yes
Flaherty	U	30	2	Yes
Keating	U	36	6	Yes
McGahon	U	47	1	Yes
Manning	U	40	1	No
O'Leary	U	47	18	No
Owen	U	38	2	Yes
Shatter	U	32	2	Yes
Skelly	U	42	1	No
Average		39.6	3.4	

U = largely urban; R = largely rural; (u) = significant urban element.

Unlike Labour conservatives, most sat for urban constituencies. Their average age in 1983 was 50 years and 3 months and mean length of Dáil service 12 years and 6 months. The second key division for analysis occurred on 26 February 1986 on the second stage of the Labour Party bill on divorce. There was a party whip in force, though the knowledge that Garret FitzGerald was about to begin consultations with the Churches on the matter and would bring forward a bill after Easter, persuaded most party members to vote against. However, eleven Fine Gael deputies felt so strongly on the issue that they voted in favour of the bill and they are considered to be the more liberal element of the party. Analysis revealed that ten of them sat for urban constituencies, their mean age in mid-1983 was just over 39 years and 6 months and on average they had served just over 3 years and 4 months in the Dáil. They thus tended to be more urban oriented, younger, and less politically experienced than their conservative colleagues, though both groups had considerable local authority experience in common. With the exception of the type of constituencies they represented, these contrasts tended to be more marked than within the Labour Party.

Emerging from this analysis, therefore, are tendencies for more conservative social values and voting behaviour to be associated with rural background and age, and conversely, more liberal values to be linked with an urban context and youth. The referenda results of 1983 and 1987 bore out these patterns.

THE REFERENDA: RESULTS AND ANALYSIS

The two referenda will be discussed together, partly because both subjects being voted upon concerned the sensitive subject of sexual mores in contemporary Ireland, and partly because the patterns of attitude and behaviour which emerged were strikingly similar. The government lost in both polls. The Taoiseach's advice not to support the anti-abortion amendment was ignored and by 66.5% to 32.5% on a turnout of 54.6% the amendment was passed. Similarly the coalition's divorce proposals were rejected by 63.1% to 36.3% on a turnout of 62.7%. It is proposed to discuss the patterns of turnout and voting for and against these two measures along with material from the 1981–2 general elections and the 1981 Census.

The level of voter participation attracted comment, but especially the 1983 turnout which, at 54.6% was just over half those qualified to take part and was regarded as unusually low (Girvin, 1986; Randall, 1986). This led to considerable speculation about the opinions and motivations of those who stayed at home. At the simplest level bad weather and a bus strike on polling day may have deterred some electors. It is also true that referenda in Ireland do not usually arouse the same level of voter interest as general elections. However, it depends on the issue (Girvin, 1986): in 1972 the move to delete mention of the special position of the Roman Catholic Church from the constitution brought only 50.7% to the polls and alterations to the composition of the Senate and the law on adoption in 1979 produced only 28.6% turnout. But these were non-controversial measures on which Church agreement and a broad all-party consensus had been constructed before the question was put to the public. By contrast, the attempt to replace the PR-STV electoral system with the British first-past-the-post arrangement in 1968 brought out 65.8% of voters and the referendum on EEC entry in 1972 produced 70.9%. Both matters had been subjects of vigorous debate, with no all-party agreement before the vote—the proposition for electoral reform was actually lost in 1968. Since the anti-abortion amendment in particular was notably contentious and there was no all-party agreement, the 54.6% turnout can be seen as significantly low and explanations must be sought in the realm of opinion and attitude.

One school of thought voiced by Labour leader Dick Spring contended that the majority of non-voters represented a potential 'no' vote (Randall, 1986), but examination of the results does not really bear out this argument. It begs the question why people who wished to vote 'no' in the secrecy of the polling booth did not do so. The spatial variations in the level of turnout provide some crucial insights at this point. In 9 constituencies less than half those qualified turned out to vote: two of these were in central Dublin, and Kildare and Cork North-Central also came into this group, but the greatest concentration was in 5 constituencies along the western and north-western seaboard (Fig. 6.1). Since these are deeply rural areas long renowned for their conservative attitudes it is highly unlikely that their non-voters were potential 'no' voters. Rather more credible is the hypothesis that since these areas have a small population dispersed over rugged terrain with poor communications then many people simply found the task of travelling to the polling booth too difficult and stayed at home. Moreover, since it was not a general election the party machines were not at work to provide the usual free transport on polling day, though as noted elsewhere some Fianna Fáil elements were believed to be active unofficially on the pro-amendment side. The low turnout in the other 4 constituencies mentioned may have been due to their rapid population turnover in urban areas rendering the voting register particularly inaccurate. If these hypotheses are valid, two things should follow. First, the areas of low turnout in the 1983 abortion referendum should also have a low turnout in the 1986 divorce referendum. If the constituencies with the lowest turnout in 1983 and 1986 are compared there is indeed some overlap, with 7 appearing on both lists (Table 6.3). The second test concerns general election turnout. If the arguments about accessibility and the register are valid then those constituencies with the lowest turnout in the 1983 referendum should also have a relatively low turnout in the November 1982 general election. Here again, the hypothesis is partially validated. Of the 12 constituencies with the lowest turnout in 1983 and November 1982, 8 appear on both lists (Table 6.4). Overall, there was a rank correlation of +0.5334 between turnout in November 1982 and the 1983 referendum (Table 6.5).

There was also some speculation that those who did not turn out

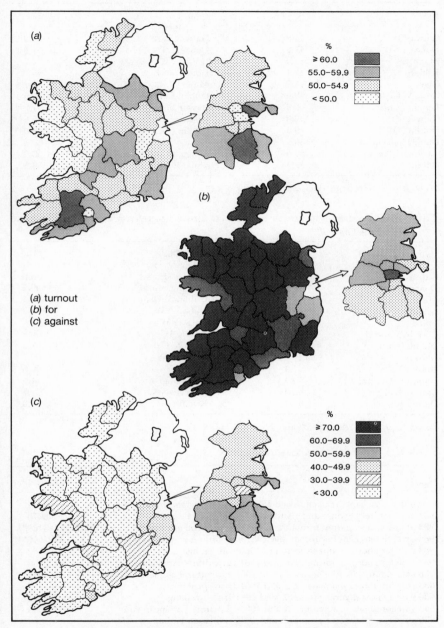

FIG. 6.1 Geography of voting behaviour, Anti-Abortion Referendum 1983

Table 6.3. *Twelve constituencies with lowest turnouts in referenda, 1983, 1986*

1983	%	1986	%
Galway W.	41.0	Galway W.	51.0
Donegal SW	47.2	Donegal SW	51.0
Mayo W.	47.9	Dublin SE	52.8
Kildare	48.4	Donegal NE	55.5
Clare	48.9	Mayo W.	55.7
Cork N. Central	49.0	Dublin Central	55.9
Dublin Central	49.6	Cavan-Monaghan	57.2
Galway E.	49.8	Kildare	57.6
Dublin NW	49.9	Dublin S. Central	58.0
Dublin S. Central	50.9	Clare	58.2
Carlow-Kilkenny	52.0	Longford-Westmeath	58.5
Dublin W.	52.3	Mayo E.	58.5

Source: *Irish Times* 9 Sept. 1983, 28, June 1986.

Table 6.4. *Twelve constituencies with lowest turnouts in referendum 1983 and general election 1982*

1983	%	Nov. 1982	%
Galway W.	41.0	Dublin SE	55.0
Donegal SW	47.2	Dublin Central	59.3
Mayo W.	47.9	Dublin S. Central	62.3
Kildare	48.4	Dublin NW	63.9
Clare	48.9	Galway W.	64.6
Cork N. Central	49.0	Dublin W.	66.8
Dublin Central	49.6	Cork N. Central	68.3
Galway E.	49.8	Dublin SW	69.2
Dublin NW	49.9	Dublin N.	70.6
Dublin S. Central	50.9	Dun Laoghaire	71.3
Carlow-Kilkenny	52.0	Donegal SW	71.7
Dublin W.	52.3	Kildare	71.8

Sources: *Irish Times* 9 Sept. 1983 and Trench, 1982.

Table 6.5. *Correlation analysis summary*

	Correlation
November 1982 general election and 1983 abortion referendum turnouts	+0.5334*
1983 abortion referendum and 1986 divorce referendum turnouts	+0.8078
1983 abortion referendum turnout and 1981 agricultural employment	+0.3189**
1986 divorce referendum turnout and 1981 agricultural employment	+0.2519***
1983 vote for abortion amendment and 1986 vote against divorce	+0.9502
1983 vote for abortion amendment and 1981 agricultural employment	+0.8838
1986 vote against divorce proposals and 1981 agricultural employment	+0.9078
1983 vote for abortion amendment and 1981 Irish-speaking	+0.5357
1986 vote against divorce proposals and 1981 Irish-speaking	+0.6317
1983 vote for abortion amendment and 1981–2 Fianna Fáil mean vote	+0.5699
1986 vote against divorce proposals and 1981–2 Fianna Fáil mean vote	+0.5662
1983 vote against abortion amendment and 1986 vote for divorce proposals	+0.9510
1983 vote against abortion amendment and 1981 agricultural employment	−0.4898*
1986 vote for divorce proposals and 1981 agricultural employment	−0.5695
1983 vote against abortion amendment and 1981–2 mean coalition vote	+0.3695**

No asterisk Significant at 0.1% level.
* Significant at 1.0% level.
** Significant at 5.0% level.
*** Not statistically significant.

in 1983 were more likely to be supporters of the constitutional amendment. Since opinion amongst voters divided roughly 2 : 1 in favour of the amendment then it is logical to assume that non-voters at the very least divided in roughly the same proportions. But Walsh (1984) suggested that non-voters were in fact slightly more in favour of the amendment than those who did go to the polls, and supports his proposition by reference to the strong positive inter-constituency correlation be found between the 'yes' vote and turnout. If valid, this again provokes questions about the motives of the abstainers. One possible explanation is suggested by the opinion polls before the 1983 referendum which revealed that a majority of respondents, though opposed to abortion, did not think it a suitable subject for a referendum (Girvin, 1986). It is quite possible that many people, subject to these cross-pressures, resolved their dilemma by abstention. Certainly Walsh (1984) concluded that the pro-amendment forces were not as successful as the anti- campaigners in getting their supporters to the polls.

It has already been noted that in both 1983 and 1986 there were considerable spatial variations in turnout (Figs. 6.1 and 6.2). Though the national turnout in 1986 was almost 8% higher than three years earlier, the overall geographical patterns were broadly similar—correlation analysis of the two levels of participation yielded +0.8078. In both years the highest turnout was to be found in two contrasting types of area: first the suburban fringes of north-eastern and south-eastern Dublin and second the rural areas of the south-west, especially County Cork and parts of Tipperary and Limerick. Explanations for these patterns are not easy. The suburban areas of Dublin voted strongly against the abortion amendment in 1983 and in favour of the divorce proposals in 1986, while both rural Cork and Tipperary were equally strongly for the amendment and against divorce. It is almost as if voters in both regions, strongly convinced of their opinions, were highly motivated to go to the polls. It certainly destroys any hypothesis of a rural–urban contrast in turnout: correlation of 1981 agricultural employment with 1983 turnout yielded only +0.3189 and with 1986 turnout, +0.2519.

The result of the referendum revealed considerable spatial variation in opinion. In the 1983 referendum, 36 of the 41 constituencies had a majority in favour of the amendment, and 5 were against. In 1986 there were 35 constituencies with a majority against the divorce proposals and 6 with a majority in favour. The spatial patterns of voting behaviour were very similar on both occasions. Rank correlation of the 1983 vote supporting the abortion amendment with the

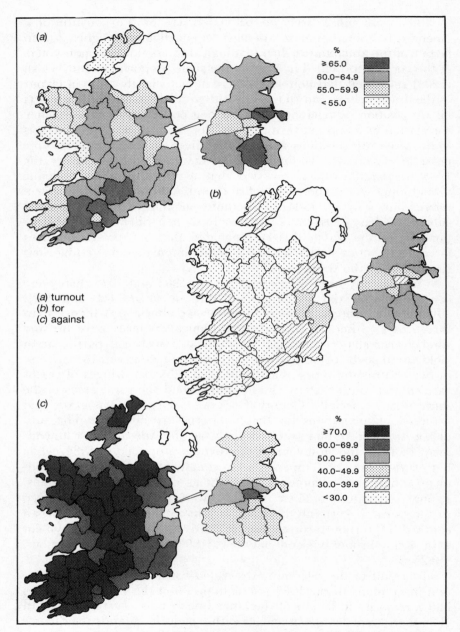

F IG. 6.2 Geography of voting behaviour, Divorce Referendum 1986

1986 vote against divorce yielded +0.9502, a very close relationship. In both cases there was a decided division of opinion between eastern and western Ireland, or perhaps more accurately between urban and rural. In both years the strongest support for strengthening or confirming the status quo came from rural constituencies in the west (Figs. 6.1 and 6.2). In 1983 8 constituencies voted over 80% in favour of the abortion amendment, 2 in the south-west and 6 in the north-west or along the border with Northern Ireland. The highest vote for the amendment (83.2%) was recorded in the neighbouring constituencies of Roscommon and Mayo East. By contrast, all 5 of the constituencies with a majority against the amendment were in the Dublin region, 4 on the south side of the conurbation (Fig. 6.1c). It is also noticeable that in other Dublin constituencies and those elsewhere in the country with a significant element of urbanization in the electorate, there was a notable 'no' vote.

A very similar pattern emerged in the 1986 poll. Once again, the traditional outlook was most strongly upheld in western, rural Ireland (Fig. 6.2c). In 16 constituencies the vote against divorce was 70% and over with a notable concentration in the western parts of the country, especially the south-west and north-west, Roscommon again being the most conservative. Once again, the Dublin region was the core of reform: all 6 constituencies with a majority for the divorce proposals were here, 4 on the south and 2 on the northern side of the conurbation (Fig. 6.2b).

These patterns clearly suggest a strong link between rural living and conservative views on sexual mores. This hypothesis was tested against a series of variables describing aspects of 'traditional' Ireland. The first was agricultural employment which in the absence of a more suitable variable was taken as a measure of rurality. Correlation with support for the 1983 abortion amendment yielded +0.8838 and with the 1986 vote against divorce +0.9078, both significant at 0.1% and both remarkably strong associations (Table 6.5) Two further variables often regarded as measures of traditionalism in contemporary Ireland are Irish-speaking and the Fianna Fáil vote. The correlation of support for the 1983 amendment with Irish speaking was +0.5357, just significant at 0.1% while the figure for association between the language and opposition to divorce in 1986 was the somewhat stronger +0.6317. The Fianna Fáil mean vote over 1981–2 showed an association of +0.5699 with support for the abortion amendment and +0.5662 with opposition to divorce (Table 6.5), both just significant at 0.1%. Clearly these results are neither as strong nor as statistically significant as some of the earlier correlations, possibly because of the fact that however conservative the party's stance on these issues, it still has a notably 'catch-all' support base. It is also true that almost all parts of the country have recorded an increase in Irish-speakers in recent years, regardless of socio-economic or demographic make-up, and some of the most notable increases have been in growing urban areas. Nevertheless, one can detect a certain clustering of traditionalist attitudes and characteristics centred in a rural, more Irish-speaking, and pro-Fianna Fáil milieu.

As already noted, in both referenda approximately one-third of voters took the more liberal viewpoint and their spatial pattern was broadly similar (Figs. 6.1 and 6.2). Correlation of the 1983 vote against the abortion amendment with the 1986 vote in favour of divorce yielded +0.951, suggesting a remarkably coherent, consistent body of opinion. It has also been noted how it was the more urban constituencies which were most liberal. This hypothesis was tested by correlation of the 1983 'no' vote and the 1986 'Yes' vote with agricultural employment: the results were −0.4898 (significant at 1.0%) and −0.5695 (0.1%) respectively, some confirmation of the importance of the urban milieu, though not a particularly strong one. Since the divorce proposals were sponsored by the coalition government it was decided to test the mean coalition vote in the 1981−2 elections against opposition to the 1983 abortion amendment: the result was +0.3695, a notably weak association scarcely significant at the 5% level. It strongly suggests that not only were the coalition parties internally divided on these issues, but so also were their supporters, though Walsh (1984) found a negative association between combined Labour and Workers' Party support in the November 1982 election and support for the abortion amendment.

Some caution is necessary in assuming an automatic link between urbanization and support for liberal attitudes in 1983 and 1986. Once again, the spatial patterns of opinion are central to the discussion. While the Dublin region contained the only concentration of constituencies to vote against the abortion amendment and for divorce reform, by no means all Dublin constituencies supported these viewpoints. In the 1983 abortion referendum there was actually a popular majority of 51.7% to 48.3% in favour of the abortion amendment in Dublin and 6 of the 11 constituencies voted for it. In 1986 there was a majority for divorce reform, but it was a narrow lead of 50.1% to 49.9% or in actual votes a lead of only 559. This time 5 of the 11 constituencies voted against divorce, and when the lists are examined, the same 5 voted for the abortion amendment (Table 6.6). The question which naturally arises is why some Dublin

Table 6.6. *Dublin constituencies voting 'yes' in 1983 and 'no' in 1986*

1983 'yes' vote	%	1986 'no' vote	%
Dublin Central	61.6	Dublin Central	60.5
Dublin N Central	57.0	Dublin N Central	55.8
Dublin S Central	56.1	Dublin S Central	54.1
Dublin W	54.4	Dublin NW	52.2
Dublin N	53.6	Dublin W	50.1
Dublin NW	52.2		

Sources: Irish Times 9 Sept. 1983 and 28 June 1986.

constituencies should be so strongly in favour of liberalization in both polls while others are almost equally strongly against. Once again, the spatial pattern of behaviour may be highly significant. In both 1983 and 1986 the more liberal constituencies were on the southern and northern fringes of the conurbation, while the more conservative tended to be in the inner-city areas and the western fringes. This suggests it is the older, more run-down, and more working-class districts of the conurbation which are the most conservative on these issues, while the relatively liberal areas are the product of more recent urban growth, especially in the higher-status suburbs, and are therefore probably inhabited by a more middle-class, prosperous, educated population which is both geographically and socially mobile.

CONCLUSION

The referenda of 1983 and 1986 revealed the relative strength of opinions in the Irish Republic on these two emotive subjects, at least amongst those who had turned out to vote. It was now clear that the traditionalists outnumbered the liberals by roughly two to one. The traditionalist viewpoint is most strongly held in the more rural areas and in the older working-class urban districts. The campaigns suggested that the traditionalist camp consists of two strands, the ideological and the pragmatic. The ideological traditionalists see Irish public life in a semi-mystical, semi-nationalist fashion. They seem to regard true Irish national culture as being inextricably bound up with conservative Irish Catholicism and the Irish legislature and legislators as duty bound to reflect these values. Such an attitude has been aptly dubbed by one commentator as 'the politics of cultural defence' (Garvin, 1986). Such people formed the backbone of the pro-amendment and anti-divorce campaigns and would probably vote as directed by the Church on any issue. The more pragmatic element in the traditionalist camp was probably influenced by the nature of the subjects under discussion in 1983 and 1986. Abortion and divorce touch on very personal issues related to sexual behaviour, reproduction, and marital relationships, topics which arouse deep emotions in any society or culture. But in Ireland they are particularly sensitive areas; since the mid-nineteenth century the Irish Catholic Church, for a variety of economic and social as well as religious reasons, has consistently stressed the virtues of chastity, self-control, and even lay celibacy (Inglis, 1987). On such issues therefore it is hardly surprising that a large number of those who voted took their cues from the Church to which almost everyone in the country claims allegiance. However, if the subjects under debate had been less personal and sensitive, not so central to Catholic teaching, and more 'political' in the widest sense, then the pragmatic traditionalists might have voted differently. In the past Irish politicians and voters have resisted Church opinions on issues such as the legitimacy of political violence and the reorganization of education. The implication is therefore that, as has been said before, Irish voters 'take their religion from Rome and their politics from home'. It was unfortunate for the reformers that the two issues on which they needed popular consent for change were so central to explicit Catholic teaching and some traditional Irish cultural values and thus drew both the ideological traditionalists and those of a more pragmatic outlook into the same camp.

The liberal viewpoint on both issues was most strongly supported in the more prosperous parts of urban Ireland, especially the southern side of the Dublin conurbation. This particular constituency seems to consist of voters who have to some extent broken loose from the customary Irish reference points of extended family, Church, and rural community ethos and adopted a more individualistic, personalized lifestyle, forming their own viewpoints by reference to individual conscience, personal discussion, and decision-making rather than automatically conforming to Church teaching or community consensus.

These divisions were reflected to some extent in the party system. The Fianna Fáil stances of opposition to the family-planning legislation and professed neutrality during the abortion and divorce campaigns were undoubtedly based on calculations of party advantage rather than principle. It has also been pointed out that the official neutrality was in fact somewhat hollow and the signals to their supporters to discomfit the Coalition were barely coded. The end result was to create a widely diffused belief that the party had aligned itself with the traditionalist viewpoint. Fine Gael and Labour by contrast adopted definite viewpoints on all three issues, especially contraception and divorce, and suffered considerable internal strains as a consequence. Analysis of the resulting voting behaviour of deputies confirmed and reflected the marked traditionalist and liberal, rural and urban divisions of opinion in the country as a whole.

7
Conclusion

The three Irish general elections and two referenda over the years 1981–6 provided opportunities for insights into the geography of Irish opinion. Certain basic patterns which emerged will be reviewed under two headings: first, elements of stability and second, elements of change.

Of the elements of stability the most significant is that the rank ordering of the political parties remained the same throughout the period, namely Fianna Fáil the strongest, with Fine Gael second and Labour third. Of these three Fianna Fáil remained dominant. It retained persistent strength throughout the country but especially in western Ireland and in some of the more working-class constituencies on the northern side of the Dublin conurbation. It was relatively weak in the east of the country, especially the southern side of the Dublin region and in Cork county and city. When campaigning the party retained its traditional stance of rejecting alliances and arrangements with all other parties and the one government it formed during this period consisted of Fianna Fáil TDs only.

Fine Gael remained the second party in Ireland despite impressive progress. It was strongest in some of the rural areas of the north and north-west midlands, in the east, especially on the south side of the Dublin conurbation, and in Cork county and parts of the city. It was in office after two of the elections in this period but in both cases it required a coalition partner to achieve a majority government and, despite a notably good performance in November 1982 and the rhetoric of some of its more enthusiastic partisans, it was still unlikely to be able to govern on its own for the foreseeable future.

The Labour Party also retained its traditional position as the third party of the Irish political system, only picking up a fraction of votes and seats and serving in government as the junior partner in coalition with Fine Gael. It retained its notably regional and class-based pattern of support, with its greatest strength in eastern and southern Ireland and only patchy support in the north and west. It was also quite localized in its strongholds of the south and east: stronger in rural than urban areas, and even then confined to places where agricultural employees were numerous and well known, and hardworking candidates were active.

Labour's great rival for the left-wing vote, the Workers' Party, was even more localized, being confined to some of the more working-class urban areas. Like Labour it left quite a few constituencies uncontested, mostly in the more rural and prosperous parts of the country. Its support increased gradually but steadily through all three elections and this led to some speculation that it would eventually overtake Labour as the party of the left and the latter would fade away or merge with it. However parties are long-lived creatures and Irish Labour had suffered worse electoral defeats and survived, and seemed likely to do so again.

The supporters of the H-Block/Provisional Sinn Féin contested two of the three elections in this period. They had one of the most distinct regional patterns of support: their great strength lay in constituencies bordering Northern Ireland and in areas with a tradition of militant republicanism. This however was no new development since it had been these areas which had strongly supported Sinn Féin candidates in the election of 1957. It also remained true that this vote could only be mobilized in times of tension over the Northern question as in 1981, the year of the hunger-strikes. When such issues had faded this vote returned either to abstention or to Fianna Fáil. There was little prospect of Provisional Sinn Féin becoming a serious national rival to Fianna Fáil for the nationalistic vote.

At the sub-constituency level there is plenty of evidence that kinship, locality, patronage, and factionalism still play a significant role in voting behaviour. Indeed there are even indications that in the period under discussion they became marginally more important. They also seemed to be particularly vital in securing the election of Labour and Workers' Party deputies and independents, though it has been shown that they play some role in the election of most deputies regardless of party. The electoral system itself plays a role allowing these factors full play and the redistribution of seats and boundaries in 1980, with its increase in the number of 4- and 5-seat constituencies by lowering the quotas in many constituencies made relatively small shifts of votes more significant and local factors relatively more influential. The parties realized this and were at pains during this time to maximize their vote by fielding candidates with strong local links.

But in many ways this was merely the traditional pattern of Irish electoral influences reasserting themselves. Since the very beginnings of popular democracy in the nineteenth century local and personal factors had characterized Irish voting and provided the bread and butter of political debate in the constituencies. Just occasionally they would be overwhelmed by national issues as in 1885 or 1918–23 and candidates with national reputations could be elected in any constituency in the country, but with the passage of time and the ebbing of political excitement localism and personality would reassert themselves as the norm (B. Farrell, 1975; Hoppen, 1984). Consequently the slight rise in candidates with local links over this period is totally in line with Irish political tradition.

Given these regional strongholds, the enduring significance of kinship, locality, personality, and faction, and an electoral system which maximizes voter choice and is so sensitive to voter movement, it would seem on the face of it that the Irish political system contains considerable potential for disruption and the emergence of new parties on the basis of region, locality, and personality. Indeed, this did actually happen in the period under review with the founding of the Progressive Democrats in late 1985 and early 1986.

In fact, such disruptions are relatively rare events and the question which must be answered is why the factors cited above have not been the basis for much more frequent individual and group breakaways and the formation of new parties. The answer is that there are certain strong forces at work which channel all these factors into support for the existing national parties. The first of these is the nature of the original cleavage between the two main parties and the potent force of their appeal to their followers. It has been shown that it was a deep divide on nationalistic and constitutional issues and these by definition have a national appeal. Thus from the outset both parties drew in supporters regardless of age, gender, class, region, or locality. Moreover, this appeal was strengthened by the trauma of civil war, a searing experience in the history of any state. Military conflict deepened and embittered the divisions between the parties and sanctified them in blood for several generations (Hopkinson, 1988). It also seems possible however that out of sheer self-interest some socio-economic groups did prefer one party to another: the more prosperous elements tended to be pro-Treaty because they had most to lose from continuing instability while the Irish-speakers, more traditionalist elements, and small farmers were more anti-Treaty because that side expropriated so much of the mystical symbolism of an economically and culturally self-sufficient Irish nationalism.

A second powerful factor was the considerable freedom of manoeuvre which this original divide bequeathed to both parties. They were able to adjust their policies as they saw fit on a broad range of issues and thereby contain potential sources of disruption. Nationalistic cleavages do not predetermine policies on social and economic affairs beyond a vague commitment to do the best for the country and its people. Thus both parties had remarkable freedom to adapt their programmes as events and ideas developed. They could both quite easily take on board new ideas on social welfare, the state role in economic development, and public ownership. In this way they could occupy ground normally associated with the Labour movement without any of their supporters or opponents claiming inconsistency or ideological betrayal. This meant there was little room for breakaway or regional parties. If they did manage to establish themselves the existing parties could easily appropriate their ideas, siphon off their support, and consign them to the margins of the political scene and eventually to oblivion. Thus, since the foundation of the state, if Fianna Fáil is accepted as the direct heir of the anti-Treaty group and Fine Gael as descended from Cumann na n Gaedheal, no new party has managed to establish itself as a permanent feature of the Irish political scene.

A further factor which restrains the influence of regional and particularly local factors is the Irish electoral system itself. It has already been argued that it allows the voters to give full play to the pulling power of kinship, locality, and indeed any other factor. However, it also enables them to do so without abandoning their party. In effect, Irish voters can choose not only between parties but also between candidates within the party slate and national, regional, and local influences can thus be reconciled.

But the parties themselves have also played a considerable role in defusing these potentially disruptive influences by adroit electoral management. From the earliest days the parties have sought to appease or divert such influences by allocation of patronage, distribution of government posts, choice of candidates with known family background and local links, and the nomination of geographically balanced slates of candidates. Thus every party has tried to combine national and local appeal and in so doing has managed to head off potential disruption. Given the recent tendency of both main parties to centralize power within their structures and direct nomination strategies from head office, their control over such regional and localist forces has if anything increased of late (Mair, 1987). The parties do not always succeed in these management strategies of course, hence the appearance of the occasional minor party and independent deputy in this period, but on the whole they have been remarkably skilful in their management of the electoral system.

A good deal of comment during this period was focused on the patterns of voter movement and the rise in support for Fine Gael. Most movement seemed to occur in the Dublin conurbation, parts of the midlands, Cork City, and the border counties and in almost all cases except the last Fine Gael was the chief beneficiary. There were some suggestions, not least from some of the more enthusiastic of the party's own followers that these changes represented a significant permanent shift in Irish electoral alignments and that Fine Gael would soon be able to form a government on its own. This was almost certainly wishful thinking. Ironically, the regional patterns of support for the main parties and the voter movements which did occur tended if anything to reinforce rather than remake the Irish electoral landscape. Fianna Fáil's gains in the border counties were really some of its more republican votes coming home after flirting with H-Block/Sinn Féin candidates in 1981 and February 1982. The party's strongholds in the west and working-class Dublin had always been the core of its strength since at least 1933: they stood out more at these elections because of losses elsewhere. Equally, for Fine Gael its strength in the north and west midlands, the east, the south side of the Dublin conurbation, and Cork City were, except for the last, merely further increases in places and groups where it had been traditionally strong (Sinnott, 1987), and to some extent the return of voters who had deserted in 1977. It is also true that there is no guarantee that Fine Gael's advances are permanent. To some extent they were due to an attractive manifesto and leader, modernized and well co-ordinated organization and electoral machinery, and the disarray of its opponents. Such assets are not the permanent pro-perty of any one party. Moreover, if there is a fluid element in the electorate which was induced to move towards Fine Gael in these elections then it was equally capable of detaching itself and moving elsewhere in subsequent contests. Equally, the contest between Labour and the Workers' Party for the left-wing, urban, working-class vote would not significantly alter the political scene whichever party won. The two parties were fighting over a relatively small prize since the left vote in Irish elections has never exceeded 18% of the total even at its maximum in 1969. Nor were there any signs that either party was successfully challenging Fianna Fáil, the party which has long had the majority of the Irish urban working-class vote. Taken to their logical conclusions these foregoing arguments would suggest that the Progressive Democrats, who gained 11.8% of votes and 14 seats in the general election of February 1987 are by no means assured of a permanent place on the Irish electoral scene.

Perhaps it was the referenda of 1983 and 1986 which gave the most thought-provoking insights into the patterns of opinion in Ireland in the first half of the 1980s. Simply by their results they demonstrated the relative strength of conservative and liberal out-looks not merely on social and marital mores but also on the more general question of the relation between Church and state. They showed that about two-thirds of those who voted were still of a conservative and traditionalist Catholic viewpoint on these issues and were prepared to follow Catholic church teaching on them, even in the privacy of the polling booth. For most of this group it was still difficult to separate the ethos of the Irish state from that of traditional Catholicism. By contrast those who took a more liberal view were outvoted two to one in both referenda. Overall it meant that in the mind of many, perhaps most, of the citizens of the country it was right and proper that significant sections of the constitution should directly reflect Catholic teachings. The outbreak of claims to have seen religious statues move, weep, and speak during the same period demonstrated that the popular, peasant strand of Irish Catholicism was still strong, particularly in a period of painful economic and social change. The result was that by the late 1980s the power and influence of Catholicism in the Irish state was probably stronger than for the previous three decades because its strength had been proven twice by large majorities in bruising campaigns and few politicians would be willing to risk their political lives by taking on a Church which had so recently and decisively proven its strength.

The question which arises is why is Ireland so conservative? Superficially it seemed that the country was merely conforming to the rather conservative mood which was affecting parts of the Anglo-American world in the 1980s, partly as a reaction to the more relaxed attitudes of the 1960s and 1970s. However it seems much more likely that most of Ireland had never shared fully in this relaxation of traditional values. The new ideas had been beamed in via the media based in the Dublin region and perhaps became subjects of discussion in that area, but for much of the rest of the country they seemed like foreign customs with little relation to everyday life lived under the scrutiny of family and parish priest in the rural and small-town context. As for the liberating effects of Vatican II, it has been pointed out that they were only filtered to the Irish population in amounts carefully controlled by the hierarchy (Fisher, 1986), thereby ensuring that the existing pattern of control and influence in the church was retained as far as possible. The result was that beneath the endless discussions in the media was a deep latent stratum of traditionalist conservatism in Irish public opinion and the campaigns of the pro-amendment and anti-divorce groups, while undoubtedly skilful and well organized, merely mobilized and articulated its feelings. In this context it is significant that the only reform in this area which was achieved during this period, on contraceptive law, was carried by the Dáil alone, but when the public were consulted by referenda on abortion and divorce they proved more conservative than their legislators. Irish politicians have on occasion been accused of lack of moral and political courage in not pressing publicly for more liberal legislation on these matters, but in view of the referenda results their reluctance is understandable.

But while the Irish political scene can at times give an impression of immobility, there are also indications of changes, some of which have quite significant implications. The first of these is the fact that there was a change of government after each of the three elections under discussion. In fact these years are merely part of a longer period of unprecedented electoral mobility in Ireland. No incumbent Irish government has been re-elected since the 1969 general election. There have been previous periods of electoral uncertainty, most notably 1927–33 and 1948–57, but the current phase is much more long-lived. The basic reason may well be that growth of electoral restlessness which was remarked on earlier and the fact that there is now a gradually increasing proportion of the electorate available to be wooed by carefully crafted manifestos, attractive leaders, and well-run election campaigns.

The Irish electoral system has always been a particularly sensitive reflector of such voter movements in that it permits choice between both parties and candidates. But the redistribution of seats and boundaries in 1980 if anything increased this sensitivity by the creation of many more 5-seat constituencies, since the larger a constituency the closer the relationship between votes cast and seats won. Any shift of the voters' favours therefore is now more faithfully reflected in representation.

One implication of these changes is that a party can experience quite dramatic surges in support in one election only to find them ebbing at the next. This was certainly the experience of Fianna Fáil in 1977 when it won a record overall majority of 20 seats and passed 50% of the popular vote for only the second time in its history, and then lost office in 1981, could only form a minority government in February 1982 and lost office again in November of the same year. Conversely Fine Gael suffered a heavy defeat in 1977 and then saw its support climb to record levels at each of the elections of 1981–2. It also had the experience of seeing it decline sharply in the general election of 1987. These voter movements were influenced by a great mass of motivations but one theme which did appear in the election of February 1982 was the suggestion that in the Dublin region at least there were signs of social class groups shifting *en masse* to one party or the other in accordance with their perceived class interests. In particular it was noticed that Fine Gael's stress on fiscal rectitude in that campaign seemed to resonate with the more middle-class constituencies on the southern side of the conurbation which showed a swing to the party. By contrast in the more working-class constituencies on the northern side there was a movement towards Fianna Fáil, presumably because voters there interpreted the talk about the need for control of public expenditure to mean cutbacks in the welfare services on which they depended for a tolerable standard of living. This led to discussion about the arrival of class-based voting in Ireland, but it is not quite as straightforward as it might seem to those used to British and West European electoral behaviour. The comments already made about the flexibility of the parties and the growing restlessness of the voters are relevant here. In the Irish context class-based voting does not necessarily mean that working-class people will vote for leftist parties, instead they will shop around for the party which seems to promise most protection for their interests, and given the Irish context this can mean virtually any party which chooses to try and attract them. It also means of course that such voters may be weaned away by another party at the next election and a different pattern of class voting will appear.

The patterns of opinion revealed by the two referenda also hinted at some changes under way in Irish society. It is certainly true as noted above that Ireland remained a notably conservative country with the traditional Church viewpoint supported by about two-thirds of those who voted, but it does not necessarily follow that two-thirds of voters would wish to see Catholic ideas shaping legislation on all issues. It is quite possible that if the issues had been less sensitive and emotive, and not so directly related to matters on which there was such a great body of unequivocal Church teaching, the liberal viewpoint might have gained greater support. In actual fact it was probably something of a small victory to have the support of even one-third of those who voted. It is also interesting to note the shift of emphasis in the conservative arguments between the two referenda. In support of the anti-abortion amendment the stress was very much on a mixture of Catholic teaching, the sanctity of life from conception, and Ireland's role as an example to Europe, while the anti-divorce case depended much more on materialistic arguments about the fate of family property and the financial status of the first family in the event of divorce. The implication would seem to be that arguments based on Church teaching alone will only mobilize the laity if they touch on matters closely related to aspects of personal sexual morality. This the abortion question did, but the divorce question did not do so quite so directly, hence the shift in focus in the conservative campaign. There is also the implication that those in favour of divorce reform might have stood a better chance if they had drafted somewhat different proposals. Certainly the opinion polls before the referendum campaign got under way showed a majority in favour of allowing divorce 'in certain circumstances', and shortly after the referendum this majority reappeared in the polls. It is just possible that somewhat different proposals might have passed, though of course it is equally possible that the well organized and financed conservative elements would have found equally effective arguments no matter what was proposed.

Regardless of the results it was highly significant that these two referenda provoked public debates not merely on the merits of the proposals themselves but on the general question of the relation of church and state in modern Ireland. The last occasion on which there had been a public clash between a prominent political figure and the Catholic hierarchy had been over Dr Noel Browne's Health Bill in 1950, and even then it had been more a case of one man against the hierarchy, and a good deal of the background discussion had been conducted in private. This time however it was a case of public differences between a government and the hierarchy, with a good deal of the debate in the open between two quite strongly marked positions. As such this was good for the general health of the Irish political system and the results provided a fairly precise measure of the strength of the two viewpoints. But it was also a salutary experience for both sides, with liberal politicians possibly more cautious about their public stance on such matters in the future, and the Church for its part quite pleased with the results of the vote but somewhat unhappy about having become involved in public disputes with the secular authorities. The end product was a general feeling on both sides that in the future if at all possible such public differences should be avoided by adopting either of the time-honoured Irish approaches—ignoring such awkward issues, or consulting in private and at length to discover a mutually agreeable measure before going public.

One of the most interesting features of the pro-amendment and anti-divorce campaigns was their public domination by the Catholic laity. The clergy generally confined themselves to restatements of Church teaching on the proposals and what they believed would be their pastoral consequences and did admit, if somewhat grudgingly, that the individual in the end had the right to follow personal conscientious conviction. One or two bishops went further and at the grass-roots level considerable assistance was provided to the PLAC and anti-divorce campaigns by parish priests, but the great burden of the public campaign was carried by the laity who, especially in the anti-divorce campaign, stressed the material and social arguments against the government proposals. In some ways it was a remarkable demonstration of lay power in a Catholic country where the emphasis has always been on clerical authority with the laity relegated to comparatively modest and carefully regulated roles. Such a novel development had implications for the future which did not necessarily bode well for the Church, because lay power could be a double-edged sword. Having twice tasted power and influence in such a public manner there was no guarantee that the laity would not jib at having to subside into their traditional attitudes of deference and obedience. There was also no guarantee that the laity would always respond so readily to the summons to public battle. It was quite possible that on some future, less clear-cut issue the Church would misjudge the mood of the faithful and they would not rally in the expected manner or numbers. The result would be a notable public weakening of clerical prestige and authority, but this was the risk taken when the Church set itself in public opposition to government measures of any sort.

The spatial pattern of the opinions revealed a notable divide between rural and urban Ireland or perhaps more accurately between prosperous urban Dublin and the rest. It was certainly true that the more rural an area, the stronger the vote for the traditionalist outlook, and that as rurality diminished, the liberal view became stronger. At least two of the political parties were as deeply divided as public opinion, and their divisions followed approximately the same lines of cleavage. In both Fine Gael and Labour the more liberal deputies were younger, had not been so long in the Dáil, and were urban based, while the more conservative tended to be older, with more Dáil service and, though not always, rural based. In breaking ranks publicly the deputies concerned may well have damaged their parties' standing in the narrow partisan sense but, taking a broader perspective, they may have served the Irish political system well in that they reproduced, and articulated at the highest level, the divide which ran right through Irish society as a whole.

From this viewpoint the Fianna Fáil stance may have been tactically skilful in the short term but strategically unwise in the long run. The party was officially neutral in both referenda, though it openly opposed the contraception legislation. This stance of neutrality and the vote against the family-planning bill were undoubtedly intended to reap party political advantage. On abortion and divorce the party could claim the people were being allowed to decide for themselves. Whatever the results, Fianna Fáil would accept them and legislate accordingly. In this way the party avoided the need both to choose and enforce a party line before the popular vote, and to face the prospect of further divisions within party ranks as well as the possibility of having their approach rejected by the electorate. In the mean-time they could enjoy the internal divisions of both coalition parties and their open differences with the Catholic Church.

But regardless of the official neutrality there were various coded signals from Fianna Fáil leaders which were universally taken as encouragement for their activists and supporters to work and vote against the coalition outlook in both referenda. Party members were active in both campaigns at all levels, provoking the question 'neutral in whose favour?' The result of this stance was to create the firm impression that Fianna Fáil was quietly aligning itself with the more traditionalist viewpoint in Irish life. To some extent this would be consistent with its historic stance as the champion of traditional Irish values. In the past this has involved support for the Irish language, family farms, self-sufficiency, and rural living; it could be argued the modern equivalent is to embrace a conservative stance on social and moral issues. But this is to ignore the fact that within the party there were always some who had held the Catholic church at arm's length when it came to political decisions. Furthermore, it ignores the fact that for about twenty years after 1958 the party was also a champion of a more open attitude towards the contemporary world in terms of economic development, trade, and foreign policy, and had liberalized the censorship laws. Part of the explanation for Fianna Fáil's electoral success has always been its ability to accommodate such seemingly contradictory stances. Simply to embrace the conservative Catholic viewpoint on these issues was a radical departure. It could also be seen as dangerous in both principle and practice. In principle it could be seen as surrendering the party's independence on social and moral questions to an outside body, namely the Catholic Church. In practical terms it is worth noting that while Irish public opinion was generally conservative on two issues in the early 1980s there was no guarantee it would remain so or that it was equally conservative on other such issues. Fianna Fáil thereby risked the possibility of being seen as the Conservative and Catholic party.

This could be a notable disadvantage in the future. It has already been noted that in the first half of the 1980s there were signs that a significant section of the Irish electorate was less tied to traditional loyalties to parties and institutions. The steady advance of Fine Gael was most notable in the urban areas of the east and south; it was also by and large the urban deputies of Fine Gael and Labour who were most consistently liberal on abortion, contraception, and divorce, and in both referenda it was the most urban areas which were most liberal. There is therefore a notable divide between rural and urban Ireland on these issues. In the rural areas the traditional institutions of social control—extended family, community, local school, and Catholic parish church—still have considerable sway. In the urban areas by contrast, and above all in the Dublin region, they are less effective. Here other sources of values and lifestyles are strong and individuals are freer to think, speak, and behave as they see fit without automatically encountering censure from family, community, and church. In such surroundings life has become more varied in texture and to a certain extent Irish society has become more plural.

There are therefore almost two value systems available in modern Ireland, creating a dual culture. One system is conservative, communal, rural-oriented, still espoused by the majority of the population and supported by powerful institutions such as the Catholic Church and its more conservative adherents both lay and clerical, and by Fianna Fáil. The alternative system is more open, liberal, individualistic, and urban based, supported by the more liberal elements in Fine Gael and Labour and some elements in the middle-class professions. In a country which since independence has been remarkable for the homogeneity of its population and the almost total absence of deep divisions on grounds of culture, religion, or ethnic origin, the need to accommodate this significant urban minority is a novel challenge. To some extent the new Progressive Democrat party which emerged in late 1985 with its espousal of classical liberal views on the separation of church and state may be seen as a vehicle for this outlook, and its chief strength in the general election of February 1987 was certainly amongst the more middle-class urban electors. However it has already been noted that Irish electoral history provides cold comfort for such new parties—they either suffer electoral erosion or eventually merge with existing larger parties—and there is no reason to think the PDs will be any different. This leaves the question of where such relatively liberal voters will find refuge. Some may gravitate to Labour or the Workers' Party though they may find the ethos unwelcoming for middle-class outlooks, and besides, both these parties are opposed to the curbs in state spending which are espoused by these same middle-class groups. The only refuge is Fine Gael which under FitzGerald's leadership hesitantly assumed a social democratic tinge and had originally championed the legislation on contraception and the divorce referendum.

For those who were actually faced with personal problems concerning abortion, contraception, or marital breakdown two traditional Irish solutions were available, namely hypocrisy or emigration. By 'hypocrisy' is meant the fact that in the Irish Republic there is a long tradition of contrast between publicly stated principle and practical reality. On such matters as political unification of the island and the status of the Irish language both of which are given quite high priority in the constitution and public rhetoric, little is in fact done and in practice both are very low-level concerns. It would now seem that the same situation will prevail on abortion, contraception, and divorce. Officially the first and last are forbidden by the constitution, but in reality those who desire an abortion may obtain it illegally or, increasingly, by going to Britain. Those faced with marital breakdown may obtain separation orders or decrees of civil or Church annulment or simply desert their marriages and start new though unofficial relationships. On contraception the official Church doctrine is still to forbid all artificial methods, but sales of contraceptives together with the persistent decline in marital fertility and the average family size would suggest that in practice many, while still seeing themselves as practising Catholics, have reserved the right to follow their own conscience on this matter. In some ways this is a radical defiance of official teaching on a key issue and it is possible that such independence of mind may gradually spread into other areas of life.

The option of emigration is always available to those who find the extent of Church influence and the hypocrisy of contrast between legislation and practice intolerable. It is certainly true that emigration restarted in the early 1980s and that in contrast with earlier migrants the new generation were better educated and possibly more middle class. However it would be foolish to argue that they were motivated primarily by a desire to leave an illiberal national ethos. Lack of adequate economic openings has been the traditional 'push' factor in twentieth-century Irish migration and, given the growth in unemployment in the first half of the 1980s, it seems likely to be the main motive once again. However, when the Irish economy began to grow in the 1960s and 1970s, large numbers of migrants returned home. Given the recent evidence of traditionalist strength in the country, it is a moot point whether the emigrants of the early 1980s would be equally willing to return in the event of an economic upturn. Yet it remains true that the one-third who voted against the abortion amendment and in favour of divorce rights are an important element in Irish society, even if they are a minority. By virtue of their education and training they are often key figures in the life of the country and the source of much innovative energy and leadership. Frustration and dissembling are neither encouraging nor creative elements in a national culture and if these remain the only options, then in the long run the quality of the national life and culture will suffer. Somehow the Irish Republic needs to adjust its constitutional framework to accommodate such a minority. If this proves impossible, then another question must be asked, as it was during the divorce referendum campaign, namely how the republic could ever hope to incorporate the Unionist minority in the northeast in the event of the British administration there coming to an end. In such circumstances the Catholic hierarchy have professed themselves perfectly willing to support a federalist solution whereby special rights can be guaranteed to people living in the north-east. However this was stated in the calm, somewhat rarefied atmosphere of the New Ireland Forum discussions in 1984. Whether they would be willing to agree to such concessions in practice, especially since Irish citizens in other parts of the island might demand them as well, is another matter. What is required is a thoroughgoing revision of the Irish constitution and an 'opening out' of the national ethos in the same fashion as traditional economic policy was revamped and the national economy opened out in 1958, and this too would probably require Fianna Fáil to take the lead and carry it through, but of this there is no sign. In the meantime, it seems more likely that the Irish Republic will simply focus on the more immediate economic problems and hope that the long-term dilemmas posed by the contrast between a rigid, conservative constitution and a somewhat restless, questioning urban minority will remain quiescent.

APPENDIX: USE OF CENSUS MATERIAL FOR ECOLOGICAL CORRELATIONS

The Census of the Republic of Ireland presents its returns on the basis of local authority areas rather than parliamentary constituencies—indeed the constituencies are redrawn only after Census material has become available. However, as explained in chapter 3, since respect for local government boundaries is one of the criteria which influence the formation of constituencies, it is possible to aggregate Census returns up to constituencies in most cases. The manner in which statistics were compiled is outlined below.

1. Ten constituencies consisted of single counties or amalgamations of entire counties and Census returns for these could be used directly or easily amalgamated. This applied to:

   Carlow-Kilkenny
   Cavan-Monaghan
   Clare
   Kildare
   Laois-Offaly
   Louth
   Sligo-Leitrim
   Tipperary North (North Riding)
   Wexford
   Wicklow

2. Two constituencies consisted of subdivisions of counties, the boundaries following those of Urban Districts (UDs) and former Rural Districts (RDs). In such cases the statistics from the local government areas may be amalgamated as follows:

   Donegal North-East: Inishowen, Letterkenny, Millford, and Stranorlar RDs, plus Buncrana and Letterkenny UDs.

   Kerry North: Killarney, Listowel, and Tralee RDs plus Listowel and Tralee UDs.

3. Three constituencies consisted of amalgamations of UDs, RDs, and subdivisions of RDs—in the latter case the data for the RDs was assigned to both constituencies. This applied to:

   Cork East: Fermoy, Mallow, Midleton, Mitchelstown No. 1, Youghal No. 1 RDs and part of Cork RD, plus Cobh, Fermoy, Mallow, Midleton, and Youghal UDs.
   Cork South-West: Bandon, Bantry, Castletown, Clonakilty, Dunmanaway, Skibbereen, Skull RDs and part of Kinsale RD plus Clonakilty, Kinsale, and Skibbereen UDs.
   Mayo East: Ballina, Ballinasloe, Claremorris, Swinford RDs and part of Castlebar RD, plus Ballina UD.

4. Four constituencies consisted of parts of more than one county. This applied to:

   Limerick East: Croom, Kilmallock, Limerick No. 1 RDs, Limerick CB, and, from Co. Tipperary, Tipperary No. 2 RD.
   Meath: Co. Meath plus Delvin RD from Co. Westmeath.

Roscommon: Co. Roscommon plus part of Glennamaddy RD from Co. Galway.
Tipperary South: Tipperary South Riding plus Clonmel RD from Co. Waterford.

5. Three constituencies consisted of counties except for small areas assigned elsewhere:

Galway East: Ballinasloe, Loughrea, Mount Bellew, Portumna and Tuam RDs, Ballinasloe UD and part of Glennamaddy RD (statistics for latter assigned to both Galway East and Roscommon).
Longford-Westmeath: Co. Longford plus Co. Westmeath except for Delvin RD.
Waterford: Waterford Co. Borough and Waterford Co. except for Clonmel No. 2 RD.

6. Six constituencies consisted of remainders of counties after areas assigned elsewhere:

Cork North-West
Donegal South-West
Galway West
Kerry South
Limerick West
Mayo West

7. Five constituencies consisted of parts of large urban areas plus some surrounding rural areas:

Cork North Central: part of Cork CB plus part of Cork RD (Census data for the entire CB and RD amalgamated).
Cork South Central: part of Cork CB plus part of Cork and Kinsale RDs (Census data for CB and Cork RD amalgamated, data for Kinsale RD assigned both here and Cork South-West).
Dublin North: considered as Census area 'Dublin North County'.
Dublin South: considered as Census area 'Dublin South County'.
Dun Laoghaire: considered as Dun Laoghaire CB.

8. Eight Dublin City constituencies consisted almost entirely of sub-divisions of Dublin CB. Census data for Dublin CB assigned to all of these constituencies:

Dublin Central
Dublin North Central
Dublin North-East
Dublin North-West
Dublin South Central
Dublin South-East
Dublin South-West
Dublin West

REFERENCES

Andrews, J. H. (1960) 'The "Morning Post" Line', *Irish Geography*, 4, 99–106.
—— (1968) 'The Papers of the Irish Boundary Commission', *Irish Geography*, 5, 477–81.
Arnold, B. (1984) *What Kind of Country? Modern Irish Politics 1968–1983*. Jonathan Cape, London.
Ayearst, M. (1971) *The Republic of Ireland: Its Government and Politics*. Hodder & Stoughton, London.
Barritt, D. P., and Carter, C. F. (1972) *The Northern Ireland Problem: A Study in Group Relations*, 2nd edition. OUP, Oxford.
Bax, M. (1976) *Harpstrings and Confessions: Machine Style Politics in the Irish Republic*. Van Gorcum, Assen.
Beale, J. (1986) *Women in Ireland: Voices of Change*. Macmillan Education, London.
Bell, J. Bowyer (1979) *The Secret Army: The IRA 1916–1979*. Academy Press, Dublin.
Beresford, D. (1987) *Ten Men Dead: The Story of the 1981 Irish Hunger Strike*. Grafton, London.
Bew, P. (1982) 'The Irish Election', *Marxism Today*, 4, 99–106.
Bogdanor, V. (1984) *What is Proportional Representation?* Martin Robertson, Oxford.
Boland, K. (1982) *The Rise and Decline of Fianna Fáil*. Mercier Press, Cork.
—— (1984) *Fine Gael: British or Irish?* Mercier Press, Cork.
Brennan, P. (1982) 'Garret's Gregory Deal', *Magill*, 6:2, 51.
Brown, T. (1981) *Ireland: A Social and Cultural History 1922–1979*. Fontana, London.
Browne, V. (ed.) (1981) *The Magill Book of Irish Politics*. Magill, Dublin.
—— (ed.) (1982a) *The Magill Guide to Election '82*. Magill, Dublin.
—— (1982b) 'How the Fine Gael Whiz Kids Sold us a Taoiseach', *Magill*, 6:3, 4–16.
—— (1983a) 'How Charlie Won the War: The Battle for Leadership of Fianna Fáil', *Magill*, 6:5, 10–16
—— (1983b) 'Oliver J. Flanagan: the Bitterness Erupts', *Magill*, 6:8, 6–8.
—— (1986) 'Who's to Blame?', *Magill*, 10:2, 4–16.
Bunreacht na h Eireann (1985) (Constitution of Ireland). Government Publications Sales Office, Dublin.
Busteed, M. A. (1975) *Geography and Voting Behaviour*. OUP, London.
—— (1982) 'The 1981 Irish General Election', *Parliamentary Affairs*, 35:1, 39–58.
Busteed, M. A., and Mason, H. L. (1970) 'Irish Labour in the 1969 Election', *Political Studies*, 18, 373–9.
—— (1974) 'The 1973 General Election in the Irish Republic', *Irish Geography*, 7, 97–106.
Butler, D. E., and Stokes, D. (1969) *Political Change in Britain: Forces Shaping Electoral Choice*. Macmillan, London.
Carty, R. K. (1981) *Party and Parish Pump: Electoral Politics in Ireland*. Wilfrid Laurier University Press, Waterloo, Canada.
Census of Population of Ireland (1981), vol. 1. Stationery Office, Dublin.
—— (1984) vol. 2, Ages and Marital Status. Stationery Office, Dublin.
—— (1985a) vol. 4, Principal Economic Status and Industries. Stationery Office, Dublin.

—— (1985*b*) vol. 6, Irish Language. Stationery Office, Dublin.

—— (1986) vol. 7, Occupations. Stationery Office, Dublin.

Chubb, B. (1963) 'Going about Persecuting Civil Servants: The Role of the Irish Parliamentary Representative'. *Political Studies*, 11, 272–86.

—— (1970) *The Government and Politics of Ireland*, 1st edition. OUP, London.

—— (1978*a*) Appendix A: 'Procedures for Voting and Counting the Votes in Force in 1977', in H. R. Penniman (ed.), *Ireland at the Polls: The Dáil Elections of 1977*. American Enterprise Institute, Duke University Press, Washington DC.

—— (1978*b*) 'The Electoral System', in ch. 2, H. R. Penniman (ed.), *Ireland at the Polls: The Dáil Elections of 1977*. American Enterprise Institute, Duke University Press, Washington DC.

—— (1982*a*) Appendix C: 'The Dáil Electoral System as it stood in 1980', in Chubb (1970).

—— (1982*b*) *The Government and Politics of Ireland*, 2nd edition. Longmans, London.

Coakley, J. (1980) 'Constituency Boundary Revision and Seat Re-Distribution in the Irish Parliamentary Tradition', *Administration*, 28:3, 291–328.

Coogan, T. P. (1980) *The IRA*. Fontana, London.

—— (1984) 'Brookeborough: The Raid that Created a Martyr'; 'IRA Revival: A New Generation and a New Campaign', *War in Peace*, 3:31, 616–17; 609–11.

Cooney, J. (1986) *The Crozier and the Dáil: Church and State 1922–1986*. Mercier Press, Cork.

Corish, P. (1985) *The Irish Catholic Experience: A Historical Survey*. Gill and Macmillan, Dublin.

Coward, J. (1982) 'Fertility Changes in the Republic of Ireland During the 1970s', *Area*, 14:2, 109–117.

Dáil Eireann Constituency Commission Report (1980). Stationery Office, Dublin.

Droop, H. R. (1869) *Papers of the Juridical Society*, III, part XII, 469.

Dunne, D., and Kerrigan, G. (1984) *Round Up the Usual Suspects: The Cosgrave Coalition and Nicky Kelly*. Magill, Dublin.

Dwyer, T. R. (1980) *Éamon de Valera*. Gill and Macmillan, Dublin.

Electoral (Amendment) Act (1980) Stationery Office, Dublin.

Electoral Reform: Fairer Voting in Natural Communities (1982). Poland Street Publications, London.

Fanning, R. (1983) *Independent Ireland*. Helicon, Dublin.

Farrell, B. (1969–70) 'Labour and the Irish Political Party System: A Suggested Approach to Analysis', *Economic and Social Review*, 1, 477–502.

—— (1970) 'Dáil Deputies: The 1969 Generation', *Economic and Social Review*, 3, 309–27.

—— (1975) 'Irish Government Re-observed,' *Economic and Social Review*, 6, 405–14.

—— (1983) *Sean Lemass*. Gill and Macmillan, Dublin.

—— (1985) ch. 14, 'Ireland: From Friends and Neighbours to Clients and Partisans: Some Dimensions of Parliamentary Representation under PR-STV' in V. Bogdanor (ed.), *Representatives of the People? Parliamentarians and Constituents in Western Democracies*. Gower, Policy Studies Institute, Aldershot.

—— (1987*a*), ch. 1, 'The Context of Three Elections', in H. R. Penniman and B. Farrell (eds.), *Ireland at the Polls 1981, 1982, and 1987: A Study of Four General Elections*. American Enterprise Institute, Duke University Press, Washington DC.

—— (1987*b*) ch. 5, 'Government Formation and Ministerial Selection', Penniman and Farrell (eds.), op. cit.

Farrell, B., and Manning, M. (1978) ch. 6, 'The Election', in Penniman and Farrell (eds.), op. cit.

Farrell, D. M. (1984) 'Age, Education and Occupational Backgrounds of TDs and "Routes" to the Dáil: The Effects of Localism in the 1980s', *Administration*, 32, 323–41.

—— (1986) 'The Strategy to Market Fine Gael in 1981', *Irish Political Studies*, 1, 1–14.

Farrell, M. (1976) *Northern Ireland: The Orange State*. Pluto Press, London.

—— (1983) 'The Extraordinary Life and Times of Sean McBride: Part II', *Magill*, 6, 4, 24–37.

Fisher, D. (1986) ch. 13, 'The Church and Change', in K. A. Kennedy (ed.), *Ireland in Transition: Economic and Social Change since 1960*. Mercier Press, Cork.

Fisk, R. (1985) *In Time of War: Ireland, Ulster and the Price of Neutrality 1939–1945*. Paladin, London.

FitzGerald, G. (1968) *Planning in Ireland*. Institute of Public Administration, Dublin.

—— (1973) *Towards a New Ireland*. Torc, Dublin.

Forester, M. (1972) *Michael Collins, the Lost Leader*. Sphere, London.

Gageby, D. (1979) 'The Media', in J. J. Lee (ed.), *Ireland 1945–1970*. Gill and Macmillan, Dublin.

Gallagher, M. (1975) 'Disproportionality in a Proportional Representation System: the Irish Experience', *Political Studies*, 23, 501–13.

—— (1976) *Electoral Support for Irish Political Parties 1927–1973*. Sage Professional Papers, Contemporary Political Sociology Series, London.

—— (1978–9) 'Party Solidarity, Exclusivity and Inter-Party Relationships in Ireland 1922–1977, the Evidence of Transfers', *Economic and Social Review*, 10, 1–22.

—— (1979a) 'The Impact of Lower Preference Votes on Irish Parliamentary Elections 1922–1977', *Economic and Social Review*, 11, 19–32.

—— (1979b) 'The Pact General Election of 1922.' *Irish Historical Studies*, 21:84, 404–21.

—— (1980) 'Candidate Selection in Ireland: The Impact of Localism and the Electoral System', *British Journal of Political Science*, 10, 489–503.

—— (1982) *The Irish Labour Party in Transition 1957–1982*, Manchester University Press, Manchester.

—— (1984) '166 Who Rule: The Dáil Deputies of November 1982', *Economic and Social Review*, 15, 241–64.

—— (1985) *Political Parties in the Republic of Ireland*. Manchester University Press, Manchester.

—— (1986) 'The Political Consequences of the Electoral System in the Republic of Ireland', *Electoral Studies*, 5:3, 253–75.

—— (1987) 'Does Ireland Need a New Electoral System?', *Irish Political Studies*, 2, 27–48.

Gallagher, T. (1981) 'The Dimensions of Fianna Fáil Rule in Ireland', *West European Politics*, 4:1, 54–68.

Garvin, T. (1974) 'Political Cleavages, Party Politics and Urbanisation in Ireland: the Case of the Periphery-Dominated Centre', *European Journal of Political Research*, 2, 307–27.

—— (1977–8) 'Nationalist Elites, Irish Voters and Irish Political Development: a Comparative Perspective', *Economic and Social Review*, 8, 161–86.

—— (1978) 'The Destiny of the Soldiers: Tradition and Modernity in the Politics of de Valera's Ireland', *Political Studies*, 26, 328–47.

—— (1981a) *The Evolution of Irish Nationalist Politics*. Gill and Macmillan, Dublin.

—— (1981b) 'The Growth of Faction in the Fianna Fáil Party, 1966–1980', *Parliamentary Affairs*, 34:1, 110–23.

—— (1982) 'Change and the Political System', in F. C. Litton (ed.), *Unequal Achievement: The Irish Experience 1957–1982*. Institute of Public Administration, Dublin.

——(1986) *Irish Press*, 27 June.

Girvin, B. (1986) 'Social Change and Moral Politics: The Irish Constitutional Referendum 1983', *Political Studies*, 34, 61–81.

Grogan, V. (1978) 'Towards the New Constitution', in F. C. MacManus (ed.), *The Years of the Great Test 1926–1939*. Mercier, Cork.

Gudgin, G., and Taylor, P. J. (1979) *Seats, Votes and the Spatial Organisation of Elections*. Pion, London.

Hand, G. F. (1969) Introduction to *Report of the Irish Boundary Commission*. Shannon.

Hare, T. (1857) *The Machinery of Representation*.

—— (1859) *Treatise on the Election of Representatives Parliamentary and Municipal*.

Hogan, J. (1945) *Election and Representation*. Cork University Press, Cork.

Holland, M. (1983) 'Dublin's New Dealer', *New Statesman*, 31 Dec., 104:2702, 8–9.

Hopkinson, M. (1988) *Green Against Green: The Irish Civil War*. Gill and Macmillan, Dublin.

Hoppen, K. T. (1984) Elections, Politics and Society in Ireland 1832–1885. OUP, Oxford.

Horner, A. A. (1986) 'Rural Population Change in Ireland', in P. Breatnach and M. E. Crawley (eds.), *Change and Development in Rural Ireland*. Geographical Society of Ireland, Special Publications No. 1. Cardinal Press, Maynooth.

Horner, A. A., and Daultrey, S. G. (1980) 'Recent Population Changes in the Republic of Ireland.' *Area*, 12:2, 129–35.

Industrial Development in Ireland. (1980) IDA, Dublin.

Inglis, T. (1987) *Moral Monopoly: The Catholic Church in Modern Irish Society*. Gill and Macmillan, Dublin.

Johnson, J. H. (1963) 'Population Changes in Ireland, 1951–1961', *Geographical Journal* 129, 167–74.

—— (1978) 'Population Changes in Ireland, 1961–1966', *Irish Geography*, 5:5, 470–7.

Johnston, R. J. (1979) *Political, Electoral, and Spatial Systems*. OUP, Oxford.

Joyce, J., and Murtagh, P. (1983) *The Boss: Charles J. Haughey in Government*. Poolbeg Press, Swords, Co. Dublin.

Katz, R. S. (1981) 'But How Many Candidates Should we Have in Donegal? Numbers of Nominees and Electoral Efficiency in Ireland', *British Journal of Political Science*, 11, 117–22.

Kennedy, F. (1986) ch. 9, 'The Family in Transition' in K. A. Kennedy (ed.), *Ireland in Transition: Economic and Social change since 1960*. Mercier Press, Cork.

Kerrigan, G. (1982) 'Goodbye Mick, Hello Dick', *Magill*, 6:2, 53–4.

—— (1983a) 'Labour: The Cutting Edge of Coalition', *Magill*, 6:7, 6–9.

—— (1983b) 'The Moral Civil War', *Magill*, 6:12, 6–16.

Knight, J., and Baxter-Moore, N. (1972) *Northern Ireland: The Elections of the Twenties*. Arthur McDougall Fund, London.

Komito, L. (1984) 'Irish Clientelism: A Reappraisal', *Economic and Social Review*, 15, 173–94.

Laffan, M. (1983) *The Partition of Ireland 1911–1925*. Dundalgan, Dundalk.

Laver, M. (1986a) 'Ireland: Politics with Some Social Bases: An Interpretation Based on Aggregate Data', *Economic and Social Review*, 17:2, 107–31.

—— (1986b) id., *Economic and Social Review*, 17:3, 193–213.

—— (1986c) 'Party Choice and Social Structure in Ireland', *Irish Political Studies*, 1, 45–55.

Laver, M. (1987) 'Measuring Patterns of Party Support in Ireland', *Economic and Social Review*, 18:2, 95–100.

Lee, J. J. (1979*a*) 'Continuity and Change in Ireland, 1945–1970', in J. J. Lee (ed.), *Ireland 1945–1970*. Gill and Macmillan, Dublin.

—— (1979*b*) 'Sean Lemass', in J. J. Lee (ed.), op. cit.

Lipset, S. M., and Rokkan, S. (1967) 'Cleavage Structures, Party Systems, and Voter Alignments: An Introduction', in S. M. Lipset, and S. Rokkan (eds.), *Party Systems and Voter Alignments: Cross-National Perspectives*. Free Press, New York.

Longford, Earl of, and O'Neill, T. P. (1970) *Éamon de Valera*. Hutchinson, London.

Lyons, F. S. L. (1973) *Ireland Since the Famine*. Fontana, London.

—— (1979) *Culture and Anarchy in Ireland 1890–1939*. OUP, Oxford.

McCracken, J. L. (1958) *Representative Government in Ireland: Dáil Eireann 1919–1948*. OUP, London.

McDowell, M. (1981) 'Irish Budgetary Politics', *National Westminster Bank Quarterly Review*, August, 22–35.

McMenamin, P. (1975) 'The Industrial Development Process in the Republic of Ireland', in J. Vaizey (ed.), *Economic Sovereignty and Regional Policy: A Symposium on Regional Problems in Britain and Ireland*. Gill and Macmillan, Dublin.

McVey, E. (1981) 'How PR Works: An Easy Guide', *Irish Times*, 10 June.

Magill (27 June 1985) 'Say Goodnight Dick', *Magill*, 8. 16. 10–14.

Mair, P. (1977–8) 'Labour and the Irish Party System Revisited: Party competition in the 1920s', *Economic and Social Review*, 9:1, 59–70.

—— (1978) 'The Anatomy of the Political: The Development of the Irish Party System' *Comparative Politics*, 11. 1. 445–65.

—— (1981) 'Analysis of Results Dáil General Election, 1981', in T. Nealon and S. Brennan, *Nealon's Guide: 22nd Dáil and Seanad*. Platform Press, Dublin.

—— (1982) 'Muffling the Swing: STV and the Irish General Election of 1981', *West European Politics*, 5, 76–91.

—— (1986) ch. 19, 'Districting Choices under the Single-Transferable Vote', in B. Grofman and A. Lijphart (eds.), *Electoral Laws and their Political Consequences*. Agathon Press, New York.

—— (1987) ch. 4, 'Party Organisation, Vote Management and Candidate Selection: Towards the Nationalisation of Electoral Strategy in Ireland', in H.R. Penniman and B. Farrell (eds.), *Ireland at the Polls 1981, 1982, and 1987: A Study of Four General Elections*. American Enterprise Institute, Duke University Press, Washington DC.

Mair, P., and Laver, M. (1975) 'Proportionality, PR and STV in Ireland', *Political Studies*, 23, 491–500.

Manning, M. (1970) *The Blueshirts*. Gill and Macmillan, Dublin.

—— (1972) 'Irish Political Parties: an Introduction.' *Studies in Irish Political Culture*, 3, Gill and Macmillan, Dublin.

—— (1978) ch. 4, 'The Political Parties', in H. R. Penniman (ed.), *Ireland at the Polls: The Dáil Elections of 1977*. American Enterprise Institute, Duke University Press, Washington DC.

—— (1979) 'The Farmers', in J. J. Lee (ed.), *Ireland 1945–1970*. Gill and Macmillan, Dublin.

—— (1986) 'The Pride of Balaghaderreen (James Dillon)', *Magill*, 9:7, 34–8.

Mansergh, N. (1934) *The Irish Free State: Its Government and Politics*. George Allen & Unwin, London.

Marsh, M. A. (1981) 'Electoral Preferences in Irish Recruitment: the 1977 Election', *European Journal of Political Research*, 9, 61–74.

—— (1985) ch. 7, 'Ireland', in I. Crewe and D. Denver (eds.) *Electoral Change in*

Western Democracies: Patterns and Sources of Electoral Volatility. Croom Helm, Beckenham.

Meenan, J. (1978) 'From Free Trade to Self-Sufficiency', in F. C. MacManus (ed.), *The Years of the Great Test 1926–1939.* Mercier, Cork.

Messenger, C. (1983) 'Border War: The 1950s Raids by the IRA', *War in Peace* 3:31, 612–15.

Mitchell, A. (1974) *Labour in Irish Politics 1890–1930.* Irish University Press, Dublin.

Moss, W. (1933) *Political Parties in the Irish Free State.* Columbia University Press, New York.

Murphy, J. A. (1969) 'The Irish Party System 1938–1951', in K. B. Nowland and T. D. Williams (eds.), *Ireland in the War Years and After 1939–1951.* Gill and Macmillan, Dublin.

—— (1975) *Ireland in the Twentieth Century.* Gill and Macmillan, Dublin.

—— (1979) 'Put Them Out! Parties and Elections 1948–1969' in J. J. Lee (ed.), *Ireland 1945–1970.* Gill and Macmillan, Dublin.

Nealon, T., and Brennan, S. (eds.) (1983) *Nealon's Guide 24th Dáil and Seanad: 2nd Election '82* (Platform Press, Dublin 1983).

Nevin, D. (1978) 'Labour and the Political Revolution', in F. C. MacManus (ed.), *The Years of the Great Test 1926–1939.* Mercier Press, Cork.

New Ireland Forum (1984) No. 12 Irish Episcopal Conference Delegation Public Session, 9 Feb. 1984, Dublin Castle. *Report of Proceedings.* Stationery Office, Dublin.

Nic Ghiolla Phadraig, M. (1976) 'Religion in Ireland: A Preliminary Analysis' *Social Studies* 5, 113–80.

Nolan, W. (1986) ch. 3, 'Some Civil and Ecclesiastical Territorial Divisions and their Geographical Significance', in W. Nolan (ed.), *The Shaping of Ireland: The Geographical Perspective.* Mercier, Cork.

Nowlan, K. B. (1978) 'President Cosgrave's Last Administration.' in F. C. MacManus (ed.), *The Years of the Great Test 1926–1939.* Mercier, Cork.

O'Byrnes, S. (1986) *Hiding Behind a Face: Fine Gael under FitzGerald.* Gill and Macmillan, Dublin.

O'Faolain, S. (1980) *The Irish.* Penguin, Harmondsworth.

O'Leary, C. (1979) *Irish Elections 1918–1977: Parties, Voters and Proportional Representation.* Gill and Macmillan, Dublin.

O'Leary, O. (1984) 'Rome Rule', *Magill,* 8:4, 6–7.

—— (1985a) 'Take me Home, Country Roads: With Dick Spring in Kerry', *Magill,* 8:7, 40–6.

—— (1985b) 'Newman: The Mullah of Limerick', *Magill,* 8:9, 24–33.

—— (1985c) 'Peter Prendergast: The National Handler', *Magill,* 8:10, 8–11.

—— (1985d) 'Irreconcilable Differences' (Oireachtas Committee on Marriage Breakdown), *Magill,* 8:11, 28–33.

—— (1986) 'Irish Voters are Divided against Divorce Legislation', *Listener,* 115: 2965, 7–8.

O'Malley, J. (1983) 'The Election', in T. Nealon and S. Brennan (eds.), *Nealon's Guide: 24th Dáil and Seanad: 2nd Election '82.* Platform Press, Dublin.

—— (1987) ch. 2, 'Campaigns, Manifestoes and Party Finances', in H. R. Penniman and B. Farrell (eds.), *Ireland at the Polls 1981, 1982, and 1987: A Study of Four General Elections.* American Enterprise Institute, Duke University Press, Washington, DC.

O'Reilly, E. (1986) 'The Legion of the Rearguard', *Magill,* 9:9, 8–14.

O'Toole, F. (1986) 'An Apostle's Creed', *Magill,* 9:10, 16–36.

Paddison, R. (1976) 'Spatial Bias and Redistricting in Proportional Representation Election Systems: A Case Study of the Republic of Ireland' *Tijdschrift voor Economische en Sociale Geografie*, XVII. 4. 230–41.

Parker, A. J. (1982) 'The Friends and Neighbours' Voting Effect in the Galway West Constituency', *Political Geography Quarterly*, 1, 243–62.

—— (1983) 'Localism and Bailiwicks: the Galway West Constituency in the 1977 General Election.' *Proceedings of the Royal Irish Academy*, 83c, 17–36.

—— (1984) 'An Ecological Analysis of Voting Patterns in Galway West, 1977', *Irish Geography*, 17, 42–64.

—— (1986) 'Geography and the Irish Electoral System', *Irish Geography*, 19, 1–14.

Pringle, D. G. (1986) ch. 12, 'Urbanisation in Modern Ireland', in W. Nolan (ed.), *The Shaping of Ireland: The Geographical Perspective*. Mercier, Cork.

Randall, V. (1986) 'The Politics of Abortion in Ireland', in J. Lovenduski and J. Outshoorn (eds.), *The New Politics of Abortion*. Sage, London.

Roche, M. (1983) 'The Secrets of Opus Dei', *Magill*, 6:8, 16–36.

Rottman, D. B. (1986) ch. 10 'Crime and the Criminal Justice System', in K. A. Kennedy (ed.), *Ireland in Transition: Economic and Social Change since 1960*. Mercier Press, Cork.

Sacks, P. M. (1970) 'Bailiwicks, Locality and Religion: Three Elements in an Irish Dáil Constituency Election', *Economic and Social Review*, 1, 531–54.

—— (1976) *The Donegal Mafia: An Irish Political Machine*. Yale University Press, New Haven and London.

Sinnott, R. (1978) ch. 3, 'The Electorate', in H. R. Penniman (ed.), *Ireland at the Polls: The Dáil Elections of 1977*. American Enterprise Institute, Duke University Press, Washington DC.

—— (1984) 'Interpretations of the Irish Party System', *European Journal of Political Research*, 12, 289–307.

—— (1987) ch. 3, 'The Voters, the Issues and the Party System' in H. Penniman and B. Farrell (eds.), *Ireland at the Polls 1981, 1982, and 1987: A Study of Four General Elections*. American Enterprise Institute. Duke University Press, Washington DC.

Smith, R. (1985) *Garret: The Enigma: Dr Garret FitzGerald*. Aherlow, Dublin.

Taylor, P. J., and Johnston, R. J. (1979) *Geography of Elections*. Penguin, Harmondsworth.

Thornley, D. (1978) 'The Blueshirts', in F. C. MacManus (ed.), *The Years of the Great Test 1926–1939*. Mercier Press, Cork.

Trench, B. (ed.) (1982) *Magill Book of Irish Politics, 1983*. Magill Publications, Dublin.

Trench, C. C. (1984) *The Great Dan: A Biography of Daniel O'Connell*. Triad Grafton, London.

Van Hatten, M. (1985) 'Pressures on Labour Increase' *Financial Times*, 2 July.

Walsh, B. M. (1978) 'National and Regional Demographic Trends', *Administration*, 26, 162–79.

—— (1979) 'Economic Growth and Development, 1945–1970', in J. J. Lee (ed.), *Ireland 1945–1970*. Gill and Macmillan, Dublin.

—— (1984) 'The Influence of Turnout on the Results of the Referendum to Amend the Constitution to Include a Clause on the Rights of the Unborn', *Economic and Social Review*, 15:3, 227–34.

Walsh, D. (1986) *The Party: Inside Fianna Fáil*. Gill and Macmillan, Dublin.

Walsh, J. A. (1979) 'Immigration to the Republic of Ireland, 1946–1971', *Irish Geography*, 12, 104–10.

Whyte, J. H. (1966) 'Dáil Deputies: Their Work, its Difficulties, Possible Remedies', Tuairim Pamphlet 15, Dublin.

—— (1974) 'Ireland: Politics without Social Bases', in R. Rose (ed.), *Electoral Behaviour: A Comparative Handbook*. Free Press, New York.

—— (1979) 'Church, State, and Society, 1950–1970', in J. J. Lee (ed.), *Ireland 1945–1970*. Gill and Macmillan, Dublin.

—— (1980) *Church and State in Modern Ireland, 1923–1979*, 2nd edition. Gill and Macmillan, Dublin.

Wickham, J. (1986) ch. 4, 'Industrialisation, Work and Unemployment', in P. Clancy, S. Drudy, K. Lynch, and L. O'Dowd (eds.), *Ireland: A Sociological Profile*. Institute of Public Administration, Dublin.

Williams, T. D. (1978) 'De Valera in Power', in F. C. MacManus (ed.), *The Years of the Great Test 1926–1939*. Mercier Press, Cork.

Younger, C. (1970) *Ireland's Civil War*. Fontana/Collins, London.

INDEX